Y0-BUU-974

CHILDCRAFT

CREATIVE PLAY AND HOBBIES

Childcraft

IN FIFTEEN VOLUMES

•

VOLUME EIGHT

CREATIVE PLAY AND HOBBIES

FIELD ENTERPRISES EDUCATIONAL CORPORATION
Merchandise Mart Plaza • Chicago 54, Illinois

CHILDCRAFT

Reg. U. S. Pat. Off.

Copyright © 1954, U. S. A.
by Field Enterprises, Inc.

Copyright © 1949 by Field Enterprises, Inc.
Copyright © 1947, 1945, 1942, 1939 by The Quarrie Corporation
Copyright © 1937, 1935, 1934 by W. F. Quarrie & Company

THE CHILD'S TREASURY

Copyright © 1931, 1923 by W. F. Quarrie & Company

International Copyright © 1954, 1949
by Field Enterprises, Inc.
International Copyright © 1947
by The Quarrie Corporation

———————

All rights reserved. This volume may not be
reproduced in whole or in part in any form
without written permission from the publishers.

———————

Printed in the United States of America

FJA

CONTENTS

v

These Are the Authors

Catherine Corley Anderson

suggests things boys and girls will like to make with pieces of cloth, in SEWING FOR FUN (page 241). She tells you just how to take different kinds of stitches, how to cut materials, how to follow a simple pattern, and how to make trimmings. This author, who is also an artist, was formerly art instructor for the Chicago Park District and has written a dozen books about things to make.

Bernice Wells Carlson

PLANNING A PARTY (page 75) helps you give a party you and your friends will enjoy. This chapter has easy-to-carry-out ideas for invitations, games, favors, decorations, and things to eat. Whether your party is built around a birthday or a holiday, or is a costume affair, whether it is for two-year-olds or ten-year-olds, this chapter will give you suggestions. Among the books this author has written are *The Junior Party Book*, and *Make It Yourself, Handicraft for Boys and Girls*.

David Dushkin

as Director of the Dushkin School of Music, Winnetka, Ill., showed how you can create good music with simple homemade instruments. In MAKING MUSICAL INSTRUMENTS (page 262) he describes how you can use materials around your house to make tomtoms, tambourines, castanets, xylophones, and similar music makers. He tells how you can play on them, too. This author has written music for piano and recorder.

Paul Engle

Professor of English at the State University of Iowa, brings you new ideas about making up stories and poems, in WRITING OUR THOUGHTS (page 163). He shows you how to have fun writing letters, invitations, or your own newspaper or magazine. Here you will find help in making your stories or verses more interesting, in choosing the words that say just what you mean, and in telling other persons what you are thinking about.

Alice M. Hoben

writes about PUPPETS AND MARIONETTES (page 231). She explains how you can make the simplest puppet that is really just a knotted handkerchief, as well as the more complicated marionettes that have papier-mâché heads, wigs, and beards, and are controlled by strings. She tells, too, how you can make a stage and give a puppet show. This author, who has written several books for children, teaches at the Washington Square Reading Center in New York City.

Caroline Horowitz

in GAMES FOR OUTDOORS AND INDOORS (page 1) describes running games, singing games, games to play with homemade equipment, quiet and active games, games for two to play, or for a larger group. You will find her directions clear and easy to follow. This author has also written *The Good Time Book*, *A Boy's Treasury of Things To Do*, and other books about play.

Carolyn S. Howlett

and Isabel Smith give you new ideas for PAINTING AND DRAWING (page 149) that will make you eager to try your hand with paint and brushes, finger paints, crayons, colored chalk and pencils, charcoal, and clay. Ways of using these materials are explained, too. This author is Professor and Head of the Department of Art Education, and also Head of the Junior School at the Art Institute of Chicago.

Marguerite Ickis

offers you a variety of good ideas for MAKING THE MOST OF YOUR HOME (page 48). You will like her suggestions for making your own room more attractive and orderly, for turning basements and back yards into play places with easily made equipment, and for setting up outdoor games, as well as doing simple outdoor cooking. The author is instructor in Recreation at Teacher's College, Columbia University, in New York City.

Clara M. Lambert

tells you about CHOOSING A HOBBY (page 109). She describes hobbies that give you a chance to make things, to find new friends and learn new facts. You will find here, too, good ideas for making collections and keeping them in order. The author, who is Director of Teacher Training for the Play School Association in New York, has written many books for children, including *Manhattan Now and Long Ago* and *Skyscrapers*.

Ruby Bradford Murphy

shows you that bad weather or a rest in bed need not keep you from having fun, if you follow the suggestions in QUIET PLAY (page 35). You will find things to do and to make if you are alone or if you have company. There are word games and guessing games. This author has written many books for boys and girls, including *Who's Who in Mother Goose Land* and *Streamliner*.

Martha Parkhill

gives you many ideas for attractive and useful things to make in ADVENTURES IN HANDWORK (page 210), which she wrote with Dorothy Spaeth. These two authors also wrote the book *It's Fun to Make Things*. They tell you how to make place cards, Christmas tree ornaments, belts, mittens, earrings, fans, and decorations that will be attractive presents. You can build birdhouses and bird feeding stations from the simple directions they give.

Josephine Van Dolzen Pease

brings you entertaining GAMES FOR TRAVEL (page 66) and good ideas for making your train, plane, bus, or automobile trip more interesting. Some of the games center around what you see out of the window, some are paper-and-pencil games, others need only two or three players with lively imaginations. *This Is the World*, *The Happy Book*, and *It Seems Like Magic* are among this author's many books for boys and girls.

Irma S. Rombauer

makes cooking an exciting adventure in COOKING UP FUN (page 193), the chapter she wrote with Jane Crawford Torno. Here you will find out how to use kitchen equipment safely and correctly, how to make tasty sandwiches and fruit drinks, lunches, and simple but delicious meals for the family. This author also wrote *Cookbook for Boys and Girls*, and is co-author of *The Joy of Cooking*.

Isabel Smith

Art Instructor at the Junior School of the Art Institute of Chicago, wrote PAINTING AND DRAW-

Frontispiece from R. C. Miller, FPG

ING (page 149) with Carolyn S. Howlett. These two authors give you new ideas for using paints and brushes, finger paints, crayons, colored chalk and pencils, charcoal, and clay. They suggest ways to use different materials to tell a story, to express ideas or feelings, or to recall a sight you enjoyed.

Moyne Rice Smith

knows a great deal about PLAYMAKING AND PLAY ACTING (page 130), for she is Director of the Junior Community Players of Princeton, N. J. She tells you what steps to take in choosing a play you want to give, in preparing the scenery, costumes, and properties, and in making up your program and tickets. You will like the stories she suggests that lend themselves to play acting.

Dorothy Spaeth

gives you many ideas for attractive things to make as presents or for your own use in ADVENTURES IN HANDWORK (page 210), which she wrote with Martha Parkhill. You will have fun putting together odd scraps of material to make decorations, fans, Christmas tree ornaments, place cards, purses, mittens, belts, and earrings. You will find directions, too, for birdhouses and bird feeding stations. These two authors also wrote the book *It's Fun to Make Things*.

Jane Crawford Torno

wrote COOKING UP FUN (page 193) with Irma S. Rombauer. Cooking will become an exciting adventure when you find out how to prepare delicious sandwiches and refreshing drinks, hamburgers, hot dogs, and desserts for yourself and your friends, and even entire meals that your whole family will enjoy. You can use kitchen utensils and equipment carefully and cook without waste if you follow the suggestions in this chapter.

Lawry Turpin

author of MAKING TOYS AND PLAYTHINGS (page 174), tells you what tools you will need for simple woodwork, and gives you clear, step-by-step directions for using them to make games, puzzles, a sand box, teeter-totter, building blocks, kites, and even a table and chairs. This author has had long experience in teaching boys and girls how to work with wood, and has written *Toys You Can Make of Wood*.

GAMES
FOR INDOORS
AND OUTDOORS

CAROLINE HOROWITZ

H. Armstrong Roberts

Outdoor games like "Run, Sheep, Run" or "Hide and Seek" are not only fun but help to build strong, healthy bodies.

"LET'S PLAY" are magic words that make it possible for us to enjoy many happy hours of fun and pleasure. We love to play games, whether we are young or old. For some years Caroline Horowitz has made a study of games we like best. Author of *The Good Time Book, A Girl's Treasury of Things-to-Do, A Boy's Treasury of Things-to-Do,* and many other popular books, she tells how to play many of our best-loved games. There are games for indoors and outdoors. There are games for groups and there are games for just you and a playmate.

SOMETIMES you may think that nothing can make you happy except a certain game which you see in a store. "If only I had that game," you say. But many times you could make the same game, or one like it, in a few minutes.

Spinning a top is a game you can play by yourself. Did you ever make a top by cutting out a circle of cardboard and pushing a short pencil through the middle of the cardboard? This top spins wonderfully. You make the cardboard circle by turning a cup upside down on a piece of cardboard and running your pencil around the cup. Then you cut along the pencil line. Be sure that the hole for the pencil is in the center of the cardboard.

There are many other games you can make for yourself and your friends that are just as easy. You can make wonderful games with clothespins, beans, boxes, toothpicks, paper bags, peanuts—all sorts of simple things that are easy to

1

A homemade top which is easy to make

get. When you know how to play these simple games, you will find yourself making up new ones—games which are a little different and sometimes even better than the old ones.

Games for You and a Playmate

When you play the first of these games, you will have to watch closely and listen carefully. Sooner or later you will make a mistake, but that will make the game even more fun.

Simon Says Thumbs Up. Two or more can play this game. The players face the leader, or "Simon," and obey his orders. He holds his fists in front of him. Then he begins the game by calling out "Simon says 'Thumbs up.' " Or "Simon says 'Thumbs down.' " If it is "Thumbs up," he straightens up his thumbs. At "Thumbs down," he turns his thumbs downward. You do the same in either case.

But watch out. He will give his orders faster and faster. If he says merely "Thumbs up" or "Thumbs down," you are not to obey, even if his own thumbs are up or down. If you make a mistake, you drop out of the game. The one who stays in longest wins. Then it is the turn of the winner to be "Simon."

Pease Porridge Hot is a hand-clapping game for two. Face your partner, and say the following poem:

> Pease Porridge hot,
> Pease Porridge cold,
> Pease Porridge in the pot
> Nine days old.
>
> Some like it hot,
> Some like it cold,
> Some like it in the pot
> Nine days old.

When you say "Pease," you clap your hands against your knees. When you say "Porridge," you clap your hands together. When you say "hot," you clap your right hand against your partner's right hand. On "Pease," you clap your hands against your knees again. On "Porridge," you clap your hands together again. On "cold," you clap your left hand against your partner's left hand.

Again, on "Pease," you clap your hands against your knees. On "Porridge," you clap your hands together. On the word "in," you clap your right hand against your partner's right hand. On the words "the pot," you clap your hands together. On "Nine," you clap your hands against your knees. On "days," you clap your hands together. And on "old," you clap your left hand against your partner's left hand. Do the second half of the poem in the same way. See how fast you can do it without making a mistake.

Circle Tit-Tat-Toe. Draw a circle, 6" in diameter, on a piece of paper. Divide the circle just as you would if you were cutting a pie into eight portions. Then draw a small circle in the center of the large one.

Write a number in each part, arranging your numbers so that a high number is placed next to a low number. A good arrangement would be: 1, 4, 6, 3, 7, 2, 8, 5. Write 10 in the small center circle.

Each player takes a turn. The first player holds his pencil about one foot above the paper, closes his eyes tight, and moves his pencil around in the air, as if he were drawing a circle with it. The pencil should be kept high, while the player recites the following rhyme:

Tit-Tat-Toe, Around I go;
If I miss, I miss in this!

Then with his eyes still closed, the player lowers his pencil point and puts it on the paper.

If the pencil point lands in a portion numbered 5, the player gets 5 points; if it lands in a portion with 2 in it, the player gets 2 points. If he is lucky enough to land in the small circle marked 10, he gets 10 points.

As soon as he lands in a portion, he puts his initials in it and neither player can score in it again. Each player takes turns and when all the portions have been used, the one who has the greater number of points wins. If you want a longer game, you can make a bigger diagram with 16 or even 32 portions.

The Minister's Cat. Start this game by saying, "The minister's cat is an *active* cat." Or you can choose any other word beginning with the letter A. Then your friend has to describe the minister's cat with a word beginning with the letter B. For instance, he might say, "The minister's cat is a *big* cat." And so the game goes on, with each player taking the next letter in the alphabet. If you like, you can agree not to use certain letters, such as X.

If two persons are playing and one person cannot think of a word begin-

"Tit-Tat-Toe" played in a circle

ning with the next letter of the alphabet, he loses. But if there are more than two playing, anyone who gets stuck must drop out of the game. The last person left wins. You can go through the alphabet as many times as you like.

Sidewalk, Porch, and Back-Yard Games

Many of the best-liked games are those which are played outdoors. Some of them do not require much space.

Jacks or Jackstones. Jacks are usually used for this game. But if you should be on the beach, or in the country, and do not have any Jacks, you can play the game with five smooth little stones, just as they used to play it long ago.

You start by playing Onesy. You throw 5 Jacks on the ground or table. Then you throw one into the air. While it is still in the air, you pick up one of the Jacks from the ground. You must catch the Jack which you threw up, before it touches the ground, with the same hand which holds the picked-up Jack. You may now lay that Jack to one side. Continue in this way, until you have picked up each of the four Jacks, one at a time.

Now you are on Twosy, and pick up 2 Jacks at a time. On Threesy, you pick up 3 Jacks at a time, and then 1 Jack. Or, if you like, you can pick up 1 Jack first and then 3 Jacks at a time. On Foursy, you pick up all 4 Jacks at one time.

If you should drop a Jack during play, fail to catch the thrown-up Jack, or touch a Jack that you were not picking up, you lose your turn. When your turn comes again, you continue where you missed. That is, if you missed while playing a Threesy, you play Threesy over again, but you get credit for everything that you did correctly before that. The winning player is the one who first completes ten games correctly.

You can play Jackstones with a ball, if you like. In that case, you throw the ball up instead of the Jack and let it bounce once before you catch it.

You can also play "Knock, Knock." In this game, you throw the ball up, pick up the Jack, and knock twice on the ground with it before you catch the ball. To play "Around the World," you throw up the ball, pick up the Jack, and, holding it in your hand, wave your hand around the ball while it is still in the air. Playing "Pick-a-Back," you catch the ball first on the back of your hand. Then you bounce it up, turn your hand around, and catch it in your palm.

Hopscotch is a good game to play on the sidewalk. You can mark the diagram shown with chalk on cement. Or you can make a fine hopscotch game by marking the spaces with a pebble or stick on the damp sand of a beach. There are 10 spaces as shown on page 5.

H. Armstrong Roberts

These two friends are playing an exciting game of "Jack-stones" on the front step.

You stand in front of 1 and throw a Potsy into Box 1. This Potsy can be a small flat stone, or even a flattened bottle cap. Next, you hop on one foot into the box and kick the stone out of the space. This is called playing Onesy. You must not step on any of the lines at any time. You must not put your other foot down except in certain boxes.

Now throw the Potsy into Box 2, hop into Box 1, and then hop into both Box 2 and Box 3 at the same time. Do this by placing your left foot in Box 2 and your right foot in Box 3. Jump completely around, so that your left foot is in Box 3, and your right foot is in Box 2. You will now be facing Box 1. Get on one foot again, and kick the Potsy into Box 1, and then out of the lines.

Throw your Potsy into each box in turn, and then kick it out, in reverse order. Whenever a box is the full width of the diagram, you may not put down your other foot. When a box is half the width of the diagram, you may rest one foot in one box, and the other foot in the other box. But when you are kicking the Potsy out, you must hop on one foot until you have kicked it through each of the numbered boxes and out. When you reach Box 10, you may kick the Potsy out of the other end of the diagram, instead of kicking it back through each of the numbered boxes.

If you fail to throw the Potsy into the correct box, or if you should step on a line, you give up your turn to the next player. When your turn comes again, you begin with the number you missed.

As soon as you complete all the boxes, pick out a box which will belong to you. You write your initials in it. Now the other players may not step into your box at all. They must skip over it. But you

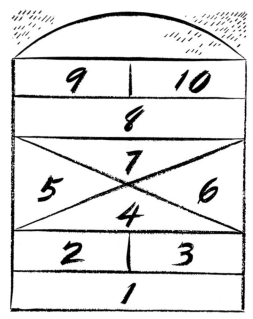

Hopscotch is a grand game which you can play on the sidewalk or the driveway.

can rest with both feet on the ground when you are in your own box. When all the boxes are filled with initials, the player who has the most boxes wins the game.

Teacher Ball. Two lines are made for this game. One, called the goal line, is about 20 feet ahead of the second line. All the players except one stand behind the second line. One player, the Teacher, stands a short distance away and throws the ball to the first player. If the player catches it and then throws it back, he is entitled to a reward. He says, "How many steps?" The Teacher then gives him as many "Baby Steps," "Lady Steps," or "Giant Steps" toward the goal line as he thinks the player deserves. He might say, for instance, "One Baby Step, two Lady Steps, and one Giant Step." The player then must say, "May I?" and the Teacher answers,

"Yes," before the player may take his steps. If he should forget to say any of these words, he loses his steps.

After a player makes a step with one foot, he brings his other foot up even with it. A Giant Step is the longest step a player can make. A Lady Step is a middle-sized step. A Baby Step is measured by placing the heel of one foot against the toe of the other foot. After a player takes his steps, he waits while the Teacher throws the ball to each player in turn, and gets back to him. The first player to reach the goal line wins the game and becomes the Teacher for the next game.

Steal Sticks. Draw two long lines across your play space, about 30 feet apart. The space between the lines is the battleground. The space behind each line belongs to the team guarding it. Some distance behind each line draw a

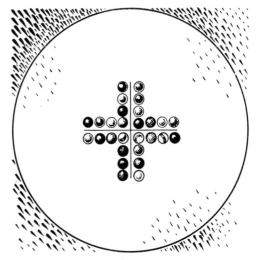

"Ringer" is an interesting marble game.

box about 5 feet by 10. Place 5 sticks in each box. Each team tries to steal the sticks from the other team's box.

As soon as a player crosses his own line into the battleground, he may be tagged by a player from the other team. He can run back behind his own line for safety, but, if he is tagged, he becomes a prisoner and must stand in his opponent's box with the sticks until he is rescued. He can be rescued only if one of his teammates runs over and tags him without himself being tagged. If he is tagged on the way, he also is made a prisoner.

The team that has no prisoners in the enemy's box and steals all five sticks first, wins the game.

Marbles. "Ringer" is one of the most popular of all marble games. Draw on the ground or on the sidewalk a circle about 10 feet across. At the center, draw two short lines crossing at right angles. Along these lines each player places an equal number of marbles. Each tosses or shoots a marble at a line. The player

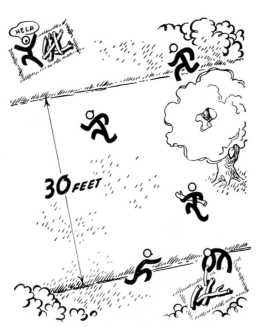

"Steal Sticks" calls for skill and speed.

"Baby in the Hole," a marble game

whose marble rolls nearest to the line is the first player. He chooses any spot on the edge of the ring, and aims his "shooter," a large, smooth marble, at the other marbles in the ring. Those he knocks out of the ring belong to him, and he keeps on shooting until he fails to knock out one or more marbles. At his first miss, he loses his turn. The game goes on until all the marbles have been knocked out of the ring and won. This is a more friendly game if the marbles are returned to their owners, than if you play for "keeps."

Another popular marble game is "Baby in the Hole." Dig a small hole in the ground and draw a line about 15 feet away. The players, in turn, toss three marbles toward the hole. The one whose marble comes nearest the mark will have the first chance to flip a "baby" into the hole. The next nearest plays next, and so on. The marbles are left where they fall. The first player, using four fingers of either hand, tries, with a flip of the wrist, to sweep one of the

marbles, or "babies," into the hole. If he does so, he wins the marble, and has another turn. As soon as he misses, the next player in line tries his luck. The game goes on until all the marbles are in the hole.

Sidewalk Tennis. Pick out four squares in a row on the sidewalk. They should all be the same size—about 4 feet square. Number them from 1 to 4.

One player stands at each end of the squares. The first server stands in front of the first square. He bounces a tennis ball in the first square, then strikes it with the palm of his hand. The ball must land in the third square. If it lands anywhere else, the opponent takes the ball and serves. The player to whom the ball is served stands back of the fourth square. As the ball bounces, he returns it, striking it with the palm of his hand. He must return it over the center line. If he fails to do this, the server scores one point. If the return is perfect, the ball, on the first bounce, is batted back

You only need a ball and a partner to play a fast game of sidewalk tennis.

Keystone

One of the healthiest of all games is rope skipping. What girl has not played "Pepper, Salt, Mustard, Cider" to the merry hum of a fast-twirling rope.

and forth over the center line until a player misses. If the server misses, he loses the ball to his opponent. Otherwise he scores a point on his opponent's miss. The first to score 21 points wins the game.

Sidewalk Checkers. Each of the two players uses twelve checkers. One set is red; the other, black. Pick a smooth 4-foot square on the sidewalk. Arrange the checkers, the red on one side, the black on the opposite side. The game starts as one of the players, Red, for example, snaps one of his checkers into the square with his index or middle finger. Black then shoots one of his, trying to knock the red man out of the square. The players take turns shooting. Each tries to knock his opponent's checkers out of the square.

It is not necessary to shoot all your checkers, one after another. If you have a checker in the square, you can shoot that checker at one of your opponent's.

If you happen to hit one of your own men, you merely waste your turn. The player who shoots all his opponent's men out of the square wins.

Skipping Rope. There are many ways of having fun with skipping ropes. Two jumpers can take turns seeing how many jumps they can make without tripping or missing. They can turn the rope, first, forward, then backward.

Turn the rope forward for five jumps, then backward for five jumps. Run forward five steps, turning the rope on each step. If there are five or six jumpers, two of them can turn the rope. One is the First Ender; the other, the Second Ender. When one of the jumpers misses, he takes the place of the First Ender, who then becomes a jumper, while the Second Ender becomes First Ender. The rope should be turned toward the jumper.

In "Lady, Lady, Turn Around" the jumper sings and suits the action to the words:

Lady, Lady, turn around,
Lady, Lady, touch the ground,
Lady, Lady, show your shoe,
Lady, twenty-three—skidoo.

At "Skidoo," he jumps out, and before the rope is turned around again, the next player jumps in and repeats the performance.

For "Follow the Leader," two players turn the rope. Another, chosen as the leader, jumps into it in any way he likes. The others follow in turn, each doing exactly what the leader did. The first to

8

fail takes one end of the rope and becomes the Second Ender.

In "Pepper, Salt, Mustard, Cider," the object is to keep jumping, up to the count of 100, as the rope is twirled faster and faster. The players keep time to the rope beats and sing:

Pepper, salt, mustard, cider, vinegar!
Ten, twenty, thirty, forty, fifty, sixty,
Seventy, eighty, ninety, one hundred!

The two players who miss on the lowest counts must take the ends of the rope.

"Calling In" is an exciting skipping-rope game. Each player, in turn, makes three jumps. Then he calls out the name of one of the others. The one called must jump in as the other jumps out, before the rope is turned again.

Tug of War. The players divide into two evenly matched teams. The members of each team hold opposite ends of a rope about 25 feet long. Each team tries to pull the other over a line drawn across the field. In the middle of the rope, a handkerchief is tied just above the line. When a signal is given, the tug of war begins. The team which first pulls the whole rope to its side of the line wins the game.

Duck on a Rock. Choose a large rock. Each player finds a smaller stone, or duck. Standing behind a line about 20 feet from the rock, each player, in turn, throws his duck, and tries to land it as near the rock as possible. The one whose duck lands farthest from the rock is IT. He places his duck on the rock and stands aside. The other players, standing 20 feet away, take turns. They throw their ducks and try to knock IT's duck from the rock. Each player, after throwing, must run out, pick up his duck, and try to get back to the goal before IT can tag him. The first to be tagged becomes IT for the next game.

If the duck is knocked off, IT must replace it before he can tag anyone. A player may not be tagged until he has picked up his duck. If caught in a tight place, he may stand with one foot on his duck and be safe until he has a better chance to run for home.

Shinny. Two leaders are chosen, and each, in turn, chooses his team from the other players. Goal lines are drawn about 75 feet apart. The game is played with a block of wood, called a puck, or with a tin can. Sticks shaped like a hockey stick, or the letter J, are used to strike the puck.

To start the game, a player from each side stands in the center of the field, facing the enemy's goal. The puck lies between them. At a signal, each player tries to put the puck in motion by hitting it toward the enemy's goal. The object of the game is to knock the puck across the enemy's goal line. Each goal counts a point. After each point, the puck is returned to the middle of the field.

Games with More Equipment

Some of the best games require more equipment than you can carry easily in your pockets. But most of the equipment for these games is easy to make.

Top Games. "In the Box" is an exciting top-spinning game to play with a friend. Get a flat box about the size of a suit box. With a ruler and crayon, draw three lines lengthwise and three lines across the inside top or bottom of the box. This will give you 16 oblong spaces. Number the spaces from 1 to 8, mixing up the numbers.

"In the Box" is a good top game.

Take turns spinning your tops in the box. When a top stops spinning, its point will be either on a line or in one of the marked spaces. If it is on a line, you have another turn. If it lies in one of the spaces, you score the same number of points as the number in the space. The player first scoring 100 points wins.

"Top-Tat-Toe" is a jolly top game that can be played on the sidewalk or on hard ground. Use a cord with a stick or a piece of chalk tied to one end. Draw a circle four inches across. Around this, from the center, draw five more circles. Lengthen the cord two inches for each one. You now have a target. Number the circles from 1 to 6, beginning at the outer one.

The first player spins his top and tries to make it land as near the center as he can. Wherever the point of the top comes to rest, he scores the number of points marked in the circle in which it stops.

The player then writes his initials in the circle. No other player can get any points for landing his top in that circle. Each player spins in turn whether he makes any points or not. The game continues until all the circles have been initialed. The player who then has the most points wins.

Ringtoss. Two or more can play this game. You can buy it, but you will have more fun making one for yourself.

Take a piece of clothesline a yard long. Then cut it into three strips, each 12 inches long. Bend each strip in the form of a circle, and place the ends together. Where the ends meet, wind adhesive tape over them to hold them together. These are the "rings."

You can use three clothespins for pegs. Punch holes in the top of a flat cardboard box and push the heads of the pins through. To hold the pegs in place, paste a few strips of adhesive tape across the heads of the clothespins on the under side of the box.

Write the number 5 on the box cover in front of the middle clothespin, and

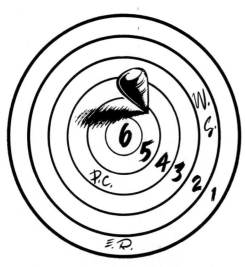

Playing "Top-Tat-Toe" with a top

Taking turns in playing "Ringtoss" with homemade equipment

the number 3 in front of the other two.

Stand about eight feet away from the pegs and toss three rings, one after another. Try to ring one of the pegs, or "make a ringer." You score five points if you ring the middle peg, and three for ringing one of the others.

After you have tossed three rings, the next player takes his turn. The game can be made 50 points. In the chapter, "Making Toys and Playthings," you will find directions for making an amusing ringtoss peg and wooden rings.

Tenpins sets usually have three balls and ten wooden "pins" shaped like bot-

tles. But if you take two clothespins and slip one into another in the form of an X, they will stand by themselves and make excellent "pins." Arrange ten of these double clothespins on the floor in the shape of a triangle, as shown in the diagram.

Stand about 10 feet away and roll a ball at the tenpins. Aim for the one in the middle. Your turn ends when you have rolled three balls, or the same ball three times. Any pins that have been knocked down are then set up for the next player. You score as many points as the number of pins you knock down

How you can use clothespins to play an exciting game of "Ten Pins"

The beanbag game develops accuracy.

with the three balls. For example, if you knock down 5 pins, you score 5 points. When each player has had ten turns, the one with the high score wins.

A small wooden ball, an old golf ball, or even a rubber ball may be used. It should always be rolled—never thrown or bounced.

Beanbag Game. The chapter, "Sewing for Fun," shows how to make beanbags. It is more fun to play the game if you have two or three beanbags, but it can be played with one.

For a score box, use a hatbox or a cardboard box. Turn the box upside down. Cut three round holes in it, as shown. For the first, use a teacup as a guide; for the second, a saucer; and for the third, a small plate. Number the holes 1, 3, and 5, beginning with the largest.

Place a cushion or book under the back of the box so that it slopes toward you. Stand 8 feet away and toss three beanbags at the box. Try to toss them into the holes. You get one point for sinking a bag into the first hole; three for the middle hole; and five for the smallest. Each player, in turn, has three throws. Keep on playing until someone

reaches a total score of fifty points.

The chapter, "Making Toys and Playthings" shows how to make a Humpty Dumpty beanbag board with one hole.

Fish Pond is a good game you can buy or easily make. All you need is a shallow cardboard box about 2 inches high, a sheet of cardboard, scissors, crayon, string, a few pins or hairpins, and short sticks.

Draw a side view of a fish, about 3 inches long, on cardboard. Cut it out, and use it as a pattern to make 20 cardboard fish. Punch a hole in the nose of each fish. Also write a number, from 1 to 10, on the tail of each fish. Then mix them up. Cut slits an inch long in the top of the box. Place the fish in the slits, tail first, so that only their heads stick out.

Bend a pin or a hairpin into the shape of a hook and attach it to the end of a short pole by a string about 2 feet long.

Each player gets a chance to hook a fish. When all the fish have been

This "Fish-Pond" game will give you a chance to hook all the fish you can.

National Recreation Assoc.

Equipment for playing table tennis will furnish hours of real fun and pleasure.

caught, the score is added up. Each player scores the number of points shown on the tails of the fish. For example, if he hooks a fish with number 4 on the tail and one with number 6, he wins 10 points.

Ping-Pong or Table Tennis. You can play ping-pong on any large table. A regular ping-pong table is 9 feet long and 5 feet wide. Some tables can be enlarged by making an extra top of wallboard. You will need balls, net, paddles, and table top. But you can make this equipment, except for the balls. The net, about 6 inches high, is stretched across the middle of the table. The players, either one or two on each side, take their places at the ends. When four are playing, the partners take turns serving.

To serve, you hit the ball so that it first bounces on your side of the net, then clears the net, and bounces on the other side. The receiver, to whom you serve the ball, must strike it with his paddle on the first bounce and send it back over the net. The server or his partner then tries to return it on the first bounce.

If the receiver fails to hit the ball on the first bounce or to send it over the net, or if he bats it off the table, the server scores one point. If the server misses the ball on the return, or hits it into the net or off the table, the point goes to the opponent. The ball is batted back and forth over the net until someone misses. The server serves the ball five times, once after every point is won or lost. Then the receiver serves five times. If the ball touches the net as it is served, it must be served again. During the play, however, if it lands correctly, even if it touches the net, it is good.

The side first scoring 21 points wins.

With the score tied 20 to 20, a side must score two points in succession to win.

Table Croquet is played in the same way as lawn croquet. But it is played on a large table with checkers for balls. You snap the checkers with your finger. Rules for playing croquet are given in the chapter, "Making the Most of Your Home."

You can make wickets by bending pieces of picture wire and pushing the ends into corks or empty spools. Pegs can be made by gluing five checkers together. Paint your checkers different colors, and use one color for each player.

Start the game by placing your checker half way between the peg and the first wicket. Then you snap your finger against the side of your checker and try to shoot it through the first two wickets. Snap the checkers through the remaining wickets, following the same order as in lawn croquet.

Card and Table Games

Checkers, dominoes, jackstraws, and many simple card games will furnish entertainment indoors for rainy days or winter evenings. In some of these as many as ten players may take part.

Anagrams is an interesting game for from two to ten players. It is played with small squares of wood or cardboard. Each square has a letter of the alphabet on one side. The squares are placed, face down, in the center of a table.

The first player draws four squares and turns them letter side up in front of him. If he can spell a word of at least three letters with them, he does so. He then draws again. If he can add this letter to his word, he draws again. He keeps on drawing until he cannot use the letter in his word. Then he places the square, face up, in the center of the table. The next player draws four squares. He can use these, together with the letter the first player has discarded, to make a word. He can draw as long as he can use the letters. Then he discards in the center. The players can use any of the discarded letters.

Any player may steal a word from another by adding one of his own letters to it. A word cannot be stolen, however, merely by changing it from singular to plural, for example, by adding S to MAST. But, with a P, a player can

WICKET 7
HALFWAY PEG
WICKET 6
WICKET 8
WICKET 5
WICKET 4
WICKET 9
WICKET 3
WICKET 2
WICKET 1
STARTING PEG

Table croquet can be an exciting game.

"Checkers," or "Draughts," is easy to learn. It has been played for hundreds of years.

Frederic Lewis

change MAST to STAMP and take the other player's word.

A player can change or string out any of his own words by adding S or any other letter or letters from the center. But he can steal a word only with the turned-down letter he has drawn.

You can make a rule that a player loses his turn if he takes more than one minute to make a word. The first player to make and keep ten words wins.

Old Maid. From a deck of playing cards take out all the queens, except the queen of spades. If there are more than seven players, use two decks. Deal the cards one at a time. It makes no difference if one or two players hold more cards than the others.

The players then sort out any pairs they may hold, and throw them in the middle of the table.

Now the picking starts. The player to the left of the dealer spreads his cards face down and the dealer selects one of them. If the card he draws makes a pair with one he holds, he discards the pair. The player to his left then draws a card from the hand of the next player, and so on around the table. The object of the game is to get rid of your cards. The first to do so drops out of the game and is the winner. The others keep on playing.

One player will be stuck with the queen of spades, or the Old Maid. Since it cannot be matched, one unfortunate player will be left with it at the end. He is the loser. Each player at every draw must discard his pair, if he has one, even if in doing so only the Old Maid remains.

Pitch, or High Low Jack. From two to seven players may take a hand in this game. Six cards are dealt to each. The remaining cards are left in the deck. The player to the left of the dealer sizes up his hand. Then he makes a bid, or declares the number of points he thinks he can make. He cannot make more than four. But he can "pass," which means to bid nothing; or he can bid any number up to four. If he bids four, no other player can bid higher, but if he makes a lower bid, the player to his left may bid higher, and so on around the table.

The player making the high bid leads, or "pitches." He lays a card face up on the table. All cards of the same kind, or suit, are trumps. That is, if he lays down a heart, hearts are trump cards. The other players in turn follow suit if they have any trumps. If not, they play a low card.

The one who plays the highest card takes the trick, or all the cards on the table. Then he leads a card which he hopes will take the next trick.

The other players follow suit or play a trump if they have one. Otherwise, they play any of their cards, usually a low one. If no trumps are played, the highest card of the suit led takes the trick. But if the trick is trumped, it goes to the player who put on the highest trump.

In scoring points, the highest trump card played counts one. The jack of trumps counts one, as does the lowest trump card played. Another point is added for "game." This is scored by the player having the highest total in cards. In counting "game," only the face cards and the tens have any value. Aces count 4; kings, 3; queens, 2; jacks, 1; and tens, 10 points.

If you are dealt a hand in which you find the ace, king, jack, and two of any suit, you can safely bid four.

But as not all the cards are dealt, any card can be "high," and sometimes both "high" and "low." The point for "low" goes to the player holding that card, and not to the one who has taken it in a trick. The game can be seven or eleven points. The jack, if high, counts two, but it is not always in the play. If two players tie for "game," the point is not scored.

Authors. If you do not have a game of Authors, you can easily make one by using index cards. These you can buy at a paper supply or dime store. Cut the cards down evenly so that each will be 2½ inches wide and 3½ inches long. You will need 52 cards.

Select a list of thirteen of your favorite authors and write the names of four books by each. Divide the cards into sets of four. In the upper right-hand corner of each card of the same set, print a letter of the alphabet.

Near the top of each card of a set, print in big letters the name of one of the authors. Print the name of one of his books above this. Below the author's name, print names of three other books by the same author. At the top of the second card of the set print the name of the author's second book, and the names of the other three at the bottom. Do the same with the third and fourth cards, having the name of a different book at the top of each. Prepare the other twelve sets in the same way.

The dealer then shuffles the cards and deals them, one at a time, as far as they will go. The game can be played by three players, but it is more fun when there are five or six. It does not matter if one player gets an extra card.

The object of the game is to complete as many "books" as possible. A book is one of the sets of four.

The player to the left of the dealer may have from one to four cards of the same set. If he has four, he shows them and places the "book" on the table in front of him. But whether he has or not, he may ask a certain player for a card which will complete or help him to complete a book.

If he happens to hold the *Tom Sawyer* card by Mark Twain, he may ask for *Huckleberry Finn*, *The Innocents Abroad*, or *The Mysterious Stranger*.

If the player he asks has the card wanted, he must give it to the asker, who may keep on asking for certain cards until he fails to get the card for which he asks. Then the player to his left takes his turn.

The game can be played also with a deck of playing cards. A book would be any four of a kind, such as aces, kings, tens, and so on.

Dominoes may be played by two, three, or four persons. The dominoes are spread, face down, on the table and shuffled. If there are two players, each picks seven dominoes. If three or four persons are playing, each takes five dominoes. Stand the dominoes on edge in front of you so the white dots cannot be seen by the other players. The leftover dominoes are kept together in a "bone pile" conveniently placed on the table.

Each domino has two groups of dots, divided by a line. You use either side in play. The object of the game is to get rid of your dominoes.

The player holding the highest double, with dots the same on both sides, lays it, face up, in the center of the table. Suppose it is a double 6. The player to his left must match it with a domino having six dots on one side. Perhaps he has a 6 combined with a 4. If so, he places his domino, face up, with the 6 against the first player's domino. The next player can add to either domino, so he must have either a 6 or a 4. If he does not, he must draw from the bone pile until he gets a domino with 6 or 4 dots on one side. If he lays down a domino with a 6 at one end and a 3 at the other, the next player must match either the 4 or the 3. The doubles are laid crosswise, but the others are laid end to end. Any player may try to block the others by making both ends of the row the same number. This gives the next player only one choice, and often sends him to the bone pile.

The player who first plays all his dominoes is the winner. He gets as many points as there are dots on the dominoes

Ewing Galloway

What better game for two or more persons to play on a rainy day than a game of dominoes!

still held by the other players. You can play for 50 or 100 points.

Five-in-a-Row, like checkers, is a game for two persons. It can be played on a checkerboard, but a board divided into 100 squares is better. You can make one of these boards out of plywood or cardboard. Divide each side into ten equal parts, and with your ruler draw lines both ways from one side to the other. You can use buttons of two different colors for "men."

The object of the game is to place five of your men on the board in a row. The row may be crosswise, lengthwise, or on a diagonal. You may use as many men as you wish and you can place them on any squares on the board. But you can only place one man on the board at each turn. You use your men to block the other player's rows, as well as to form your own "Five-in-a-Row." For more "Checkerboard Fun," turn to the chapter, "Games for Travel."

Chinese Checkers is played on a board shaped like a six-pointed star. The board is divided into triangles by lines running straight across and diagonally. At the corner of each triangle there is a hollow. Marbles of different colors are used instead of checkers. Each player has ten marbles, all the same color.

At the beginning of the game, you place your marbles in the first ten holes in the point of the star in front of you. Your opponent does the same. To win the game, you must get all ten of your marbles into your opponent's starting holes before he gets his into yours.

You take turns moving one of your marbles one hole at a time, following the lines on the board. A move may be made in any direction, but only into an empty hole. But if the hole on the other

Six players, each with ten marbles, can play the game of "Chinese Checkers."

side of an occupied hole is empty, you may "jump" your marble into it, as you jump in playing checkers. But the marble jumped remains on the board.

As many as six persons can play Chinese checkers, each trying to get his marbles into the point of the star opposite him.

Tiddlywinks. Each player is given four tiny disks and a larger disk, all the same color. Buttons may be used for disks if you have nothing better. Make a starting line on the floor about five feet from a small cup. Then each player, in turn, tries to jump one of his smaller disks into the cup. This is done by pressing on the edge of a small disk with the larger one. A player snapping one of his tiddlywinks into the cup has an extra turn. The first player to get all four disks in the cup wins the game.

If a tiddlywink lands on top of one of

another color, the lower one may be taken out and placed beside the one that is on top. If a disk lands on one of the same color, the player must snap it out as best he can.

Jackstraws. You can buy jackstraws, but it is interesting to make your own. Take fifty wooden toothpicks. Dye some of them red, others yellow, others blue or green, and leave some white. For a hook, bend a hairpin into the shape of the letter J. Put the straight end of it into the eraser at the end of a pencil, for a handle. In some straw games, the straws may be shaped like guns, spears, or axes. Each has a different value in scoring. Your red toothpicks could count 5; your blue, 3; the green or yellow, 2; and the white, 1. Set your own values.

The straws are dumped in a bunch on

H. Armstrong Roberts

the table. The players take turns trying to remove one of the straws with the hook, without moving any of the others. The player who succeeds in doing so gets another turn. When the last straw has been hooked, the player whose straws count the most wins the game.

Hearts. Any number of players, from two to seven, may play this game with one deck of cards. The object of the game is to get rid of your hearts or to avoid taking any trick on which hearts have been played. The player taking in the fewest heart cards wins. However, if one player can capture all the hearts, he wins.

The cards are dealt out evenly. Any cards left over are laid face down in the center of the table. These, called the "widow," go to the player taking the first trick.

The player to the left of the dealer starts the game, or "leads." If he is cautious, he will usually play a low card, as there may be some hearts in the widow.

Other players must follow with a card of the same suit if possible. The high card of that suit takes the trick. If a player has no card of the suit led, he can play any card. Usually, he will get rid of a heart or another high card that would be likely to take a trick. The player taking the trick leads again, and keeps on leading until someone else takes a trick. The play goes on until all the cards have been played. Sometimes the queen of spades, known as the Black Betty, is made to count as 13 hearts.

Lotto. Each player is given a card with 15 numbers on it, and each card has a

This little girl has challenged Grandmother to play a game of "Jackstraws."

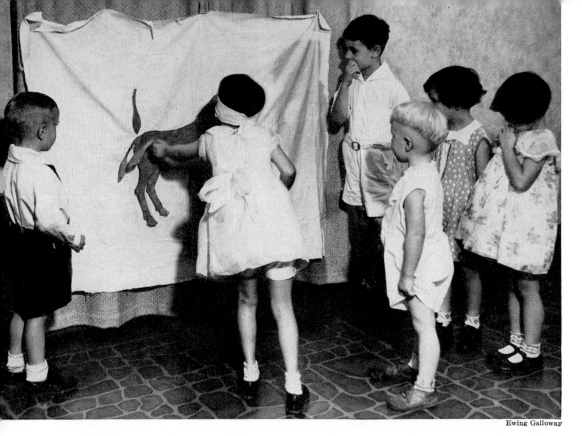

Ewing Galloway

"Pinning the Tail on the Donkey" has brought gay laughter to many a happy party.

different group of numbers. Each player also gets a set of blank disks. One player, known as the Caller, has a set of numbered disks. These are placed, face down, on a table.

When the players are ready, the Caller picks up one of the numbered disks, reads it, and calls out its number. The player having that number on his card covers the number with one of his blank disks. The Caller keeps turning up numbered disks and calling their numbers until one of the players has covered all the spaces on his card. The first to do so calls out "Lotto," and is the winner. "Bingo" is also played in this way.

Party or Group Games

When you go to a party or invite your friends to one, you expect to play games. Everyone can take part, and by the time you have played two or three games, you will be having a good time.

Button, Button, Who's Got the Button? The players sit in a circle, with the one who is IT in the center. Each player in the circle holds his hands with the palms together and the fingers pointing out. One of them holds a button between his hands.

He starts passing the button by slipping his two hands between the hands of the next player, and dropping the button into his neighbor's hands. Or he can pretend to drop the button if he likes. The next player, if he has the button, or pretends to have it, does the same, and so on, around the circle. IT tries to guess who has the button. If he guesses right, the one caught with the button takes his place.

Passing the Ring is played in the same

way as "Button, Button, Who's Got the Button?" except that a ring is passed instead of a button.

Any ring will do. Slide it onto a long piece of string and tie the ends of the string together.

The players form a circle, holding the string. One player covers the ring with one hand and slides it or pretends to slide it to the next one. IT, standing in the center, tries to guess who has the ring. If he guesses correctly, the player who has the ring becomes IT.

Pinning the Tail on the Donkey is always a favorite game at parties. Take a sheet of wrapping paper and draw on it a picture of a large donkey without a tail. Then attach the picture to the wall with pins, thumb tacks, or adhesive tape. Cut out as many paper tails as there are players, and run a pin through each tail.

Each player is blindfolded, in turn, and given a tail. He is then turned around three times to make him a little dizzy before he tries to pin the tail on the donkey.

By the time all the players have had their turns, there may be tails on the donkey's nose or ears, and others on the wall. The player who pins the tail nearest its proper place wins the game.

Pussycat's Whiskers is a variation of the donkey game. Draw a picture of a pussycat on wrapping paper, with a small circle for the head and a larger circle for the body. Make the eyes, nose, and mouth with crayons, but do not draw whiskers. Attach the pussycat to the wall. Blindfold and turn each player as in the donkey game. Give each a crayon of a different color. The one who can draw the whiskers nearest their proper place wins.

Putting the whiskers on the cat is like pinning the tail on the donkey.

Animal Calling. All you need for this game is a deck of cards. The players sit around a table. Each decides what animal he wants to be in the game. One player may choose to be a dog, another a cat, or another a kangaroo. Each must be a different animal and tell everyone else what he is.

Deal out all the cards as equally as possible. Everyone keeps his pile of cards, face downward, in front of him. The first player starts by turning up his top card and laying it, face up, in front of his pile. The player to his left turns his top card, face up, and so on, each player taking his turn. The excitement comes when one player turns up a card that matches the upturned card of another player. Then they both try to remember each other's animal name. The first one who calls it out wins all the other player's upturned cards.

All players, when they turn up their cards, must turn the cards AWAY from them. Otherwise, they could see their cards before the other players could. If a player loses all his cards, he is out of the game. The games goes on until one player, the winner, has all the cards.

Charades is a wonderful party game. Each player takes a turn in acting out a word or a sentence without making any sounds. He may announce the number of syllables there are in the word, or the number of words in the sentence. But he may not shape the syllables or words with his mouth. Only motions and gestures are allowed.

The players are divided equally into two teams. Suppose there are five players on each team. The players on Team 1 write five different words on as many slips of paper. These are kept secret from the members of Team 2. The players on Team 2 do likewise.

One of the players on Team 2 is now handed one of the slips of paper prepared by Team 1. He glances at it, but may not show it to his teammates. He is given four minutes in which to act out his word or sentence. His teammates try to guess what it is that he is trying to tell them. If they guess correctly within four minutes, they score five points. The members of Team 1 know the answer, so wrong guesses of the other side, and the antics of the player trying to act out the word, are amusing. After the time is up, or the right answer is given, Team 2 hands a slip of paper to a player on Team 1. He must then act out the word or sentence on it. The team guessing the most words wins the game.

Try acting out such words as infancy, in-fan-sea; decorate, deck-oar-ate; and handkerchief, hand-cur-chief. You will want to think of many new ones. Sentences used in Charades are often prov-erbs, such as: "A stitch in time saves nine;" "Make hay while the sun shines;" "Curiosity killed the cat;" "A barking dog never bites." Advertising slogans are also often used.

Twenty Questions is a guessing game you can play with any number of persons. One player writes the name of a person, an animal, or an object on a slip of paper. He lets no one see or know what he has written. It must, however, be something or someone that is well known. One of the other players tries to guess what or who it is. He is allowed only twenty questions. The questions can be answered only by "Yes" or "No," or "I don't know." If he guesses correctly before using his twenty questions, he can choose a word for another player to guess. If there are several players, each may ask a question in turn. The first to give the correct answer wins.

Your chance of winning will be better if you begin by asking some general question, such as "Does it belong to the animal kingdom?" or "Is it a person?" Or, if a person, "Is he or she alive?"

Hide the Thimble. Count out to see who shall be IT. While the others hide a thimble or any other small object, IT leaves the room. The thimble should not be hidden inside or under anything. When it is hidden, IT is called back and given a chance to find the thimble. The other players sit in a circle. When IT comes close to the hiding place, the others call out "Warm." If he comes closer, he is "Warmer," and, if still closer, "Hot." But, if IT is far from the hidden object, he is "Cold," "Colder," or "Freezing." As soon as IT finds the object, he may join the circle. Then another player takes his place.

The game may be varied if someone

sits at the piano and plays loudly for "Hot," and softly for "Cold."

Forfeits. Before starting to play this game, write a number of stunts on separate slips of paper, some for boys to do, and some for girls. Fold the papers and place those for the boys in one bowl, those for the girls in another.

Now choose a Leader and a Judge. The Judge is blindfolded. Then the Leader collects from each of the other players a penny, a ring, a handkerchief, or something else. These are the forfeits. The girls' forfeits are placed in one bowl or tray, and the boys' in another. The Leader then picks up one of the forfeits from either tray. He holds it over the head of the Judge, who is seated, and says:

> "Heavy, heavy hangs over your head.
> What shall be done to redeem it?"

The Judge asks, "Fine or superfine?"

If it is a boy's forfeit, the answer is "Fine;" if a girl's, "Superfine."

The owner of the forfeit must now get it back, or redeem it. He can do so only by obeying the Judge's order.

The Judge draws one of the slips of paper from the boys' tray if "Fine;" from the girls' if "Superfine." The Leader opens the paper and reads it.

The player whose forfeit has been drawn then redeems it. Here are a few suggested stunts that may amuse you:

Lap up a saucer of milk without using your hands.

Push a penny across the table with your nose.

Hop back and forth across the room, holding one toe in your hand.

Eat a cracker, and before swallowing the last of it, whistle "Yankee Doodle."

Show how a horse gallops, trots, and runs.

Pretend you are a dog burying a bone.

Drink milk out of a baby bottle with a nipple on it.

Dance a jig while singing a lullaby.

Place a handkerchief on the floor and pick it up with your teeth.

Musical Chairs, also called "Going to Jerusalem," is always an exciting game for a party.

Line up a row of chairs in the middle of the room. There should be one less chair than players. If there are ten playing, line up nine chairs. Place each chair facing in the opposite direction from the ones next to it. To the music of a piano or a phonograph, the players march in single file around the chairs. When the music stops, as it may at any moment, each player scrambles for a chair. One

A rollicking game of musical chairs will bring any party to life.

will be left out. He leaves the game. Then one of the remaining chairs is removed, and the music starts again. The last one to remain in the game wins.

No one going to Jerusalem may stop, or touch a chair, until the music stops. Neither may he turn a chair around or pull it out from under someone else.

Egg and Spoon Race. In this race, you and your partner first race against another team. Stand behind a line at one end of the room, while your partner stands behind a line at the other end. Place the handle of a teaspoon between your teeth and put a hard-boiled egg in the spoon. Your partner holds a teaspoon in the same way, but with no egg in it.

When the signal is given, you run across the room to your partner, and without either of you using your hands, transfer the egg into your partner's spoon. Your partner then runs to the line from which you started. If the egg falls out of the spoon, the player carrying it must pick it up without using his hands.

After the first two teams finish, two more teams race against each other, then another pair, until all the teams have had a turn. The winners of each race are then paired off, and so on until the finals, when one team becomes the champion.

Peanut Race. Place four peanuts in a row in front of each player. The first peanut is placed three feet beyond the starting line, and the others three feet apart.

Each of the players is given a dull knife. At the starting signal, each player must run forward and pick up a peanut with his knife. Then, balancing it on the knife blade, he must run back and drop the peanut behind the line. Each does the same with the second, third, and fourth peanut. The first player to finish wins.

No one may touch any of the peanuts with his hands or with anything except the knife. He may not push the peanut against the wall or any piece of furniture to get it on the knife.

Memory Test. Lay about ten familiar objects on a table or tray. Cover them with a towel. Select such things as a teaspoon, a penny, a button, a thimble, a pair of scissors, an eraser, or a safety pin. Be sure to select ordinary things.

Give each of your guests a pencil and paper, and have each write his name at the top. Now, take the towel from the objects and leave them uncovered for four minutes.

At the end of that time, they are again covered. Each player is asked to write the names of the objects he can remember having seen. Five minutes are allowed for this. The one who has the longest correct list is the winner.

Running Games

Running games not only are great fun, but also wonderful exercise. Some of these games can be played in winter as well as in summer.

Run, Sheep, Run. The players are divided evenly into two teams. Members of one team are called the Sheep; of the other, the Hunters. Each team chooses a captain.

You select a home base. Then all the sheep, except the captain, seek hiding places. The captain goes out with his team and sees that all are hidden. Then he returns to home base and joins the Hunters, who go out looking for the Sheep. When the captain of the Sheep thinks that his flock can get back to home base without being caught, he shouts: "Run, sheep, run." The Sheep come out from hiding and make a dash for home. The Hunters also race for home. Whichever side gets all its players to home base first, plays the Sheep next.

Pom Pom Pullaway. Draw two long lines at least thirty feet apart. The player who is IT stands midway between the lines. The other players stand along one of the lines, ready to run.

The signal comes when IT calls:

"Pom pom pullaway! If you don't come, I'll pull you away."

Now the others must cross the space between the lines and try to reach the other side without being tagged by IT. Whoever is tagged first, joins IT in the tagging. The game continues, the players racing back and forth, until all are caught. The last to be caught wins the game. The first one caught becomes IT in the next game.

Hide and Seek. In this game, a tree is usually selected for HOME. The player who is IT stands there and closes his eyes. Then he counts loudly up to 100. While he is counting, the other players hide.

When IT has finished counting, he calls, "All around my base are IT. One—two—three." Then he tries to find the hiders. As soon as he sees one, he calls him by name, and says, "I spy Johnny" or the name of the one he sees.

At that signal, the two race for Home. If the hider gets there first, he shouts, "Home free!" That means that he is safe and will not have to be IT in the next game. But if IT reaches the goal first, the hider is the next to be IT, unless he is freed or unless IT is unable to find all the hiders. If he can do that,

he must quickly call, "All outs in free."

After finding the first hider, IT goes out again, and keeps on searching until he has found or freed all the players. Any hider, after the first, who reaches goal ahead of IT, may free one or more of the hiders who have been caught. He can call, "I free Johnny," "I free Mary," and so on, naming as many of the hiders as he wishes. If he frees all the hiders, the one who was IT must be IT again. The first one caught is IT in the next game.

Prisoner's Base. The players are divided equally into two teams, with a captain for each. Draw two lines about 30 feet apart. Behind each line draw a box 5 feet wide and 10 feet long. These are the prisons. The space between the lines is the battleground.

The game begins when the captain of one team sends a player to the middle of the battleground to dare, or challenge, the other team. At this, the captain of the other team sends out one of his men to tag the challenger. The challenger then starts to run back home. If he is tagged before he reaches home, he becomes a prisoner, and must stand in the box behind the enemy line.

While one player is being chased, his captain may send out another man to tag the chaser. In this way, someone is always chasing someone else. But a player may only tag an enemy player who has run out into the field before him. As soon as a player has tagged an enemy, he may not be tagged until he has touched home base and run out into the field again. Besides capturing prisoners in this game, each side tries to rescue its prisoners from the enemy. If a teammate manages to cross the battleground without being tagged, and touches a prisoner, both may return home without being chased.

A prisoner is required to keep only one foot in the box. When there are several prisoners, only one may keep his foot in the box. He and the others may clasp hands and form a chain reaching out closer to their base. Only one prisoner may be rescued at a time. The game continues until all the players on one team are in prison.

Hare and Hounds is sometimes called a paper chase. The players are divided into two teams. One team is made up of Hares, the other of Hounds.

Each Hare carries a bag filled with scraps of paper. The Hares are given a five-minute head start, but they drop bits of paper as they go. In this way they leave a trail for the Hounds to follow. But they can make false and dead-end trails to deceive the Hounds.

When the Hares have been out for fifteen minutes, they start back for a secret goal which is unknown to the Hounds. This is usually near the starting point. If they can reach the goal before any one is tagged by the Hounds, they win the game.

Tom Tidler's Ground is another tag game. Draw a long line to mark the boundary of Tom's ground. The player who is IT is Tom Tidler and stands beyond this line. The other players stand behind it. The fun starts when they run across the line and sing: "Here I am on Tom Tidler's ground, picking up gold and silver!"

While they are on Tom's ground, he tries to tag them. Those who can run back to their own side are safe. The first one tagged must take Tom's place.

Blindman's Buff. One player is blindfolded and turned around several times so he does not know which way he is facing. The other players scatter. The "Blind Man" then tries to catch one of the players and guess who he is.

Any player may go close to the Blind Man and tease him by shouting in his ear and ducking out of reach. But when this happens, the Blind Man may call out, "One, two, three—stop."

At that signal, all the players must stand still until one of them is caught. If the Blind Man can tell who the player is, the handkerchief is removed from his eyes, and the player caught becomes the Blind Man. Otherwise, the Blind Man is turned around again and the players scatter as before.

Tag. There are several ways of playing Tag. In the simplest game, one player, chosen as IT, chases the others and tries to tag one of them. Whoever he tags becomes IT in his place.

Cross Tag. If a player runs between IT and a player who is being chased, he in turn is chased. He can get out of danger only when another player crosses between him and his pursuer.

Squat Tag. The player who is IT tries to tag one of the other players as in the simple game. But any player in danger of being tagged may squat down so that he is sitting on his heels. In this position he is safe. But the moment he gets up, he may be tagged.

Nose and Toe Tag. A player is safe from being tagged in this game only when he is holding his nose with one hand and one of his feet with the other hand.

Shadow Tag is a game for a sunny day. A player is safe so long as he stands in a shadow cast by one of the other players, a building, or a tree.

Grass Tag should be played on

ground where there are only small patches of grass. A player is safe while standing on the grass.

Japanese Tag starts out in the usual way. The first player to take IT's place must, while chasing the others, keep one hand on the spot where he was tagged. The next player to be tagged does the same, and so on, to the end of the game.

Fox and Geese is sometimes called *Wheel Tag*, because the players make the shape of a wheel on the ground. The game is often played in the snow or on the damp sand of a beach.

A circle about four feet wide is marked on the ground. From the center of this circle paths are made, cutting it at six points, like the spokes of a wheel. The paths should be at least three feet wide and ten feet long. A circular path is drawn around the ends of these paths. This also is three feet wide.

One player, chosen to be the Fox, stands in the small circle in the center of the wheel, or the goal. The other

"Fox and Geese," an old favorite

players, the Geese, take places along the outer path. The Fox now tries to catch one of them. He runs out along one of the straight paths or spokes. On reaching the circular path, he may follow the Geese around on that, or along any of the other paths into which they may dodge. Neither Fox nor Geese may step outside any of the paths. The Geese, however, may jump across any space from one path to another.

Any Goose who stands inside the smaller circle or the goal is safe and may not be tagged. Only one Goose may be there at one time. If another Goose comes running into it, the first Goose must leave the goal immediately or change places with the Fox. Otherwise, the first player to be tagged becomes the Fox.

Bull in the Ring. Select a spot or a tree to be Home. About 30 yards away, the players form a circle by holding hands. One of the players, chosen as the Bull, stands inside the circle. He must now break his way out. He is not allowed, however, to duck under the other players' hands.

After he has broken through, he runs for Home, while the others chase and try to catch him. Whoever catches him before he reaches Home becomes the Bull. If he is not caught, he plays the Bull again.

Cat and Mouse. All but two players stand in a circle, holding hands. One player is chosen as Cat, another as Mouse. Mouse stands inside the circle, Cat outside. Cat tries to catch Mouse. Both may run in and out of the circle. The players try to help Mouse by raising their arms to let him in or out. They try to hinder Cat by blocking him with their arms. But they must keep their hands clasped whether aiding Mouse or blocking Cat. If Cat catches Mouse, he becomes Mouse for the next round. Cat then joins the circle and a new Cat is chosen.

Drop the Handkerchief is also called A *tisket, a tasket*. One player is chosen to be IT and to drop the handkerchief. The others stand in a circle, facing the center, but not holding hands. They must not look around as IT walks around the circle behind the backs of the players. IT holds a handkerchief, and as he walks, he sings:

> "A tisket, a tasket, a green and yellow basket;
> I wrote a letter to my love,
> And on the way I dropped it, I dropped it.
> And one of you has picked it up
> And put it in his pocket, pocket.
> It isn't you . . . It isn't you . . ."

He repeats the last line several times as he passes players. Then he drops the handkerchief behind one of the players, and calls, "It's you!" IT now runs around the circle in the same direction that he has been walking. The player at whose heels the handkerchief has been dropped turns around, picks up the handkerchief, and tries to catch IT.

If IT can reach the place left vacant by the player who is chasing him before the other tags him, he takes that player's place in the circle, and the one with the handkerchief becomes IT. But if he is tagged before getting around, he must be IT again. This game is often played without the song.

Garden Scamp. One player is chosen to be the Gardener, and another, the Scamp. The rest of the players form a circle, holding hands. The space inside the circle is the Garden. The Scamp stands in the Garden, while the Gardener stands outside.

The Gardener calls to the Scamp, "Who let you in my garden?" "No one," the Scamp replies.

The Gardener now chases the Scamp in and out of the circle. But while chasing the Scamp, he must imitate everything that the Scamp does. If the Scamp crawls on hands and knees, or hops on one leg, the Gardener must do likewise.

If the Gardener fails to catch the Scamp within a certain length of time, say five minutes, he takes his place in the circle and the Scamp chooses another Gardener. If the Gardener catches the Scamp, he becomes the Scamp and names another Gardener.

Follow the Leader. The players form in line behind the Leader and follow him as he starts to walk or run. Now they must imitate everything the Leader does, no matter how hard or how silly it may be. If the Leader flaps his arms as if he were a bird, his followers must do the same. The Leader may turn a somersault, or jump over a stone, or pretend to be playing a violin. Any player who fails to do exactly what the Leader does, is dropped from the game. The players may take turns acting as Leader.

Treasure Hunt. A treasure is hidden. It may be something funny, or something which all the players can share, like a box of candy. Clues are written on slips of paper and put in various places leading to the treasure.

The players are given the first clue. This clue leads them to the second. That clue will lead them to the third, and so on, to the treasure. The "hunters" must always put the clue back so the next players can find it.

For example, the first clue might read, "Go to the tree at the end of the lane, then look to the right." The second clue should be placed where the treasure-seekers can find it by following the directions.

A treasure hunt may be planned so that each player is out for himself. But often the players are divided into teams. Each team races to be the first to find the treasure.

Races

Backward Race. Decide on a starting line and a finish line. The racers must walk, run, or skip backwards to the finish line. They may not turn around to see where they are going. If you think this is easy, just try it.

Bear Race. You run this race on all fours. That is, on hands and feet. Your knees must not touch the ground during the race.

Walking Race. In this race, the walkers may not have both feet off the ground at the same time. Anyone breaking this rule loses. The walking race should be a rather long one. If space is small, the walkers may go over the course several times.

Heel and Toe Race is another kind of walking race. You go forward only by placing the heel of one foot against the toe of the other foot. Every step you make must be made in this way. If you leave any space between heel and toe at any step, you are out of the race.

Hopping Race. This is run by hopping on one foot from start to finish. In doing so, each person must prove that he is really hopping by holding up the ankle of one foot for the whole distance.

Wheelbarrow Race. For this race you will need a lively "wheelbarrow"—someone who can run along well on his hands. When you have found such a wheelbarrow, take hold of his ankles, and wheel him along as fast as you can. If a large group of boys and girls are entering this event, divide them into groups. Or have one pair race against another. The winners can then race against each other until one pair becomes the champion wheelbarrow team.

Three-legged Race. This is another race in which you will need a partner. The left leg of one partner is tied to the other's right leg. Be sure you are tied securely for, if the cord falls off, you must take time out to tie it on again. If you have enough space, four or five couples can race at once.

Sack Race. Each person gets into a potato sack or a big laundry bag, the top of which is tied, securely, around his waist. One-two-three-GO! Now jump as fast as you can to the goal.

Potato Race. Four or five potatoes are placed on the ground, the first about four feet beyond the starting line and the others four feet apart, stretching ahead of the first. Each player is given a tablespoon.

To win the race, a player must pick up the potatoes, one at a time, in the spoon, and carry them back to the starting line. The potatoes may be picked up in any order—the last one first, or any other way. But no one is allowed to push a potato against his shoe or any other object in order to get it into the spoon.

Singing Games

Nobody wins in a singing game, except in "London Bridge," but these games are as much fun as others, and sometimes more fun than others are.

Ring-Around-a-Rosy is a simple game, in which the players hold hands and dance around in a circle, singing:

Ring-Around-a-Rosy

Ring a-round-a ro- sy, A

pock-et   full of po-sies,

All   fall down.

Ring-around-a-rosy,
A pocket full of posies.
All fall DOWN!

On the word "Down," the players
pretend to fall down, but they only
squat down, still holding hands.

Here We Go Round the Mulberry Bush.
The players, holding hands, march
around in a circle, singing:

Here we go round the mulberry bush,
The mulberry bush, the mulberry bush,
Here we go round the mulberry bush,
So early in the morning.

As the last line is sung, the players
stop marching and drop each other's
hands. Then they act out the second
verse of the song by pretending to wash
clothes.

This is the way we wash our clothes,
Wash our clothes, wash our clothes,
This is the way we wash our clothes,
So early Monday morning.

At the end of this verse, all join hands

again and march around the circle singing, "Here we go round the mulberry
bush" again. Then they sing and act out
the next verse:

This is the way we iron our clothes,
Iron our clothes, iron our clothes,
This is the way we iron our clothes,
So early Tuesday morning.

The players sing the first part of the
song again, as they do between each new
verse. Now it is time to mend the
clothes:

This is the way we mend our clothes,
Mend our clothes, mend our clothes,
This is the way we mend our clothes,
So early Wednesday morning.

After the first part of the song, again
the players go through the motions of
sweeping the floor while they sing:

This is the way we sweep the floor,
Sweep the floor, sweep the floor,
This is the way we sweep the floor,
So early Thursday morning.

Friday is cleaning day. So the players
sing and act the next verse as they get
down on hands and knees and scrub.

This is the way we scrub the floor,
Scrub the floor, scrub the floor,
This is the way we scrub the floor,
So early Friday morning.

Again the players go round the mulberry bush, and now Saturday and baking time comes. They knead the dough
as they sing:

This is the way we bake our bread,
Bake our bread, bake our bread,
This is the way we bake our bread,
So early Saturday morning.

After going around the mulberry bush

Here We Go Round the Mulberry Bush

Here we go 'round the mul- ber- ry bush, The
mul - ber - ry bush, the mul - ber - ry bush;
Here we go 'round the mul- ber - ry bush, So
ear - ly in the morn - ing.

for the last time, the players march in pairs with linked arms, as they sing:

> This is the way we go to church,
> Go to church, go to church,
> This is the way we go to church,
> So early Sunday morning.

There are many ways of playing this singing game. Some use such verses as "Hang our clothes," while others make shoes and pat fishcakes.

London Bridge. Two players are chosen, one to be called Silver, the other, Gold. But none of the others may know which is which. Silver and Gold now stand facing each other. They clasp hands and raise their arms to form an arch, or bridge. The other players march under the bridge as they sing together:

> London bridge is falling down,
> Falling down, falling down,
> London bridge is falling down,
> My fair lady.

On the word "lady," Silver and Gold bring their arms down and trap the one who is passing under the bridge. Then they rock the prisoner back and forth, and sing:

> Off to prison you must go,
> You must go, you must go,
> Off to prison you must go,
> My fair lady.

> Take a key and lock her up,
> Lock her up, lock her up,
> Take a key and lock her up,
> My fair lady.

London Bridge

Lon-don bridge is fall-ing down,

Fall- ing down, fall-ing down;

Lon-don bridge is fall-ing down,

My   fair la-   dy.

Now they whisper in the ear of the "Fair Lady," who may be either a boy or a girl, "Do you choose silver or gold?"

If the "lady" chooses silver, she says so in a whisper, and stands behind Silver. If she chooses gold, she stands behind Gold. Then the bridge is raised, and the march begins again. The game goes on in this way until everyone has been caught, and is standing either behind Silver or Gold.

Silver and Gold clasp hands. Each player throws his arms around the waist of the one in front of him, forming two chains, one on each side. Now comes a tug of war. The side pulling the other side across a line drawn between Silver and Gold wins the game.

Farmer in the Dell. One player is chosen to be the Farmer. The others form a circle, with the Farmer in the middle. Then, holding hands, they march around him, singing:

The farmer in the dell,
The farmer in the dell,
Hi ho the derry oh,
The farmer in the dell.

The Farmer then chooses a player from the ring to step inside with him and be his wife. The others march again, and sing:

The farmer takes a wife,
The farmer takes a wife,
Hi ho the derry oh,
The farmer takes a wife.

As each of the next verses is sung, a player is chosen to join the Farmer as child, dog, cat, rat, and, finally, the cheese. The rest of the verses go:

The wife takes a child,
The wife takes a child,
Hi ho the derry oh,
The wife takes a child.

The child takes the dog,
The child takes the dog,
Hi ho the derry oh,
The child takes the dog.

The dog takes the cat,
The dog takes the cat,
Hi ho the derry oh,
The dog takes the cat.

The cat takes the rat,
The cat takes the rat,
Hi ho the derry oh,
The cat takes the rat.

The rat takes the cheese,
The rat takes the cheese,
Hi ho the derry oh,
The rat takes the cheese.

Pfaffle, Black Star

A lively birthday party is never complete without some kind of singing game.

The cheese stands alone,
The cheese stands alone,
Hi ho the derry oh,
The cheese stands alone.

Everyone stands in his place, and claps his hands while he sings the last verse. The cheese then becomes the Farmer for the next game.

Oats, Peas, Beans, and Barley Grow. The players stand in a circle, with one, the Farmer, in the center, while they sing:

Oats, peas, beans, and barley grow,
Oats, peas, beans, and barley grow.

They point to each other, then to themselves, and then spread their hands

wide as they sing the next two lines:

Do you or I, or anyone know
How oats, peas, beans, or barley grow?

Now they do as each line tells them, in the next verse. They scatter seeds from a make-believe basket; they place their hands on their hips; they stamp their feet; they clap their hands; and then they turn around as they sing:

First the farmer sows his seed,
Then he stands and takes his ease;
He stamps his foot and claps his hands
And turns around to view his lands.

Now the players hold hands and face the center, as they sing:

33

Oats, Peas, Beans, and Barley Grow

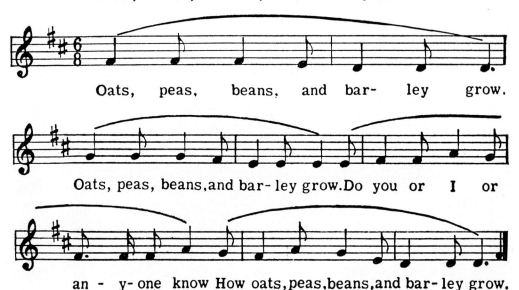

Oats, peas, beans, and bar- ley grow.

Oats, peas, beans,and bar- ley grow.Do you or I or

an - y- one know How oats,peas,beans,and bar- ley grow.

Waiting for a partner,
Waiting for a partner,
Open the ring and choose one in
While we all gaily dance and sing!

The one in the middle picks a partner,
while he and the others skip as they sing

the last verse of the song, which is:

Tra, la-la, la-la, la-la!
Tra, la-la, la-la, la-la!
Tra-la, la-la,
Tra-la, la-la,
Tra-la, la-la, la-la, la-la.

BOOKS TO READ

CARLSON, BERNICE WELLS. *Do It Yourself! Tricks, Stunts and Skits.* Illus. by Laszlo Matulay. Abingdon-Cokesbury, 1952.

COIT, LOTTIE ELLSWORTH, and BAMPTON, RUTH. *Follow the Music; A Collection of Easy Musical Games.* Illus. by Martha Powell Setchell. Birchard, 1948.

FRANKEL, LILLIAN and GODFREY. *101 Best Games for Girls 6 to 12.* Sterling, 1952. *101 Best Action Games for Boys 6 to 12.* 1952. Both illus. by John Fischetti.

HARBIN, ELVIN OSCAR. *Games for Boys and Girls.* Abingdon-Cokesbury, 1951.

HOROWITZ, CAROLINE. *Little Girl's Busybook of Play Ideas and Things-To-Do.* Hart, 1952. *Young Boy's Busybook of Play Ideas and Things-To-Do.* 1951.

MACFARLAN, ALLAN A. *New Games for 'Tween-Agers.* Illus. by Paulette Jumeau. Association Press, 1952.

MILLEN, NINA, ed. *Children's Games from Many Lands.* new ed. Friendship, 1951.

NORTH, ROBERT. *Town and Country Games.* Illus. by Garry Mackenzie. Crowell, 1947.

WEBB, MARIAN AGNES. *Games for Younger Children.* Morrow, 1947.

QUIET PLAY

RUBY BRADFORD MURPHY

SOME OF the happy times you may remember longest are those you spent in quiet play. Even when the doctor orders bed rest, and you can't go outdoors to run and play, you can amuse yourself with books, toys, puzzles, and card games. Ruby Bradford Murphy, author of books and magazine features for boys and girls, tells how to play some jolly games. Some of these you can play alone. Others need only one companion, or playmate. Still others you will want to play with a group inside on a rainy day.

A RAINY day when you have to stay indoors can be a happy one if you know how to play quietly by yourself or with a friend or two. And just before bedtime, a half hour of quiet play will be as soothing as a lullaby. Even bed rest can be a happy time, for there are many games which you can play in bed. These games can also be played when you are feeling better, but not quite well enough to go

Harold M. Lambert

The doll is a favorite playmate of almost every girl. It makes no difference what they look like or how much they cost, dolls are loved the world around.

outdoors. There are times, also, when your mother or father or some other person may be resting and you will be asked to play quietly.

It is a good idea to have a special shelf on which you can keep games and toys for quiet hours. If you are in bed, a lapboard of lightweight plywood will be useful for playing games, for making things, or for drawing and painting. If you have an old card table, saw the legs off evenly. Make them as short as you wish. This will make an excellent table for use in bed. Or, if your bed is narrow, you can place a table leaf across it on

35

the backs of two chairs. A shoe bag fastened to the head of the bed will serve for holding pencils, crayons, scissors, and small toys.

A Rainy-Day Box or a Mystery Bag will also help to keep you busy when you cannot go out to play. The box or bag should be big enough to hold such things as blocks, small bottles, buttons, beads, spools, toy planes, automobiles, trains, marbles, a mouth organ, anagrams, dominoes, a game of authors, toy animals, and a favorite doll. Fill it up some day, then put the Mystery Bag away and forget it. When the time comes to open it, it will be almost as much fun as opening a Christmas stocking.

Games for a Rainy Day

There are many quiet games which you can play with your friends on a rainy day.

What Is It? This game is a good one for guessing the objects in your Mystery Bag. As one player passes the bag, each of the others takes one object from it. But no player should let any of the others see what he has drawn. The player who drew first, describes the object which he holds. The player to his left tries to guess what it is. Suppose it

is a marble. The first player may say: "It is round and hard." If the second player cannot guess correctly, he is given another chance. He may be told, "It is used to shoot." At this point, he may guess "a bullet." "Not a bullet," the first player may say. "But its name has six letters."

If, after the third hint, the second player is still puzzled, the player to his left may guess, and so on down the line. The first player to guess the object correctly gets to describe the object which he himself holds. He gives three hints in describing the object. The player to his left tries to name the object after each hint. The game goes on until each player has had a chance to describe an object.

If you have a scorekeeper, you can make the game more interesting by giving 10 points to the one who answers correctly on the first guess; 5 points for the second guess; and 1 for the third. The player scoring the most points will be the winner.

I Am Thinking of Something is played much like "What Is It?". But in this game, no player holds anything and no one has to see the object.

The first player turns to the one on his left and says, for example: "I am

Ewing Galloway

You can build walls and garages, bridges, and little houses, by using wooden blocks.

Jigsaw puzzles will keep you amused for hours if you have to stay indoors.

Pfaffle, Black Star

thinking of something. It grows in the South."

"Bananas?" asks the second player.

"Wrong. It is used for making cloth."

"Hemp?"

"Wrong again. It has six letters, and it begins with 'c'."

Answer: *Cotton.*

The game can be varied if the players choose to describe a famous person, a character in a book, or a playmate known to all the others.

For example:

I am thinking of someone.
He was born in Virginia.
His father's name was Augustine.
He could throw a stone farther than any of his playmates. When he grew up he made a famous trip across the Delaware River.
Answer: *George Washington.*

I am thinking of someone.
He went to a fair.
He went fishing.
He met a pieman.
He was simple.
Answer: *Simple Simon.*

I am thinking of someone.
He is good at playing marbles.
He has freckles.
He collects butterflies.
Answer: *Bill.*

It is "not fair" in any of these guessing games for any players to help the one who is guessing.

For Dinner I Like is an alphabet game played much like "Minister's Cat," described in "Games for Indoors and Outdoors." The first player starts the fun by saying, "For dinner I like . . . ." He names something that begins with "a," such as apples, apricots, or asparagus. The second player must name some-

thing beginning with "b," such as beans or beets. The third player should prefer cabbage or carrots, and so on down the alphabet, omitting "x" and "z" because it is hard to find words beginning with those letters. If anyone takes longer than half a minute to name something beginning with his letter, he must pay a forfeit.

In the Zoo. This is another alphabet game. The players stand in a circle, and each in turn is given a letter of the alphabet. The "a" player begins by saying, "At the zoo I saw an . . . ." naming an animal such as an antelope or an anteater, or any other whose name begins with "a." The "b" player must have seen an animal with a name beginning with "b"—a bear, perhaps, or a badger. You may omit the letters "x" and "z," if you wish. This game can go on for hours on a rainy afternoon.

Teakettle is a word game that is always amusing. One of the players leaves the room, while the others make a list of

37

words which are pronounced alike, but which have different meanings, such as tail and tale; mail and male; or sail and sale. Try to think of others.

The player who left the room is now called back and asked questions in which TEAKETTLE is used in place of the right word. He might be asked, for example:

"Does a dog wag its TEAKETTLE?"
"Did the stranger tell a long TEAKETTLE about his travels?"
"Will you TEAKETTLE the apple?"

In each case the word, TEAKETTLE, is used for the proper word. Instead of questions, the guesser can be given a number of statements, such as:

"I bought a TEAKETTLE of shoes."
"Oh, what a delicious TEAKETTLE!"

The player whose puzzle is guessed first will be the next to take a turn.

Disappearing. The leader chooses a line from Mother Goose, or a proverb which everybody knows. On a sheet of paper, or a blackboard, he draws an x for each letter in the line, grouping the x's so that each group represents one of the words.

Suppose he chooses, "Jack and Jill went up the hill." His line of x's would look like this:

XXXX XXX XXXX XXXX XX XXX XXXX.

Each player is now given a sheet of paper on which to draw a "stick" man.

The first player then suggests a letter to put into the line instead of one or more of the x's. If he chooses "e," the leader puts in the two "e's" where they belong. One would be placed in the fourth group of x's, for "went," and the

Newman-Schmidt, Frederic Lewis

Stringing colored wooden beads on a strong cord provides fun when it is raining outside.

In playing this game, you draw a rough-looking stick man on a sheet of paper.

Each time a player gives the wrong answer, a part of his stick man is erased.

other in the sixth, for "the." The line of x's would then appear like this:

XXXX XXX XXXX XEXX XX XXE XXXX.

The second player then suggests a letter. If he suggests one which can be used, for example, "j," "i," or "l," the leader puts it in as before.

But if it is a letter that does not fit into the sentence, such as "g," the player must erase one leg of his stick man.

At his second wrong guess, he must lop off another leg. On each mistake, he removes arms, body, neck, and finally the head. If his letter can be used, he may put back one part of his man which has been erased. The player who first guesses the sentence wins. If a player has so many wrong guesses that his man disappears, he drops out of the game.

Lo, It Is Gone can be played with the objects in your Mystery Bag. One player is blindfolded while you take twelve or more small objects from the bag and

spread them on a table. The bandage is then removed from the "Blind Man's" eyes to let him have a look at the articles. After about half a minute he is blindfolded again. Then one of the objects is taken away and hidden, while the others are mixed up. The bandage is again taken off, and the players chant:

"Tell us, Blind Man, if you're able,
What is gone from the table."

The Blind Man replies:

"I will try with all my might
To tell what's gone out of sight."

He is allowed only one minute in which to answer, and is given only one guess. If he "gives up," or gives the wrong answer, either he must pay a forfeit or be blindfolded again. The missing object is then put back on the table, and mixed up with the others. The game continues until all the players have had a chance to guess.

It's in the Bag is a listening game which can be played with objects from the

Mystery Bag by any number of players. All players but one, the Leader, are blindfolded. The Leader empties the contents of the Mystery Bag on a table. Each player in turn draws one object from the bag, and is given half a minute to feel his "grab" and decide what he has drawn.

As the Leader passes the bag, each player in turn drops his "grab" into it and says, "A doll," or whatever it is, "It's in the bag."

The other players must listen carefully. Before dropping their "grabs," they must repeat what the player or players ahead of them have said, in the proper order.

The second player, for example, would say, "A doll. It's in the bag." Then, dropping his own grab, would say, "A bottle," or whatever he had, "It's in the bag." The third player, if he had a toy automobile, would say, "A doll. It's in the bag. A bottle. It's in the bag. A car. It's in the bag."

A player must drop out of the game if he fails to name his own "grab" correctly or if he fails to repeat, in the right order, what the players ahead of him have said. The game may continue until each player has had a second or third "grab."

The game called, "Memory Test," in "Games for Indoors and Outdoors" may also be played with objects in your Mystery Bag.

Games for One Player

A peg game can amuse you for hours when you are playing alone. Many good ones can be bought, but it is easy to make one of the best of these games.

Lone Wolf. Use a sheet of cardboard to make a board. Take a penny and a pencil. With the penny as a guide, draw seven rows of circles on the cardboard. The first two and the last two rows should have three circles each. The three rows in between should have seven circles each. The circles in all the rows should be the same distance apart. Arrange them in the form of a cross, like the picture. Use 32 pennies for counters. Buttons will do if you do not have that number of pennies.

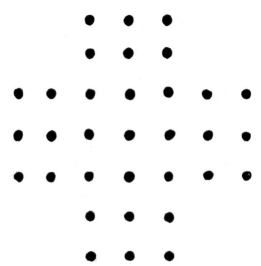

"Lone Wolf" can be played on cardboard with buttons, or it can be played on a board with wooden pegs in the holes.

Place the pennies, or buttons, on the circles, leaving the middle circle vacant. The object of the game is to jump your men, one at a time, until only one of them remains on the board in the center circle.

You may jump your men up or down, that is, vertically. Or you may jump them straight across, or horizontally. But you cannot jump them in a slanting direction, or diagonally. Each man that is jumped over is taken from the board.

Your first jump must land one of your men in the center. You keep on jumping and removing men until only one man, the Lone Wolf, remains in the center, or until you can make no more jumps. This game can be played also by jumping wooden pegs from hole to hole in a board. The holes are arranged in the same way as the circles.

Hidden Words. Print a long word, or somebody's name, if it is long enough, at the top of a sheet of paper. See how many words you can make out of it. If a letter is used only once in the word you select, you can use that letter only once in each hidden word you list. There are many hidden words in the name WASHINGTON. These include:

ant	hit	shin	ton
ash	host	shot	tin
gas	hot	show	tow
ghost	how	sing	town
gnat	in	sow	twin
go	is	stow	two
got	it	swan	want
hang	nag	tan	was
has	not	than	wash
hat	sag	thin	washing
hint	sang	thing	wish
his	saw	this	won

Select other words and find the hidden words in them. After you have found all you can, try to arrange them in alphabetical order. This is also a good game to play with your friends. Select a long word and see which player can find the greatest number of hidden words in it.

Picture Writing. The Egyptians of long ago had no alphabet. They wrote by drawing pictures. One of their pictures was that of an ox head. As time went on, different nations copied this and changed it. After many changes had been made, the picture looked like our letter A turned sideways. That is how we got the first letter of our English alphabet.

Now, suppose you wanted to spell your name in pictures and see how it would look. This is how it is done. For each letter draw a picture of something, the name of which begins with that letter. If your name is Ruth, you can start by drawing a picture of a ring for R. For U, why not a picture of an umbrella? For T, a tree; and for H, a hat. Your name would look like this:

Ring   Umbrella   Tree   Hat

How good are you at picture writing?

Make picture writings of your friends' names and have them guess the names the next time you see them.

Mix 'em and Match 'em will be most fun if you cover up the Solution which follows, for this is a puzzle as well as a game. On a strip of cardboard draw an oblong with pencil and ruler. Divide the oblong into ten equal parts by drawing lines from one side to the other. Beginning at the left, number the spaces from 1 to 10.

Now take six toothpicks. Break two of them in half. You will now have four long and four short toothpicks. Place one of the long ones in Space 1; a short one in Space 2; and so on until the first eight spaces are filled.

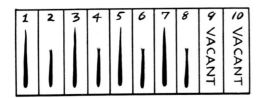

"Mix 'em and Match 'em" can be a clever puzzle as well as an interesting game.

Move the toothpicks or "men" two at a time. Try to arrange them so that the first two spaces will be vacant and so that the long and short men lie side by side as in the second picture. This can be done in four moves. Try to do it without looking at the solution.

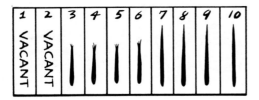

Solution:
1. Move 2 and 3 to spaces 9 and 10.
2. Move 5 and 6 to spaces 2 and 3.
3. Move 8 and 9 to spaces 5 and 6.
4. Move 1 and 2 to spaces 8 and 9.

Games with Playing Cards. There are many good card games of solitaire with which you can amuse yourself by the hour. *Twins* is one of the easiest of these to play. Deal two rows of five cards each, face up. Usually, there will be two cards alike, or a pair. Often there will be more than one pair of "twins." You may have a pair of aces, kings, tens, or fours, and so on. There may even be three or four of a kind.

Now, from the pack in your hand, deal two cards at a time. Lay these face up on any two cards on the board that match or make a pair.

After you have done this, another pair will probably be waiting to be covered. Deal two more cards and cover the new pairs. You go on in this way, making new pairs and covering them. But if, at any time, there are no pairs or "twins" to cover, you have lost the game. You win if, after dealing all the cards, you have five sets of "twins" on the table.

For *Clock Solitaire*, deal the cards face down so as to make thirteen stacks of four cards each. Arrange twelve of the stacks in a circle and imagine that each stack is a number on the face of a clock. Number 12, of course, will be at the top, and Number 6 at the bottom. Place the odd stack in the center.

Turn up the top card of the center stack. If it should be a 3, for example, slip it, face up, part way under the No. 3 stack. Then turn up the top card of the No. 3 stack and place it, face up, part way under the stack where it belongs. If it should be a jack, it would go under the 11 pile; if a queen, under the 12 pile; and if an ace, under the 1 pile.

Keep on turning up cards in the same way. Slip them face up under the piles their numbers match. If you turn up a king, it goes face up at the bottom of the center stack. The game ends when the fourth king is turned up. If you have turned up all the other cards before the fourth king comes up, you win.

Play for a Shut-in

There should always be some playthings in your Mystery Bag to keep you happy and amused, even when you must stay in bed. Small trains, automobiles, airplanes, and dolls are wonderful company when you are playing alone. And with small building blocks, you can make a house, a garage, or even an airport. Dominoes make especially good building blocks if you are building on a small tray or a board in bed.

Drawing with Crayons. A set of crayons or colored pencils and a supply of drawing paper will help you to amuse yourself. Take an old magazine and, with crayon or pencil, fill in the A's, O's, P's, and Q's. Or you can make them into funny faces. If you have a book illustrated only with line drawings, you might color the pictures. A picture-book boy, for instance, might have a brown cap, yellow hair, red cheeks and lips, a red jacket, green pants, and black shoes and stockings.

Trace any picture from a book or a magazine on paper which you can see through. Then, by placing carbon paper over a plain sheet of paper, you can transfer your picture. Place your thin paper, on which you have traced, over the carbon paper. And draw over the lines again. You can color the picture if you wish.

If you would rather draw your own pictures, you can look out of the window, and draw a landscape. Or you might set up a doll, a toy dog, or a vase of flowers as models.

Transferring Pictures, called *decalcomania*, is another interesting way of making pictures. You can transfer these pictures to paper, china, glass, or eggs. Pictures to transfer can be bought at dime stores and toy counters, and they have many uses. You can decorate your letter paper with them, make scrapbooks with them, and make Easter eggs.

Coloring pictures with crayons is one way to entertain yourself when mother says you have to stay in bed.

Clay, or Plasticine, Modeling is wonderful quiet play. A tray makes a good surface on which to work. It also helps to keep the clay from scattering. All you need for tools is a spatula and an orangewood stick. Or you may want to model entirely with your hands. By rolling, pinching, punching, and pulling a mass of plasticine, you can model almost any kind of animal or object.

Try easy things first. Model an apple or a pear. Or you can make the parts of an animal separately and stick them together with toothpicks. By rolling a lump of clay between the palms of your hands, you can make bodies, heads, and tails. Your hippopotamus may look

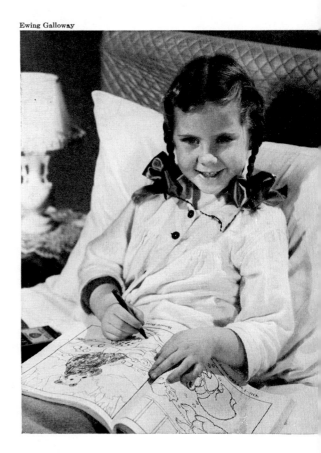

Ewing Galloway

Kaufmann-Fabry

Clay or plasticine will give you a good opportunity to test your skill in modeling various animals or other objects.

A large colored picture can be cut out, pasted on cardboard, and then cut up to make a jigsaw puzzle. When mounting the picture, avoid using too much paste. Smooth out any wrinkles in the picture. Then let it dry thoroughly before cutting it into a puzzle.

Scrapbooks. You can make your own scrapbook by making the cover from stiff cardboard. Use drawing or notebook paper for leaves. If you do not have a punch to make holes in your paper, plan to use notebook paper with holes in it. Plan your cover to fit. The cover should be an inch wider on all sides than the leaves. Decorate the cover with pictures cut from an old magazine or with crayons. Or you can paste wallpaper, cloth, or oilcloth on the outside. Make three holes in the cover to match the holes in the paper.

If your paper does not have holes, you should make one in the middle of the left side. Make the others near the top and bottom. The holes should be about ¾ of an inch from the edge. Have your mother or father help you make the holes. A punch, sharp scissors, a nail, or a drill can be used. Fit the leaves between the covers, and mark with a pencil the places for punching holes. Make matching holes in both the cover and pages. Then run heavy string through all the holes to tie the scrapbook together. Shoe laces are good to use for this purpose.

When you have finished making the scrapbook, the fun of cutting out pictures and pasting them in begins. You can follow a certain plan. Suppose you

more like a dog than a hippopotamus, the first time you make one. Perhaps, after making a plasticine zoo, you would like to try making puppet heads. Turn to the chapter, "Puppets and Marionettes." Then model a head from the clay. Make a hole in the bottom and add a sacklike garment as shown in the directions for hand puppets. You will have a puppet with which you can perform many amusing tricks.

Cut-outs. Old magazines have many uses. In some you will find paper dolls with clothes which you can cut out. If you see a colored picture you like, perhaps you can cut it out, paste it on a sheet of stiff paper, and hang it in your room.

decide on a travel scrapbook. If you have visited interesting places on vacation trips, you can easily find pictures of these places. Or you can fill the book with pictures of American scenes or those of any foreign country. For example, in a Mexican scrapbook you could paste pictures of boys and girls, burros, Indians, colorful markets, old Spanish churches, cities, and mountains. You can fill a scrapbook with pictures of anything in which you are especially interested. Make one of pets, flowers, wild animals, birds, insects, reptiles, trees, trains, or transportation. A train book could include pictures of all the models from the early locomotives to the latest Diesel engines. A picture scrapbook would make a wonderful present for a boy or girl in a foreign country to receive from you.

You may want to begin cutting and pasting at once without first making a scrapbook. Attractive scrapbooks can be made from almost any five- or ten-cent notebook. But, of course, these will not have loose leaves. Be sure you do not paste these too full or they will not lie flat.

Growing Things are always interesting to watch. You can plant a sweet potato in a wide-mouthed glass jar partly filled with water. Make sure that the potato is fresh. Stick toothpick legs in it to keep it from falling to the bottom of the jar. Within a few days you will see it sprout, and soon your potato plant will grow roots and leaves.

Carrots and other root vegetables also will sprout if placed among pebbles in a dish of water. Lima beans grow rapidly too. Soak them for an hour or more, then plant them in sandy soil. Keep the soil moist, but not too wet. Soon you

Kaufmann-Fabry

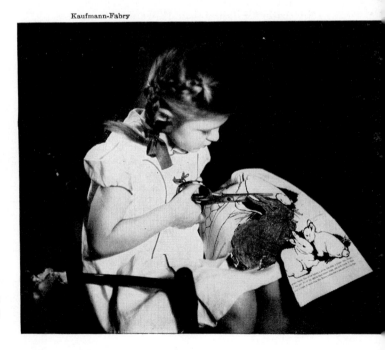

Cutting out various pictures from old magazines will provide endless hours of pleasure.

Joseph Adams, Frederic Lewis

Many boys and girls like to make toys or put things together when they have to stay indoors because of bad weather.

dyed blue or green with blue or green ink.

Place a clinker from a furnace in the center of a shallow bowl. Or you may use a rough stone instead of a clinker. Sprinkle a handful of salt over the clinker or stone. Dampen the salt with water. As the salt dissolves, it will form tiny crystals. These will look like small red, blue, or green flowers. Add a little more water now and then, but be careful not to pour it over the flowers, for if you do, they will dissolve. But, if the crystals are washed off from the clinker, they will form new crystals, or flowers. Sometimes the salt garden will grow over the garden wall—the rim of the bowl. For this reason, the clinker should not be placed in too small or too shallow a bowl.

Making Things. In the chapters "Ad-

will have the beginnings of beanstalks which will brighten up your room.

A Sponge Garden is always interesting to watch. Soak a medium-sized sponge in water. Then wring the sponge out, leaving a little water in it. Place it in a shallow dish. Sprinkle it with timothy seed or flaxseed, and keep it moist. One funny garden is easy to make. Model a large, funny head out of plasticine. Flatten the top and press it down to make a shallow bowl. Fill the bowl with sandy soil and plant grass seed. Within a few days, green "hair" will begin to grow. Every day the green hair will bring many laughs from those who see it.

A Crystal Garden is planted, not with seeds, but with salt. Coarse salt is best for this purpose. It can be dyed red with mercurochrome or red ink. Or it can be

Making valentines is an interesting pastime if you have to stay indoors.

Century

ventures in Handwork" and "Sewing for Fun," you will find directions for making many things out of odd scraps of cloth and felt. And there are many other things, such as valentines and place cards, which you can make out of paper in your hours of rest. The chapter "Planning a Party" explains how to make some of these. You will need quiet time, too, in which to do your drawing and painting.

With quiet games to play and with so many things to make and do, your quiet play should be a happy time.

BOOKS TO READ

BIRDSONG, JUNE SUMNER. *Children's Rainy Day Play; A Guide for Mothers.* Illus. by Helen Disbrow. Laurel Publishers, Scranton, Pa., 1953. (Books for Better Living series.)

HORWICH, DR. FRANCES R., and WERRENRATH, REINALD, JR. *Ding Dong School Book, The.* Illus. by Katherine Evans. Rand, 1953.

JACOBS, FRANCES E. *Finger Plays and Action Rhymes.* Photographs by Lura and Courtney Owen. Lothrop, 1941.

LEWIS, ROGER. *Sculpture; Clay, Soap and Other Materials.* Illus. by the author. Knopf, 1952.

NEWKIRK, LOUIS VEST, and ZUTTER, LA VADA. *You Can Make It; Things to Do with Scissors and Paste.* Silver Burdett Co., 1944.

PARKER, CORNELIA STRATTON. *Your Child Can Be Happy in Bed; Over 200 Ways Children Can Entertain Themselves.* Illus. by Heda Teitcher. Crowell, 1952.

SCHLOAT, G. WARREN, JR. *Playtime for You.* Scribner, 1950. *What Shall I Do?* Scribner, 1949.

Kaufmann-Fabry

MAKING
THE MOST OF
YOUR HOME

This girl is happily engaged playing in a corner of her bedroom with her two dolls and beautiful dollhouse.

MARGUERITE ICKIS

NO MATTER how small your home, or what type it may be, there must be some place, if only a nook, in which you can play. If you cannot have a room of your own, perhaps you can have your own corner somewhere. If you are lucky enough to have a back yard, then you can fix it up for all kinds of fun and play. Marguerite Ickis, Instructor in Recreation at Teachers College, Columbia University, and the author of several books on arts and crafts, gives practical aids on how you can make your home a rich place for living.

HOME is the most important place in the world. It is the place where you live. You eat, you sleep, you learn, and you grow in your home. But, best of all, home is the place where you play. When you are playing happily, you are not just keeping busy. For creative play trains your hands and your mind. And outdoor play builds strong, healthy bodies. Playing helps you to learn to get along with others. It helps you to play fair and to be a good sport. You learn that you cannot always win in any game. And you learn that teamwork, good manners, and unselfishness are important.

A Place to Play

Home may be a one-room apartment, or it may have rooms to spare and a large yard in which to play. But it is still the center of your living. Regardless of how big it is, or how small, you can make the most of it as a place to play. For you can live in a mansion or a castle and still have no place to play. Or you can live in one room and have a delightful corner where you keep your toys, and where you can play to your heart's content. Your mother and father will be your most enthusiastic helpers in making a special place which can be called your own.

Your Own Room. If you are one of the lucky boys or girls who has a room of his own, it will be easy for you to make the most of it. You may want a table or a desk. You may also want shelves for your books and playthings, a small chair,

48

an easel, a wall blackboard or a bulletin board, and perhaps a screen. You can make many of these things yourself out of orange and apple boxes. The chapter on "Making Toys and Playthings" shows how to make a bookcase, a chair, a bulletin board, and a screen. Perhaps you would like to decorate the walls with a special color, or even with pictures which you have drawn or painted. If your mother and father are willing for

An easel and some crayons will enable you to draw many interesting pictures.

you to do this, you will need their help, for it is a big job.

If your special interest is model airplanes, you can stretch a string across the room by tacking the ends to the picture molding. From the string, you can hang your favorite models which will be zooming in the sky to greet you every morning. If you have a piece of picture wire long enough, it makes an even better way to hang your planes. You can

You are very fortunate if you have a place where you can keep the toys and things with which you love to play.

attach the wire by winding it around the heads of two tacks on opposite sides of the room. The top shelf of your bookcase can hold your train models, or dolls, if one of these is your hobby.

If you have a closet, you can keep one corner as a special place for toys. There, too, you can hang your football helmet and your catcher's glove. A closet is also a good place to keep doll furniture and clothes. A special place to keep your toys will help you to be neat and orderly. It will even add to the safety of your home. For many accidents are caused by toys carelessly left around. Bright-colored linoleum, or any smooth covering for your floor, makes toy trains and cars run easier. Besides, it is easy to keep clean.

A Play Corner. If you do not have a room of your own, ask your mother and father to set aside a sunny corner for you in some part of the house. Your play nook should be near a window, and should be screened off from the rest of the room. A folding card table may be

Harold M. Lambert

This picture shows how a corner of one rumpus room was fixed up for the particular use of the children of one family.

Percy H. Prior, Jr.

used instead of a screen. It can stand on edge, with two of the legs open to support it, or it can stand on all four legs with a cloth draped over it reaching to the floor. This would provide you with a tent or a cave. You should also have a box in your special corner in which to keep your toys.

The Porch. Apartment houses often have small porches or sunrooms. There you can play out of doors in rainy weather, and out of the sun when it is hot. If the porch is big enough, there may be room at one end for a swing or a hammock. Perhaps you can put a small sandbox in one corner. Or you can make a workbench which will fold against the wall. You may have room for a bulletin board and a ringtoss game. The chapter, "Making Toys and Playthings," shows how to make these things. With the consent of your parents, perhaps you could paint a checkerboard and a hopscotch court on the floor. Or you could make a temporary court with chalk. Here, also, you can play tenpins, or produce puppet shows. Perhaps the sunny side of the porch could be shaded with a bright awning. Window boxes with

flowering plants add to the attractiveness of this outdoor playroom.

The Attic. An old-fashioned attic makes an ideal playroom. There you can roller skate if your floor is smooth enough, and if your parents have no objections, or you can put up an electric train. Attic trunks are often full of old costumes which can be used for dressing up or for play-acting. Or trunks and boxes can be moved out of the way to make room for a ping-pong table or a playhouse.

The Basement can easily be made into a rumpus or game room. At one end of the room you could build a stage or a puppet theater. You could build shelves along the walls for your hobbies. A swing, a pair of rings, and a punching bag might be hung from the beams. A small handball court, a wall blackboard, and a ping-pong table are only a few suggestions for the basement rumpus room.

The Back Yard is the best place of all to play. How can you make yours into a playground if you are so fortunate as to have one? If most of the space is now in gardens, you may have to choose between garden and playground. Or you

Percy H. Prior, Jr.

These useful pieces of furniture were made from orange cases, nail kegs, and odd pieces of lumber by a family group for their own special use.

could plant flowers and vegetables in borders along the edges. Is there a big tree with spreading branches in the yard? If so, perhaps you can hang a swing from one of them, or nail a birdhouse to the lower branches. Is there a garage? If so, to what uses can it be put? Have a family meeting and map out a plan. Who wants what? Johnny may want space for a horizontal bar or for pole vaulting or broad jumping. Susie may want a place for a dollhouse, a badminton court, or for croquet. Mother and Dad may want to keep the flower garden, or a shady corner for chairs.

First of all, the back yard should be a place for active play—for running and jumping, and for all sorts of active games. The back yard is also a perfect place for a sandbox. But this should be placed in a corner or at one side so it will be out of the way.

Making a Plan for the Back Yard

You can do as the landscape gardeners do, and draw a diagram of your yard to scale—one inch to one foot. If your yard is large, you will need a large piece of wrapping paper on which to draw your plan. Measure the yard, and the space

Ellis O. Hinsey

Making mud pies in a sandbox

Use the garage as an outdoor workshop.

taken up by garage, driveway, flower beds, and trees.

In drawing your plan, decide how much equipment and what kind you have room for, where it should go, and how much open space should be left for games. Who is to use the playground? Should there be a place where little brother or sister can play without getting in the way of others? Do you want a place where girls can play by themselves, or a place to be used by boys alone? Where should the flower beds go? Have you marked off a space for outdoor cooking and where a table can be set for campfire meals and picnic lunches?

Where will you keep your pets? Have

A workbench with a vise can be hinged to the wall and let down when not in use. A tool chest can serve as a seat.

you planned for a birdbath? It so, directions for making one will be found in the chapter, "Adventures in Handwork." Can a circular bench be built around the trunk of the big tree? Is there a driveway running from the street to the garage? If so, how much space does it take? Is it stone, cement, or cement strips? If cement, is it large enough to be used for shuffleboard?

Is there room in the garage for a tool chest, a workbench, or to store playground equipment? Can the window sill be used as a puppet theater stage, or would you prefer a flower box or a gay awning there? Can you play handball or bounce-ball against one of the walls? Have you thought of fastening a weather vane to the peak of the roof?

How will you plant, or landscape, the back yard? Do you wish to have a lawn in the center, or pack the ground hard? A hedge around the yard will attract birds, and will add color to the grounds. What flowers do you want in the borders? Peonies, iris, tulips, asters, zinnias, pansies, and nasturtiums are hardy plants for a border flower bed. And would you like hollyhocks for the sunny side of the garage?

It may be best, in planning your back yard playground, to place the equipment, such as swings, bars, and sandbox, along the sides and leave the central space open for court games, such as deck tennis and badminton.

Back-Yard Play

There are many kinds of equipment suitable for use in your back yard for everyday play. These include swings, rings or trapeze, teeter-totter, slide, sandbox, horizontal bar, playhouse or tent, ladders, barrel, benches and stools, and a beach umbrella.

Of course, you can't have all these if your space is small. You will have to select. But if there is a vacant lot in your neighborhood, and several families join forces, the lot could be cleared and made into an attractive playground. This has been done in many crowded cities.

A Tent. Almost every boy and girl wants a tent. You will not need to reserve a place for it on your working plan because it can be taken down when not in use. A tent can be made by draping an army blanket over a clothesline. You can tie the four corners of the blanket to pegs driven in the ground, or you can anchor the corners with rocks. A burlap sack opened out can be used as a flap. Another kind of tent can be made by nailing a piece of canvas to the side of the garage, stretching it out, and tying it to pegs driven into the ground.

A Playhouse. You may even have an opportunity to make a playhouse. This can be made out of a large packing case or, better still, a piano box. Cut out a door and windows. The door can be made to swing on leather hinges. Use cellophane for window panes, or leave the windows open and shade them with dainty tie-back curtains. You might also like to have small flower boxes in the windows. You could even plant a small flower or vegetable garden in the yard of your playhouse.

A Barrel of Fun. The younger members of the family will probably want a tunnel, or something they can crawl through. A barrel with both ends knocked out makes a good tunnel. It would be fun to roll in it, too, as the little pig did when it had to escape from

A large barrel open at both ends will give many hours of active play and fun.

the wolf and rolled away in a churn.

Several empty kegs will also be useful in the back-yard playground. A smooth plank laid across the tops of two kegs will make a bench. Or they will make a bridge across which the younger boys and girls will like to walk. Two logs laid close together lengthwise on the ground, with two short logs laid across them and nailed down, will make a rustic bench or stool. The sides of the upper logs should be planed to make them flat.

Kegs sawed in the middle can be used for stools. Put a plank on the kegs and you have a fine little bridge.

This ramp can be used for climbing, for sliding, or for crawling underneath.

If there is a big tree in the yard, a circular bench built around it will provide a restful place for quiet games. A table for outdoor meals, for clay modeling, or for playing games, should also be included in your equipment.

For a slide, a ramp can be made of three strips of five-ply plywood. Use hinges to fasten the pieces together. Place them over a strong box as a sup-port for the center. When not in use, this slide can be folded and easily stored.

A simple teeter-totter can be made by laying a plank over a sawhorse. Be sure that the plank has been planed and sandpapered to make it smooth. The same plank, with a hole in the center, can be used for a merry-go-round if it is balanced on the flat top of a big log in which a spike has been driven. Directions for making a teeter-totter you will be proud to have indoors as well as out-side, will be found in the chapter "Making Toys and Playthings."

Swinging and Climbing. Swings always help to make a playground out of your yard. They may be hung from trees or from the crossbar of standards anchored in cement. If you have no better place, perhaps you could put hooks in the frame of your garage doorway and hang a swing there. Be sure to place a hook on the inside of the garage wall so

Frederic Lewis

There is no fun on a hot day like that of having a cool, outdoor shower in a canvas bath.

Even an eighteen-month-old baby can have fun on a swing in the back yard.

Press Syndicate

that you can pull the swing out of the way of the car.

Equipment to climb on will furnish many hours of healthful play. If you like to climb, make a lattice.

You can make one yourself if you have a hammer and nails, a plane, and a saw. You can add a coat of paint if you want it to be attractive. The lattice can also be used as a screen to shut off part of the yard for different kinds of play. Cut the crosspieces about 5 feet long. Nail the pieces to three uprights—one at each end and one in the center.

A horizontal bar for climbing can be set up at different heights between two firmly anchored uprights. But do not depend on a broomstick for this bar or that of a trapeze. A metal bar, or a hickory bar, which you can buy at a sporting goods store, is safer to use.

Special Games and Sports

Besides other play equipment, most

A lattice such as this can be used for climbing and to separate play areas.

boys and girls want some permanent equipment for games in their yard. Pegs can be driven into the ground for quoits or ring toss, and a board for your bean-bag game can be made. Learn how to make a ring-toss game in "Games for Indoors and Outdoors."

Handball is played against a wall and on a handball court. The wall should be about 20' wide and 16' high. The handball court is the same width as the wall. It is about 34' long. Draw a back line parallel to the wall 34' away and two side lines to make the court. Now draw another line across the field, about 16' away from the wall. This is called the short line.

When a player serves, neither he nor any other player may step between the short line and the wall. He bounces the ball once, and as it comes up, he hits it against the wall with the palm of his hand. He must hit it hard enough so that when it bounces off the wall, it will land between the short line and the back line. If it bounces between the short line and the wall, or outside either of the side lines, it is no good. If the first serve is no good, the server gets a second chance. If it is good, his opponent must hit it back against the wall. Then the server must hit it against the wall again.

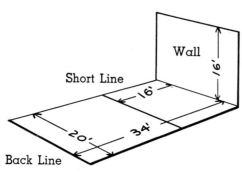

Plan for a Handball Court

Each player hits the ball in turn, until one player fails to hit the ball against the wall properly. In that case, his opponent becomes the server. If the player misses after his opponent has served, his opponent makes a point. The first player who makes 21 points wins the game.

Four players play as two teams, with two on each team. When the first server's turn is over, his partner serves next. When his partner loses his turn, each of the two members of the other team has a turn as server.

Bounce-Ball can be played in a smaller space than handball. You can play it

against the side of the garage if your parents are willing. Draw a line 8 feet from the wall. Stand behind the line. Bat the ball with your hand against the wall and try to catch it on the rebound without stepping over the line. If you catch the ball before it hits the ground, you score one point. A catch from a bounce counts nothing. Keep on serving until you miss. Then the next player takes his turn. Stepping over the line counts as a miss.

Here Goes up for Monday is a game for seven players. Each is named for a day of the week. "Sunday" throws the ball high against the wall. As he does so, he calls out, "Here goes up for ——," naming any other day of the week. The player named must catch the ball on the rebound and on the fly. If he catches it, he takes his turn at serving.

If he misses, a point is scored against him. He must then pick up the ball and throw it at one of the other players who, as soon as the ball is missed, scatter in all directions. If one of them is hit, he also loses a point, but takes his turn at serving. The game can go on as long as you like. The player with the fewest points against him wins. A small blackboard either on an easel or nailed to the side of the garage can be used as a scoreboard.

Croquet is a game that everyone in the family can enjoy. You will need a smooth space, with the grass cut short. The regular game requires a space 30' wide and 60' long, but these measurements may be cut down to fit the size of your yard.

For a regulation court, set two stakes 2½' in from the two ends of the court. Put the first wire, or wicket, the length of the mallet handle from the first stake, and the second wicket a mallet handle

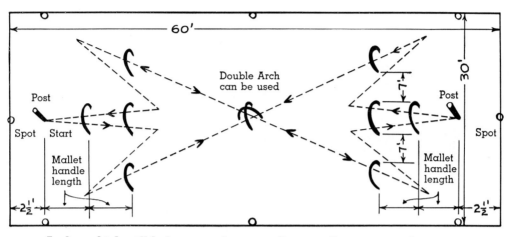

A plan which will help you to lay out a Croquet Court in your back yard

length from the first. The center wicket should be exactly in the middle of the court, between the two stakes.

The outside wickets should be set in a line with the second wickets and about 7′ or 8′ from them, on each side. Mark a boundary line with a white string. To play the game, strike your ball so that it goes through all the wickets in the order shown in the diagram. The first player to hit the last stake wins the game.

The first player places his ball between the stake and the first wicket. Then he hits it with the mallet, trying to get it through the first two wickets. If he does, he has two turns to get through the side wicket, and after that, one more turn every time he gets his ball through a wicket. If he fails, he loses his turn. If the ball goes out of bounds, he loses his turn. He plays it from the boundary line the next time.

Clock Golf is another interesting game that can be played in the middle of the yard. This is a good game for all ages and it is excellent training for golf. Draw a circle 24′ across. But it can be smaller if necessary. Sink a tin can inside the cir-

cle about 4′ from the edge. Make the rim level with the ground. Divide the circle by driving in small stakes, just as though you were marking the face of a clock.

Start at the stake that would be 1 on a clock's face, and try to hit a golf ball into the tin can. Use a golf putter or a croquet mallet. If you hit the ball in the

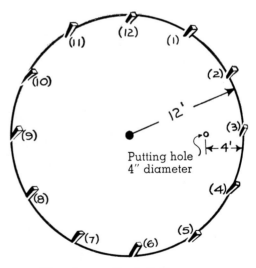

Plan for a Clock-Golf course

2	9	4
7	5	3
6	1	8

How to prepare a Bull Board

can the first time, you can go on to the place where 2 is. If you miss, leave your ball where it is. The other players take their turns, and try to hit the ball into the tin can. Keep on playing around the clock. The first to complete the twelve shots successfully wins the game. You can play this game another way by counting your strokes. The player with the fewest strokes wins.

If the game becomes too easy, move the tin can to some other place in the circle. But be sure to fill in the hole left by the can. The stakes should be pounded all the way into the ground, and the tops painted white so you can see them. If the stakes are not driven even with the surface of the ground, they should be taken up each time you finish playing.

Bull Board, as played on ships, is another good game for the yard, and it is easy to make. You will need a board about 3′ long and 2′ wide. Mark off the board into nine equal spaces, and paint the lines. Paint a number on each space, so that each column down and each column across adds up to fifteen. But first mark the numbers in chalk or pencil. The spaces at one end may be numbered 2, 9, and 4. Those at the other end, 6, 1, and 8. And those in the middle, 7, 5, and 3. Place a log, or brick, under the back of the board so that the top is about 8″ off the ground.

The game is played with ten disks. Rubber disks about 1″ wide and 5″ across are the best. Rope rings of the same size may be used instead. They will last longer if varnished. To start the game, the players line up, and the first player throws five disks at the board, from about 15 feet away. He adds up the points he has scored. If a disk overlaps two spaces, the higher one counts. The players take turns, and the first to score 100 points wins. If a player steps over the mark when tossing a disk, the throw does not count and the disk must be taken off the board.

Shuffleboard should be played on a smooth surface, such as a paved walk, a driveway, or a wooden floor. You can copy the drawing with chalk, or, if you want a permanent shuffleboard, use paint. In this game, you hit or push flat, round pieces of wood, called *disks*, with a special kind of pole, called a *cue*. This cue has a stick handle about 5 feet long, ending in a head about 3½″ wide. The disks should be about 1″ thick and 6″ across. Use eight disks, four painted blue

How to lay out a Shuffleboard plan

and four painted red. Each player needs a cue for himself.

When two persons are playing against each other, they stand on the same side of the court. They stand next to each other behind the base line, facing the court. One player uses the red disks and the other player uses the blue disks.

The player on the right plays first. He places one of his disks in the "10 off" space in front of him, and pushes it with the wide end of his cue. He tries to shoot his disk into one of the numbered spaces at the opposite end of the board. After each player has shot his disks, the opponents add the numbers in the spaces where their disks rest to find out their scores. You may not step on or over the first line of the court when you shoot. Anyone who does this loses 5 points.

After the first player has shot one disk, the second player gets his turn and shoots one disk. They take turns in this way. If one player's disk hits the other player's disk into a scoring box, that is just lucky for the one whose disk is pushed into the scoring box. If his disk gets pushed out of a scoring box by the other player's disk, that is his bad luck. What counts is where the disks are after they have all been shot. Disks which are on a line do not count. Disks which land between the two dead lines must be taken off the court immediately.

Fifty points wins the game. But you must finish a game even after one player reaches fifty points. If each player ends with more than fifty points, the one who has the greater number of points wins.

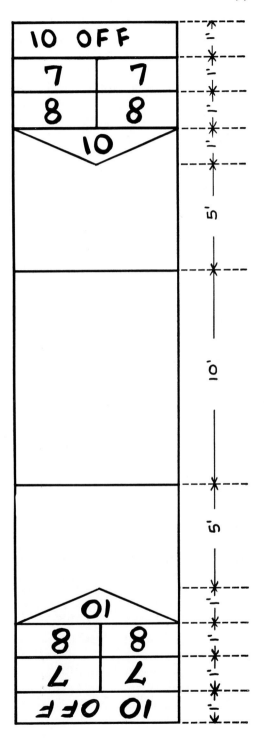

If there are four players, they play two on a team. One person from each team stands at one end of the court and one player from each team stands, facing them, at the other end of the court. First the players at one end shoot all their disks, just as if they were playing without partners. Then they make a record of the scores made. Now the two players who are at the other end of the court use the disks and play against each other in the same way. When they have shot all their disks, each player adds his scores to his partner's scores. The team that makes fifty points first wins. Or if both teams have more than fifty points, the team with the greater number of points wins.

High Jumping. Standards for high jumping and pole vaulting are easy to make. Two light poles, 6' to 8' long, can be anchored in large cans or small buckets filled with cement. First, bore holes into the uprights, beginning about 3' from the ground. Make the holes 1" apart to hold the pegs across which a light crossbar is laid. These lighter standards can be moved from place to place and used for hanging nets for badminton, volley ball, or paddle tennis.

For pole vaulting, an old gymnasium mat can be used to break the fall. Or, if your parents give permission, an oblong piece of ground can be dug out and filled with coarse sawdust. A block of wood 12" to 16" square should be sunk into the ground to hold the sharp end of the pole. A bar of wood sunk into the ground will serve as a takeoff for the broad jump.

Tether-Ball is an interesting game which you can play in your yard. You will need a pole that stands 10' above the ground. If you have a pole for climbing, it can be used. Paint a white line around it 6' from the ground. Attach a stout cord to the top of the pole. Tie a tennis ball covered by a knitted or crocheted bag to the other end of the cord. The ball should hang 2½' from the ground.

On the ground around the pole draw a circle 6' in diameter. Draw a line straight through the circle, crossing the center. The two players each have a wooden paddle or a tennis racquet. The players stand opposite each other on the edge of the circle, and bat the ball with their paddles. The object of the game is for one player to wind the cord around the pole above the white line. The other player tries to interfere by hitting the ball in the opposite direction. The game is over when one player completely winds the cord above the white line. Then unwind it and start all over. The first player to get a score of eleven points wins.

Basketball can be played with only one goal. Attach a hoop as a goal to the side of the house or garage. A peach basket with the bottom knocked out may be used instead of a regular basket.

This basketball game, in which as few as three can play, is called *knock-out*. The first player shoots from a line 15 feet away from the goal. Then each player in turn shoots from the place where he catches the ball. If the ball goes through the basket, the next player must catch it before it hits the ground. If he misses, he is "knocked out" of the game. Each time a player makes a basket he receives one point. The player who first makes 15 points wins.

Badminton, Deck Tennis, and Paddle Tennis can be played on a space about 40' long and 16' or 20' wide. You can

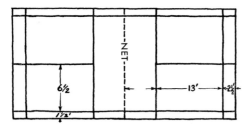

Plan for a Badminton (Doubles) Court

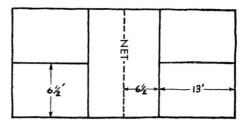

Plan for a Badminton (Singles) Court

cut down the size of the court even more and still have a good game. The main difference in these games is the height of the net used. If you do not have a net, you can use a rope.

For *badminton*, the net is placed 5' above the ground. You may decide that game is either 15 or 21 points. If the score reaches 13 all, or 13 for both sides, the side which has 13 points first can, if it wishes, set the game and scores back to 5. If the score reaches 14 all, the player who gets 14 points first has the choice of setting the game back to 3, or playing it on from 14. When a game is set back, the first side to get the next 5 or 3 points is the winner.

In playing doubles, or two on each side, the player in the right hand service court starts the play in each inning. He serves to the court diagonally opposite. The play continues until a fault occurs, or the player misses the ball. Only the serving team may score points. The serving team continues to serve as long as points are won. After each point is made the server changes service courts. Each partner has a turn at serving before the privilege goes to the other team, with one exception. Only one player serves on the side that begins service at the start of the game.

In playing singles, or with one player on each side, the rules are the same as for doubles, with one exception. The players always serve from the right-hand court when the server's score is 0 or any even number, such as 2, 4, 6, or 8. Service is from the left-hand court when the server's score is an odd number, such as 3, 5, or 9.

Players use long-handled rackets and shuttlecocks. The shuttlecocks for outdoor use are somewhat heavier than the indoor kind. Homemade shuttles of cork and chicken feathers, puff balls made with yarn, and sponge balls cut from natural sponge can be used. To make the cork shuttles, all you have to do is to punch holes in the cork with a nail, put a drop of glue in each hole, and insert the feathers.

Paddles, too, can be made easily. Make a lightweight paddle of plywood. The face should be 10" long, and 7" wide. Make the handle, 1¾" wide and 4" long.

Ring, or *Deck*, *Tennis* can be played in singles or doubles. For singles, the court should be 40' long and 12' wide. The doubles court is the same length, but 18' wide. The net is 4' 8" high. The game is played with rings of rope or rubber 6" across. A neutral space is marked off 3' on each side of the net.

The server stands back of the base line, and with an underhand motion tosses the ring over the net. The receiver

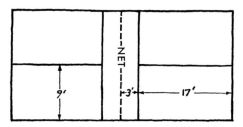

Plan for a Deck Tennis (Doubles) Court

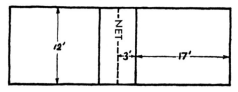

Plan for a Deck Tennis (Singles) Court

must catch the ring in the air. If he misses or steps into neutral ground, the point goes to the server. A second service is allowed if the ring hits the net and falls into the court intended for it. Only the server can score. If he fails to toss the ring over the net, the service goes to his opponent. The game ends when 15 points are scored, unless the score is tied at 14 all. In that case, the winner must make two points in a row.

Paddle Tennis. In this game, the same rules are used as in lawn tennis. Paddle tennis, however, is played on a smaller sized court, with a lower net, a shorter paddle, and a rubber sponge ball.

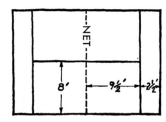

Plan for a Paddle Tennis Court

This is good training for lawn tennis. Young paddle-tennis players often play with 21 points to a game. And the players alternate service after every five points, as they do in table tennis or ping-pong.

Outdoor Cooking

Cooking in the back yard can be great fun, and food cooked out of doors always tastes especially good.

Ash Cooking. For ash or stick cooking, dig a pit at least six inches deep. Line the pit with rocks. You do not want a blaze of fire for ash cooking. Hard wood should be burned in the pit for several hours before the cooking is begun, so that there will be several inches of red coals. The rocks will hold the heat and help to keep an even temperature.

The fireless cooker principle can be used in this type of fireplace. A pot with a tight lid that fits into the pit will serve for cooking the vegetables while the remainder of the meal is being prepared. Surround and cover the pot with hot coals, and then leave it until supper is ready. All outdoor cooking pots must have handles. Circle handles like those on pails are easiest to manage. A thick pot holder should always be within reach. Baked potatoes are easy to cook in an ash fire if you place them in tin cans. A small can will hold one potato, a larger one may hold more. Wrap each potato in wet leaves, a damp paper towel, or waxed paper. Pack clean sand beneath and around the potato. Do not allow the potato to touch the side of the can or it will burn. Press the lid back over the can, then bury it in the coals for thirty or forty minutes, depending on the size of the potato.

Fish in bags is another easily prepared

outdoor dish. Cut a filet into portions, each enough for one person. Salt and spread with butter. Then wrap each portion separately in a piece of wet waxed paper. Add several layers of wet paper to each portion before putting the fish in paper bags. Let everyone place his own bag on the hot coals. When the bag begins to burn, turn the bag over, and let it cook on the other side as long as it holds up.

Banana float makes a good dessert for the open fire. Cut a ¼" strip lengthwise in the banana skin and remove the strip temporarily. Scoop out some of the banana meat and fill the hollow with marshmallows, pineapple, or any seasoning you like. Replace the strip of skin and bury the banana in the coals. It takes about fifteen minutes for the marshmallow to cook. Clean off the coals, remove the top, and eat the banana float from the skin.

To bake apples, remove the tops, hollow out the centers, and fill with nuts, marshmallows, sugar, or perhaps a little mincemeat. Replace the tops and bake the apples in the coals.

Two large sticks can be driven into the ground, and a wire strung across the coals or fireplace. Tie the apples to the wire, letting them hang about six inches above the coals. Have some thick sirup ready in a large tin can. From time to time, dip each apple in a sirup bath. They will need a number of dippings. When they are soft, they are cooked and ready to serve. They will be brown and delicious.

Stick Cooking. You may use green sticks that will not burn for stick cooking. You can also use corn poppers. A corn popper lined with tin may be used also as a frying pan.

Not the least of back-yard pleasures is cooking and eating out of doors.

Kabobs are made of squares of steak or lamb with bacon in between. They are put on the end of a sharp green stick and held over the hot coals until cooked through. You may add a piece of onion or other flavoring. Ham and pineapple, sausage and apple, chicken livers and bacon, and steak with small tomatoes can be cooked in the same way.

Bread twists made of biscuit dough about one-half inch thick wrapped around a stick and cooked slowly are delicious. Fill them with jam or fresh fruit.

A toasted marshmallow added to a sandwich made with two graham crackers and a square of sweet chocolate is called a "somare." These sweet sandwiches may be made also of two crosswise slices of apples, a peppermint drop, and a toasted marshmallow.

One-Pot Meals. A one-pot main dish is easy to prepare and serve when the family eats out of doors. The kettle should be set on two green logs or large flat rocks. When the stew is done, remove the pot from the fire and place it in an empty box at the side of the table. Surround it with branches for decoration.

Serve delicious "pocket stew" when you invite boys and girls to an outdoor meal. Cut some beef into small pieces.

Then brown them. Then put enough water into the pot to cover the vegetables that will be added. Each guest is asked to bring a vegetable. This he cleans and adds to the stew. Have an emergency pot of onions, carrots, and celery all ready and soaking in water, in case the vegetables brought by the guests are not varied enough. A "walking salad" is a good side dish for pocket stew. Roll chopped salad in a lettuce leaf and eat it sandwich fashion.

Broiling and Frying. A brick or stone fireplace is fine for broiling and frying. Lay a grill across the bricks for steaks and chops, or to hold a frying pan. For broiling, the grill must not be more than

A stone fireplace with a grill across can be used for broiling and frying.

four inches from the coals, so do not make the fireplace too high. The fire must be allowed to burn until a bed of coals is formed before you start to broil. If you want to fry, use a quick flaming fire.

Almost anything that is cooked on top of the stove can be cooked over the outdoor grill.

Tin-Can Cooking. You will need a number of empty tin cans for tin-can cooking. Save No. 10 cans, and also some large cracker, shortening, or potato-chip cans.

Cut a door in one side of each can. This is where the fuel goes in. Punch holes or bore one large hole farther up on the opposite side for draft, so the fire will burn well. Use small, dry twigs for fuel. By heating the top of a can and greasing it, you can fry on it without using a pan. Eggs, potatoes, bacon, and even pancakes can be fried this way. For quick broiling, cut out both ends of the can. Then place a metal grill or strips of tin over the top. Lay the tin strips crosswise.

If you have pancakes out of doors, use honey butter instead of having the butter and sirup separate. It is delicious and easy to make. Cream one quarter of a pound of butter and add a small jar of strained honey, beating the mixture until it is blended.

If you have trouble finding wood for the fire, you can easily make your own fuel, each piece large enough to burn for several minutes.

Use a small can. Cut a strip of cardboard twelve inches long and a little wider than the depth of the can. Twist it into a coil and insert it in the can. Melt the ends of old candles and pour the melted wax into the can until it is filled. The cardboard which extends above the can will serve as a wick. Allow the wax to harden before using. This makes good fuel.

Cone candles for the same purpose can be made from newspaper. Take a whole sheet, or two whole sheets, and wrap them tightly around a piece of heavy string such as candlewicking. At intervals of six to eight inches, beginning at the top, tie pieces of string. Clip the paper about an inch or so above each of the tied places. Spread each paper tube out at the bottom and you will have a cone. Dip the cones in melted wax and use them for tin-can fuel.

Your arrangements for outdoor cooking will not be complete without stools, benches, and a table. It is a good plan also to provide a woodpile. This should include twigs, sticks, and shavings, as well as firewood. Hard wood burns better than pine, and makes hotter coals. You may need a small cart or a wheelbarrow to carry things back and forth.

The clean-up for outdoor cooking will be easy if everybody helps. Keep two large boxes or cartons near, one for dish scrapings, the other for discarded paper napkins and the newspapers on which you have peeled fruit or potatoes. Pans should be soaked in cold water before they are washed.

A hollow filled with gravel will carry off water. Hold a leafy branch over it and pour the greasy water on the branch.

The leaves will catch the grease and the food particles. Later, you can burn the branch.

For safety, always have a small clearing around the fireplace. Keep a bucket of sand near by to put out the fire quickly, if necessary. Do not forget pot holders. All pots must have handles. Do not leave sharp edges on tin cans. Fold them over with pliers and hammer them against the sides of the can. Before lighting the fire, be sure that the pans are firmly in position. Never wear loose clothes for outdoor cooking. Always return any leftover matches to their proper place in the house.

Indoors and outdoors, summer and winter, your home can furnish you with many happy hours of play. If you make the most of your home and yard your friends will like to visit you. You and your friends can do almost everything described here. Don't expect Mother and Dad to do all the work. But they will want to share in the work as well as in the fun.

BOOKS TO READ

CROSS, GENEVIEVE. A Trip to the Yard. Illus. by Marjorie Hartwell and Rachel Dixon. Garden City Books, 1952. Backyard nature study.

HADER, BERTA HOERNER and ELMER. The Little Stone House; a Story of Building a House in the Country. Illus. by the authors. Macmillan, 1944.

HURD, EDITH THACHER and CLEMENT. Somebody's House. Lothrop, 1953.

LENSKI, LOIS. Let's Play House. Illus. by the author. Oxford, 1944. Papa Small, 1951.

MITCHELL, LUCY SPRAGUE. New House in the Forest. Illus. by Eloise Wilkin. Simon & Schuster, 1946. (Little Golden Book.)

Pinney, Monkmeyer

GAMES FOR TRAVEL

JOSEPHINE VAN DOLZEN PEASE

IT'S FUN to go traveling by airplane, train, ship, bus, and automobile. But even the most interesting trip is likely to become tiresome, especially if it is long. There will be times when you will wish you had something to do. There are many simple games you can play and things you can make which will keep you amused at these times. Josephine van Dolzen Pease, author of *The Happy Book, This Is the World,* and *It Seems Like Magic,* describes some interesting games which will help you to pass the time pleasantly.

Even though it is fun to travel, time may pass slowly if you are on a long trip. For such occasions, it is well to have some interesting games on hand.

HALF the fun of visiting new places is planning for the trip. It is always exciting to travel across the country. But after a while you may get tired of looking at the scenery. After dark, there is not much to see. At such times, you may wish you had something interesting to do. A little planning ahead of time will help to make your trip more pleasant and keep it from becoming dull.

You will enjoy the trip more if, before you start, you find out something about the place you are going to visit and the country through which you will pass. Your trip may lead you through historic places, possibly along old battlegrounds. Or it may lead you through the Indian country, with its many colorful legends. You will travel past farm lands, and perhaps visit cities which supply some of the world with manufactured goods. You will want to know something about the rivers you cross, the mountains you

66

climb, and the natural wonders you see.

You can easily find out for yourself facts about almost every city, region, or other place of interest. You may have magazines from which you can clip pictures of some of the places you will visit. Travel agencies also will supply you with picture folders. And, as you stop along the way, you can collect picture post cards. Later, these will bring back pleasant memories of your trip.

Your Fun-on-the-Way Bag

Before you start, be sure to make a list of things to pack in your Fun-on-the-Way Bag. You might include, for example: your favorite book or magazine; a doll; a toy truck, airplane, or automobile; paper cut-outs; writing paper; drawing, or construction paper; pencils; crayons; play scissors with blunt ends; a small checkerboard and checkers; a small jar of paste. You might also copy in a small notebook some of the suggestions for games which you will find in this chapter.

Looking-out-the-Window Games

When you get tired of looking at the scenery, it is time to think about looking-out-the-window games. These games can be played while you are riding in trains, buses, or automobiles, as long as you can see plainly the things you pass.

What Will It Be? In this automobile game, the players guess about the next car that they will meet on the road. The leader decides each time what to guess about. What color will the next car be? What make of car will it be? Will it be a truck or a passenger car? Will it have a man or a woman driver?

Every correct guess counts 1 point, and the player who first scores 50 points wins this looking-out-the-window game.

How Many Miles? To play this game, first choose a leader. He looks ahead at a church or a gas station, or perhaps a turn of the road. "Guess how many miles it is to that church!" he says. Or "to the turn of the road" or "to that gas station." Have the person beside the driver check the speedometer at the first and the last of the game. The speedometer will give the correct answer, and the player whose guess comes closest to the actual distance wins the game.

The Game of States. The players watch the license plates of passing cars and take turns naming the states from which the cars come. The player who is the first to name correctly thirty states, or any other number agreed upon before the game starts, is the winner.

A, E, I, O, or U. In this game each player is given one of the five vowels a, e, i, o, or u. If there are but two or three persons playing, decide what vowels you will choose. Then all the players watch the mailboxes and the road signs they pass as they drive by and read what is printed on them. Each player receives 1 point on his score every time his special letter appears. For example, if the name *Brown* is printed on a mailbox, the player whose letter is "o" would score 1 point if he saw it. The sign, "Turn Left," would give the "u" and "e" players 1 point each, if seen by both.

The player who first scores 50 points is the winner. To make this game more interesting, the players should change letters after each game.

Dogs and Cats. In this game, each player looks for certain things along the road. He gets a certain number of points on his score for each thing he sees. Unless you are especially good at adding, have an older person keep score. If you are traveling in an automobile, it is also fun for each player to count only the objects on one side of the road. Be sure to call the game off while you are going through towns and cities. A house counts 1 point; a house with a dog in the yard, 2 points; a red barn, 3 points; a barn of another color, 5 points; a cornfield, 8 points; a scarecrow, 10 points; a man fishing, 15 points; a man with a dog fishing, 20 points; a woman picking flowers, 15 points; a woman hanging out clothes, 20 points; a dog chasing a cat, 25 points.

You can add to this list other objects such as a church steeple, an oak tree, or a chicken yard. Or you can always change the number of points for each item.

The player who first calls out that he sees one of these gets the number of points allowed. If there is a tie in calling, each player receives the same number of points on his score. The first to reach a score of 100 wins the game.

Ziggity. In this game, the players watch only for white objects along the road. Each white object seen and called by its name counts a certain number of points on the scores. A white house counts 1 point; a white horse, 5 points; a white goat, 10 points; a man with a white beard, 15 points.

Whenever a player sees one of these objects he calls "Ziggity, horse," or "Ziggity, house," and so on. The first player who calls is the one who wins the points. If he makes a mistake and names the wrong thing, or if the object he names is not white, the points are taken away from his score. In case of a tie, each player receives the same number of points.

Churches and Schools. One player, or a team of two, counts the number of churches passed. Another player or team counts the number of schools. Have the game continue until a certain city or town is reached. The player or team with the highest score at that station wins the game. Another way to play this game would be to choose a side of the road or track on which you can count the objects.

When You Are Tired of Looking out the Window

If you are traveling along a country road in an automobile, singing often helps to pass the time. Your mother and father may join in the songs and you can have many happy tunes. Often, it comes in handy to know games that will not disturb other travelers. These games will also help you to amuse yourself when you visit your grown-up friends. And they are good stop-over and "waiting" games.

What Animal Am I? The player chosen to start the game decides what animal he wants to be. Then each of the other players in turn asks him one question. For example, one player might ask, "Can you swim?" Or another player might ask, "Can you fly?" "Is your color red?" Or "Do you live on land?" "Do you live in the mountains?" "Do you live in a tree?" As soon as his question is answered with "Yes," or "No," each player makes one guess as to what the animal is. The one who guesses correctly starts a new game by deciding what animal he wants to be and asking the others "What animal am I?"

I See Something You Can See. The player chosen to begin the game looks about him and decides upon something he can see that the others can see, too.

"I see something you can see," he says, and at the same time he points his finger at another player.

"What color is it?" the other player asks. The first player then gives the color of the object he has in mind. Then the other makes one guess. If he guesses correctly he may choose something for the others to guess. If he does not, the first player repeats his question and points at another player. You can keep this game going as long as you wish.

This Is My Nose. The leader of this game starts it by calling one of the other players by name. He then points to some part of his own body and calls it by a different name. He may point to his foot and say, "This is my nose," or to his knee and say, "This is my wrist."

He then begins to count up to 10. Before he gets to 10, the player named must do just the opposite of what the leader has done. If the leader has called his foot his nose, the other must point to his own nose and say, "This is my foot." If the leader has called his knee his wrist, the other must point to his own wrist and say, "This is my knee." If he does this correctly, he gets to be the leader. If he misses, the leader starts the game again. This time he calls on another player and names other parts of his body.

Rhyme Time. If you like rhymes, you are likely to be good at this game of rhyme time.

The player who starts chooses a word. Maybe he chooses "man." "I am thinking of a word that rhymes with tan," he says.

"Is it pan?" the second player asks.

"No, it isn't pan," answers the first player.

"Is it fan?" the third player asks.

"No, it isn't fan."

The player who answers correctly chooses the next word to be guessed. And so the game goes on for as long as you care to play it. A game called "I Am Thinking of Something," described in the chapter, "Quiet Play," is also an interesting stop-over game.

Snip. Snip is a letter game suitable for quiet hours on a trip. To start the game, one player points to another and says "D-O-G, Dog." Then, at once, he begins to count to 15. Before he reaches the number, 15, the player he pointed to must give a word that begins with D, something that begins with O, and something that begins with G. For example, the player pointed to may reply with *Donkey, Owl, Goat.* If he fails to name three words in time, the first player spells another word and points to another person. When a player names the three words in time he changes places with the first player, and starts the game again.

Buzz. If you know your multiplication tables, you will be a whizz at Buzz. In this merry game, the players stand or sit in line. Beginning with the one at the left, each player counts aloud in turn— 1, 2, 3, 4. When the number 5 comes up, the player, instead of calling out his number, must say "Buzz." When number 10, 15, 20, or any multiple of 5 is reached, the player on whom this number falls, does the same. The count would go: 1, 2, 3, 4, Buzz, and so on. Or you can select another number and its multiple. When the count reaches 50, the game ends. A player making a mistake drops out of the game. The last one to remain is the winner.

My Uncle Came Home. When your

arms and legs feel stiff because you have been sitting still a long time you can play "My Uncle Came Home." This game furnishes many laughs as well as good exercise. First, choose a leader.

The leader turns to the player next to him and says "My Uncle Came Home." "What did he bring you?" the player asks. "A fan," answers the leader, and starts fanning with one hand.

The player next to the leader then turns to the one next to him and the question and answer and fanning are repeated. This goes from one player to the next and back to the leader.

"My uncle came home," the leader says again. "What did he bring you?" asks the player next to him.

"A fan and a pair of scissors," answers the leader, going through the motion of fanning himself and moving the fingers of his other hand like scissors. The question and the answers, the fanning and the scissors movement go from one player to the next and back to the leader as before.

Next time around, the leader may add a pair of glasses to the list and rapidly blink his eyes. Again, shoes may have been the uncle's gift. If so, the leader starts tapping his feet. Uncle's next gift might be a hat, in which case, the leader starts nodding his head.

Each time a new article is added to the list it calls for one more motion to be made while all the other motions are continued. By the time the leader has completed the list of uncle's gifts, your head, eyes, mouth, both feet and both hands may all be in motion at the same time.

Checkerboard Fun

Here are games that may be played on trains, in hotels, on ships, or wherever there is room to hold a small board between the players.

Between the Scissors. This is a game

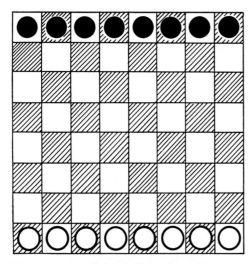

"Between the Scissors" is played by two players, each with eight checkers.

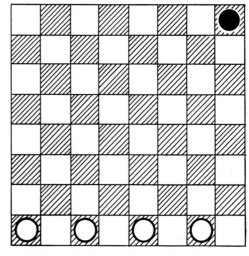

In "Fox and Geese," the black fox tries to break through the line of four geese.

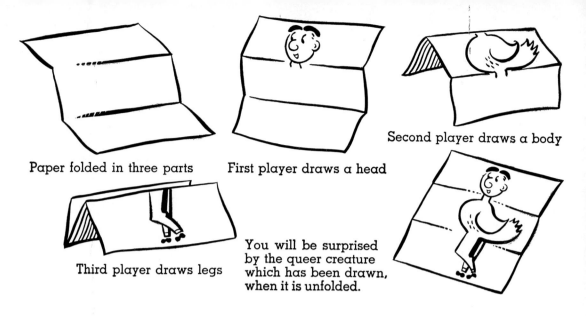

Paper folded in three parts

First player draws a head

Second player draws a body

Third player draws legs

You will be surprised by the queer creature which has been drawn, when it is unfolded.

You will have all kinds of fun making picture jokes on a sheet of paper.

for two players. The object is to take away your opponent's men one by one until he has only one left on the board.

To begin the game, each player places eight checker men on the squares directly in front of him. The board set up for playing is as shown in the illustration. The players take turns moving their men from square to square. Each player can move as far as he wishes in any direction. If a player can trap one of his opponent's men between two of his own, he may remove the man from the board. Be careful not to move one of your own men into the scissors; that is, between two of your opponent's. For, if you do, you will lose that man in your opponent's next move. Think out each move carefully before making it. In what position will it leave your men? If you wish to stop the game before one player is down to one man, the player who has the most men on the board is considered the winner.

When one player has only one man left on the board, the game is over. The player with more men is the winner.

Fox and Geese. This game is also played on a checkerboard by two players. To set up the board for playing, place a black checker, the Fox, on any of squares 1, 2, 3, or 4. Place four white checkers, the Geese, on squares as they are placed in the picture.

The object of the game is for the Fox to break through the line of Geese, or for the Geese to corner the Fox so that he cannot move.

The Geese can move diagonally forward, one square at a time. The Fox can move diagonally forward one square or diagonally backward one square. Neither the Fox nor the Geese may jump or capture men. The players should change sides after each game so that each has the same number of turns to play Fox and Geese. If the Geese are moved cleverly, they will win.

Fun with Paper

Picture Jokes. All you need for making picture jokes is a piece of paper and a pencil for each player.

The picture jokes will be easier to make if each player first folds his paper in three parts and then unfolds it.

71

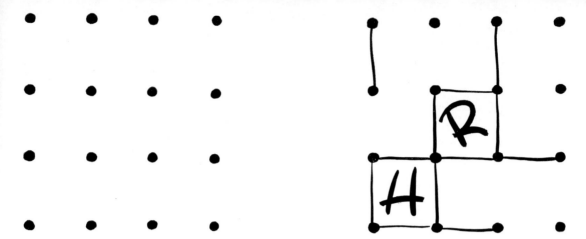

In playing "Dots and Lines," you put your initial in each square you complete.

When the paper is ready, each player draws a picture of the head of an animal or a person in the section above the upper fold. When his drawing is finished he refolds the paper so that his drawing is hidden, except the ends of the neck lines. Then the drawing is passed to the next player, who continues from the lines he can see. The second player draws the body of an animal or person, making only the lines that begin to form the legs, across the fold on the third section of the paper. He then turns the paper over so that the last player can see only the lines beginning the legs. The last player adds the legs and feet.

When the drawing is finished and the paper is unfolded you are likely to have a funny picture of a creature like none that has ever been seen.

Dots and Lines. Two players hold between them a paper on which a square made of dots has been drawn. The players take turns drawing a line between two dots in the square. The object of the game is to make as many small squares as possible. A player may draw a line straight across, or horizontally, or he may connect dots with a line up and down, or vertically. But he may not connect any dots with a slanting, or diagonal line. A player connects only two dots at a time. But if he closes up a small square he has another turn. Whenever a player closes a box, it belongs to him, and he places his initials in the square. Try never to connect the third side of a square or your opponent can make the fourth, and call the square his. The one who has his initials in the most squares after the dots are connected wins the game.

All you need for playing "Tit-Tat-Toe" is a sheet of paper and a pencil.

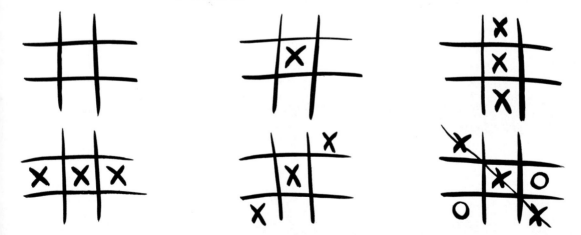

Tit-Tat-Toe. Keep this simple pencil-and-paper game in mind when you are going on a trip. Draw two sets of parallel lines crossing each other at right angles. One of the two players begins the game by marking an x in one of the nine spaces formed by the lines. His opponent marks an o in another space. The object of the game is to get three x's or o's in a row, either up and down, across, or diagonally. The player who first succeeds in doing this draws a line through his row and calls out "Tit-tat-toe." This ends the game. The players take turns in beginning the game.

Things to Make on a Trip

If you are on a train or ship, or stopping where you can have a table to work on, you can amuse yourself by making things from the materials in your Fun-on-the-Way Bag. You can cut out strings of paper dolls or make paper doilies. Or you might like to try your hand at making a drinking cup.

Paper Drinking Cup. Take a sheet of paper about 8″ square. Fold on a diagonal line so that two opposite corners meet. Hold the triangular piece with the point up, and fold over the right flap. Now fold over the left flap. Turn down the top flaps on each side, and you have your cup.

A Handy Envelope. Why not write a letter to one of your friends back home, and mail it in an envelope which you have made yourself? Cut a square of paper as shown in the illustration and fold on the dotted lines. Then open the paper flat again. Fold each side corner to the center of the paper. Fold the bottom corner to the center and paste all three corners together.

Paper Mats. It is always fun to make paper mats. You can use them for dollhouse rugs or table mats, or in many other ways. Take two squares of paper of different colors. If you have no colored paper, you can color one square with your crayons. Fold one of the squares on the dotted line as shown. Hold the paper at the folded edge and cut slits about ½″ apart through two thicknesses of paper. Stop cutting the

Paper drinking cups and envelopes come in handy when you travel.

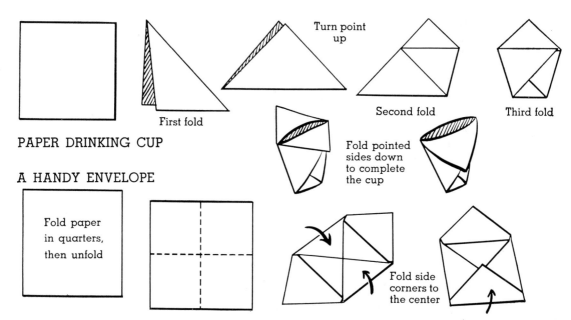

PAPER DRINKING CUP

First fold

Turn point up

Second fold

Third fold

Fold pointed sides down to complete the cup

A HANDY ENVELOPE

Fold paper in quarters, then unfold

Fold side corners to the center

Colored
strips of
paper

Thread paper
strips through
slits in sheet
of white paper

Colorful paper mats are easily made and can be used in many ways.

slits about ½″ from the edges. Cut the other square of paper into strips about ½″ wide. Lay the first square of paper flat and weave the strips back and forth between the slits until the square is full. Then paste the ends of the strips to the edges of the first square so they will not slip.

A Good Traveler

The best way to be sure of having an invitation to go on another trip is to be such a good traveling companion that everybody has more fun because you are in the party. Here are some things to remember: Keep cheerful even if you are tired of riding. Wait until a convenient time before you ask for drinks and snacks, even if you are hungry and thirsty. Enjoy doing what others want to do even if it does not always interest you. Try to like the food served to you, even if it is different from that at home. Keep your toys and your clothes picked up neatly wherever you go. Save trash for trash boxes, even if it is easier to throw it on the floor of the car or out of the window. Watch for chances to help whenever you can, and you may get to go on many happy trips to see the world in which you live.

BOOKS TO READ

HOROWITZ, CAROLINE. *It's Fun to Learn; For Boys and Girls from 5–8.* 2d ed. Hart, 1952.

KEENE, FRANCES W. *Travel Fun Book for Boys and Girls.* Seahorse Press, Pelham, N. Y., 1950.

SALAFF, ALICE. *Words Are Funny; a Riddle Book.* Illus. by Vera. Doubleday, 1952.

WOOD, RAY, comp. *Fun in American Folk Rhymes.* Illus. by Ed Hargis. Lippincott, 1952. Tongue twisters, cumulative tales, riddles, and rhymes.

ZOFF, OTTO, comp. *Riddles Around the World.* Illus. by Fritz Kredel. Pantheon, 1946.

U.S.D.A.

PLANNING
A PARTY

We all like to give parties and go to them. The fun we enjoy at birthday, Valentine, Halloween, and other parties we remember long after we have grown up.

BERNICE WELLS CARLSON

DID YOU ever give a Mother Goose, Valentine, Christmas, Cowboy, or Hobo party? If not, perhaps your father and mother will help you to plan one for your friends. You will find how easy it is to adapt some of your favorite games to various kinds of parties. Bernice Wells Carlson, author of *The Junior Party Book*, has planned parties for all kinds of occasions. In this chapter, she tells how you can plan party fun all through the year.

ENTERTAINING is an art. By giving pleasure to others you are also giving pleasure to yourself. And half the fun of entertaining is in planning the party from beginning to end.

Some time before you get your mother's consent to set a date for it, you can decide what kind of party you would like to give. The most successful parties are those which are built around one idea or theme. Cowboy and Indian parties, Washington's Birthday, Valentine, and Easter parties are each planned around an idea. Your invitations, your table decorations, favors, and games, and even the food, all tie in with the theme. All this, of course, takes planning. On your party day when you see your ideas carried out and your guests having a wonderful time, you will feel that the work of planning has been worth while.

This does not mean that you must do all the planning yourself, without the help of others. Your mother and father are the best ones to advise and help you.

Ewing Galloway

This happy boy is calling up some of his friends to invite them to a party.

ever think of giving a party in honor of some other boy or girl? Suppose a new boy has moved into your neighborhood. Perhaps you could introduce him to your friends at a party in his honor. Or perhaps one of your schoolmates is soon to go away on a trip, or is moving to another town. What could be a better good-by gift than a party in honor of that friend!

You can have parties for such holidays as New Year's, Easter, the Fourth of July, Thanksgiving, Halloween, and Christmas. You can have parties for the seasons, to welcome spring, summer, fall, or winter. Or you can have parties just because you like to have them. Sometimes these parties are the best of all.

Often your parents invite company for dinner. If the guests include a boy or girl of your own age, you can make the dinner into a party by making place cards and favors. And you can plan after-dinner games which you and the younger guest or guests can play in your own room or outdoors. Any holiday dinner will seem more festive with place cards and table decorations. You can have fun by making these yourself.

You may often invite friends to come to your home after school to play. If so, your mother may already have given her permission to serve fruit juices and cookies to make their visits seem more like a party.

Playing Host or Hostess. When you are entertaining guests in your home, you are the host or hostess. Much of the success of the party will depend on the way you act. If you are happy and at

You should never invite any guests to a party without first asking your mother's permission.

Parties for Real Fun

Parties and birthdays seem to go together. If your birthday comes in July when many of your friends are on vacation trips, perhaps you can have your party later. Or if you live in a small apartment and your birthday is in winter, you may want to celebrate your birthday quietly and wait until spring or summer for a party. Then you can play outdoors.

At your own birthday party, you are always the guest of honor. But did you ease, your guests will be happy and at ease also. And everyone will have a good time. As host or hostess, you are also the master of ceremonies. You announce the games and tell how to play them. You must be sure that no guest is left out of any game. In a game that calls for choosing, see that each player has a turn. Try to have some games in which every player has an equal chance to win. Some of your guests will be good at guessing games, others at running games. Try to have different kinds of games to satisfy all your guests.

You must decide how long to play a game. If everybody is happy, there is no reason why you should change to another game just because it is on your program. But if some of your guests would rather play something else, you should, as a host or hostess, let them have their way.

It is better to have many small and inexpensive prizes than a few expensive ones. There are many ways in which to reward winners. For example, if you are giving balloons for high scores in races, you may let the winners have first choice of colors. Or the winners may be given first place in line to enter the dining room when the refreshments are served. Again, the winners may lead a grand march, or the winner of one game may be the leader in the next. If you give any prizes at all, every guest, even if he has not won a prize, should have some little gift to take home as a souvenir of the party.

As your guests arrive, welcome them at the door and show them where to put their wraps. Perhaps one of your friends or some older person will help you. Your assistant might start one of the games while you are greeting late arrivals.

Even the gayest party must come to an end sooner or later. You can't very well tell your guests to go home, especially if they are still having fun. But the invitations have told when the party should end. As the time draws near, you can break up the party by saying, "We have time now just for one more game."

As each guest leaves, bid him good-by with a smile. Don't forget to thank your mother for her part in making the day a happy one. Then help her to clean up.

When You Are Under Six

You may not remember your first three birthday parties, but you probably enjoyed them at the time. If you have younger brothers or sisters, you might like to help plan a birthday party for one of them. For the first birthday party, one guest, one cake, and one candle will be enough. A simple sponge cake with frosting, a glass of fruit juice, ice cream, and animal crackers may be served.

Party for a Two-Year-Old. Two or more guests may come to a party for a two-year-old, and the invitations may be in the shape of some homemade toy. A cardboard cat with a bobbing head fastened on with a spreading brad would be an invitation to delight your guests. Or you can make a cotton-pussy favor.

Take a piece of cotton material $2\frac{1}{2}$

A simply made cotton-pussy favor

inches wide and 3½ inches long. Fold it in half, lengthwise, and stitch it up the sides and along the bottom. Leave the top open. You now have a long, narrow bag. Near the top, sew on two shirt buttons for kitty's eyes. Pucker the corners of the bag for ears, and pull a few long strands of heavy black thread through the material for whiskers. Stuff the bag with cotton, and tie a string around it under the whiskers for the neck. Sew a piece of yarn in place to make a tail.

Party for a Three-Year-Old. If there is a three-year-old in the family, he or she will be old enough, with a little help from you, to make the invitations to the birthday party. This party will be merrier and gayer than the last. Perhaps there will be animal crackers and cocoa to eat and drink. You might add to the fun by having balloons, soap bubbles, and "Ring-Around-a-Rosy."

Loder

After the guests have played with toys for a while, some of them may like to dance to the music of a piano or a phonograph. If you are helping with the party, you could play the music for them, or read them a story before it is time to eat.

When You Are Four or Five, your birthday party will seem like your own party because you can do so much to help get everything ready. You know how to cut and paste, so you can make your own invitations, except for the writing. If your cutting is a little jagged, it doesn't matter. Your friends will say, "Ann must have made these invitations herself," or "Bob made these." If you go to the trouble to make invitations, your guests will be looking forward to an especially interesting party.

You can look through old magazines and find pictures which you can cut out and paste on drawing, or construction, paper for the invitations. In the same way, you can make place cards. Choose pictures suitable for the season or for the kind of party you are having. Then, on your birthday, you can help set and decorate the table.

By this time you will have learned some of the singing and action games such as "Farmer in the Dell," and "Here We Go Round the Mulberry Bush." You will find the words of these songs in the chapter, "Games for Indoors and Outdoors." Other songs which you may like to sing will be found in Volume 11. If some of your guests do not care to join in a game, do not coax them. They may be having just as much fun watching the others.

Have you ever blown soap bubbles? Do you think you could do as well as this?

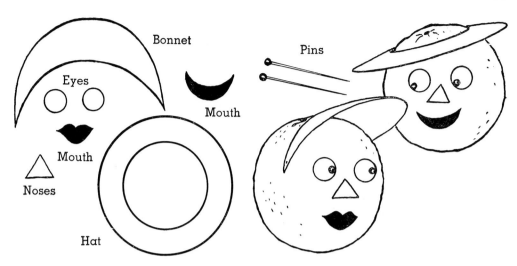

Making and pinning funny faces on oranges will give you a great deal of fun.

Kindergarten Party. One good way to celebrate a birthday is to have a party at kindergarten. With your teacher's permission, you can take cookies and animal crackers to school, and arrange to have ice cream delivered.

Perhaps your friends have never met the Orange folks. They are jolly people, and you can make them at home for your classmates. Or, if your teacher has no objections, take the "makings" of the Orange folks to school. All you need is enough oranges to go around, construction paper, scissors, and pins. Cut the eyes, nose, and mouth out of construction paper of different colors, and pin them on the oranges for faces. The orange girls will wear, on their heads, only the brims of sunbonnets. Cut them from construction paper in the shape of half moons. The orange boys will wear only the brims of hats. Cut their hats round, with a round hole cut from the center. Then slip the hats over the orange heads.

At the age of five or six, it may be most fun to have your party in the morning, from about 10 o'clock to 12:30. Then you will not have to wait all morning for the party to begin, and your guests will not be too tired when it is over. A good lunch with ice cream and cake for dessert makes a fine ending for a morning party.

When You Are Six or Over, you have had the thrill of winning games. Your playmates may like to win, too, but some of them are still too young at six to be good losers. So, instead of having contests and giving out prizes, as your older brother probably did at his party, why not have "sur-prises" for all your guests? Then everyone will have a prize. When you are over six, you can do almost everything for your own party.

Party Planning

The first step in planning a party is to select an idea, or theme. Then your invitations, games, table decorations, favors, and refreshments can carry out this theme. This would be easy to do for a

Valentine, St. Patrick's Day, or Washington's Birthday party. But you might prefer to give a Gypsy party, a Baby party, or a County Fair party. It is always exciting to be invited to a theme party of this kind.

Next, decide what boys and girls you wish to invite. Is the party to be indoors or outdoors? If it is to be in the house, how many guests can you have? Your mother will help you decide how many guests you can invite at one time. Usually you will want to invite the playmates you know best—boys and girls your own age. Make a list of them. Perhaps, you have a friend who is a little older, but who might feel out of place among the younger guests. And yet you do not wish to leave this friend out. You could give this friend a special invitation, to come to the party as assistant host or hostess.

Some of your playmates may have younger brothers or sisters who would feel hurt if they were not invited. They could not very well take part in the games, but they would enjoy the refreshments. You might invite them to come in time for lunch.

Invitations are not always needed, but they will help you to carry out your party theme. It is fun to make and receive invitations, especially if they are original and unusual. Invitations will also remind the guests of the time they are expected to arrive and leave. If you wish to know if your friends can come to your party, write "Please answer," at the bottom of your invitations.

Decorations. If your party is to be given during the Christmas holidays, you may not have to add decorations to those already in your home. At other times, crepe paper streamers or balloons may be used. Flowers are always lovely. Autumn leaves make gay-colored decorations for a fall party. A centerpiece for the table can be made of fruits or even vegetables.

Entertainment. Your next step is to select games for your guests to play. If the party is to be indoors, choose only the games you can play easily in the space you will have. Many games can be played in the living room. Your guests will not all arrive at the same time. For those who come early you can plan some game in which any number of players

Those invited to this party are getting ready to play a game of "London Bridge."

Feiler, Monkmeyer

"Blindman's Buff" is always a popular game you can play at your own party.

H. Armstrong Roberts

can take part, and which a new player can join at any time.

An active game, such as blindman's buff or a race, should be followed by a quiet game. Plan to have a quiet game just before the refreshments are served. Directions for playing many games will be found in the chapter, "Games for Indoors and Outdoors." Many of these, with slight changes, can be made to carry out your theme.

Instead of pinning a tail on a donkey, you can ask your guests to pin the ears or tail on a bunny, or pin a cap or whiskers on Santa Claus, to carry out your party theme. "A Tisket, A Tasket" can be played by sending a bunny, a shamrock, or a dolly to "my love." You can drop a cloth bunny, a paper shamrock, or a rag doll instead of a handkerchief.

"Farmer Jones's Brook" can take the place of "Musical Chairs" or "Going to Jerusalem." The "brook," a small rug, is placed on one side of the room. The players march around the room to music, each stepping on the rug in passing. When the music stops, the last player who stepped on the rug is told that he got his foot wet and must drop out of the game. At Christmas time, you can use a wreath instead of a rug, and each player must step in the center of it as he passes.

There are several ways of playing blindman's buff. At a Christmas party, Santa could be blindfolded. He has lost one of his reindeer. The other players form a circle around him. He points to one of them, and calls, "Here, Donder!" "Donder," carrying a small bell, enters the circle. Whenever Santa calls, "Don-

der" rings his bell. But he may dodge as much as he likes. When Donder is caught, Santa must tell who he really is.

Looking for hidden objects is always fun at a party. Instead of hiding a thimble, you can hide any small object in keeping with your theme.

At a patriotic party the players lined up for a relay race could be soldiers. But each of the soldiers, you explain, has lost one leg. So they must hop on one leg to the goal and back. And soldiers, of course, have to do their own mending. Who will be the first to run to the goal, thread a needle, and get back to camp?

After you have gone over your list of games, you will be surprised to see how many ways old games can be slightly changed to seem like new. Be sure to plan at least one more game than you think you will need. If you run out of games, it is not always easy to think of a new one in a hurry.

As your next step, make a list of the things you will need for the games. For

What fun it is to blow out the candles on your own birthday cake! As you grow older it becomes harder to blow out all the candles with one breath.

Keystone

those mentioned, you will need something to hide, small objects for a memory test, needle and thread, buttons, rings, pencils, and paper. Small cards, 3 inches by 5, will be easier to write on than paper, if any of your games have written answers. If your program includes races, a whistle is handy to have for starting them.

As the master of ceremonies, you will not want one guest to win too many prizes. You might limit the number of prizes to two or three for each person. If you have a prize left over, you can award it to the one guessing closest to a number written on a sheet of paper.

If you have arranged to have an entertainer at your party—a clown, a magician, a storyteller—or motion pictures, the best time for the performance will be just before refreshments are served.

Refreshments. While you are playing games, one of your younger guests may ask, "When is the PARTY going to begin?" You will know that he means,

"When are refreshments to be served?" For refreshments always help to make a party a success. If you are serving lunch or supper, the best time to do so is at the usual mealtime. The younger the guests, the more simple the food should be. Boys and girls under six usually like creamed foods, carrot sticks, sandwiches, custards, milk, and ice cream and cake that is not too rich. If you are over six, you can choose your favorite dishes and help to prepare them. Everything you do yourself makes your party more interesting.

Often you can decorate food to carry out the party theme. Or you can serve food under different names. At a Halloween party, hot chocolate becomes "witches' brew." Wieners at an Indian party become venison or bear meat.

Serve small portions, especially to younger guests. You can always arrange for second helpings. Never serve milk, water, or fruit juice in tall glasses which are easily tipped over. Perhaps you are having only light refreshments, such as ice cream and cake, for an afternoon or morning party. If so, serve soon after all the guests arrive. Then you will not spoil their appetites for their lunch or dinner.

Calendar Party for January

For invitations to a January party, paste small calendars to a 4 by 6 inch card. Circle the date of the party in red. Below the calendar write the rest of the invitation.

Because the "red-letter day" is in January, make your decorations look wintry. Even if you live in a warm climate, these icy decorations will be especially interesting. Select small, graceful branches of trees or shrubs. Spread newspapers on the kitchen floor, and place two large dishpans on the papers. Make a heavy starch, pour it into one of the pans, and dip the branches into it so that each branch is completely covered. Hold the branches, one by one, over the other pan. Then sprinkle artificial snow

or soap flakes over them. When they are dry, place the branches in vases. They will give your room the appearance of an ice-and-snow fairyland.

Make a few smaller ones to stick in corks. Paint the corks white and use them in your winter-scene centerpiece for the table.

Spread your table with white crepe paper, and make a cotton snow man for the center. Crumple wet paper into three balls, one for the head, one for the body, and one for the rest of him. Cover each ball with flour-and-water paste. Then add a thin layer of cotton. Paste or pin the three parts together. Cut eyes, nose, and mouth out of drawing or construction paper, and paste to the face. Place the small snow-covered trees around the man.

A marshmallow man with a chocolate bud hat, all pinned together with toothpicks, guards each plate. His eyes, nose, and mouth are painted on with chocolate. Melt a square of chocolate in the top part of a double boiler, over hot

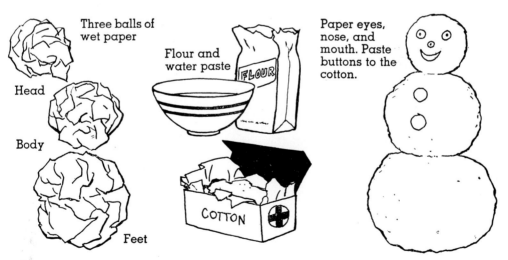

A homemade cotton snowman used as a table centerpiece for a January party

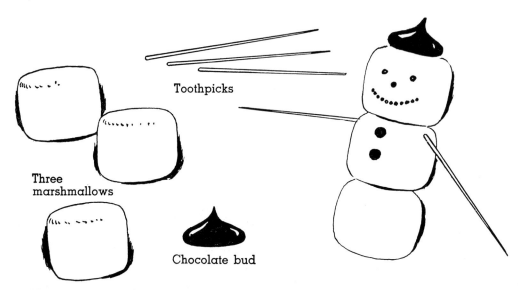

Toothpicks

Three marshmallows

Chocolate bud

How you can make a clever-looking marshmallow man with a chocolate hat

water. A toothpick can be used as a paintbrush. Set popcorn balls at each place with the place cards propped against them. Serve macaroni and cheese, green salad, milk, ice cream, and cookies.

The first game is in keeping with the first month of the year. One of the players, "Father Time," leaves the room. The others choose one of their number who, they think, will be the leader of the year. After they have made their choice, they clap their hands. Father Time comes in, and is told to kneel before the one he thinks will be the leader. If he guesses right, the others clap. If wrong, they remain silent, and Father Time has one more guess. If the second guess is wrong, another Father Time and another leader are chosen.

As this game ends, the host or hostess announces that the next game will be a series of relay races. These will represent different months. The first relay represents February, the month in which we

celebrate the birthdays of two great American patriots.

The players are divided equally into teams. Each team chooses a leader, who is given a flag. He must hold it in one hand. He places his other hand on his foot, and in this position, runs to a certain line and back. On his return, he hands the flag to the next member of his team, who must do the same.

March is too early for baseball, but there is often enough snow on the ground for snowballing. Give the leader of each team a cotton snowball. Each throws it as far as he can. A note is made of the winner, and the balls are passed to the next in line.

And who wouldn't laugh while playing the April game of your calendar party?

A foolish prize will go to the leader of the winning relay team. The winners are those who first return from threading a needle while sitting on a milk bottle. The bottle is laid on its side in the middle of the room, so all can watch.

May is the month of lambs. Each team chooses a leader. The teams line up. The master of ceremonies now announces that each team will try to reach a higher note. Middle C is sounded on the piano or any other musical instrument, and the "lambs" see who can "Ba-a-a" the highest.

"June, July, and August," says the announcer, "will be spent on the beach. You will all be crabs." A "crab" relay race is started. The "crabs" run backwards on all fours to the finish line and return.

September and October are the harvest months, and the guests must gather in the crop. To do this, the leader of each team must roll a potato across the room with his nose. Then he must pick it up, return to the starting line, and deliver it to the next harvest hand.

In November the guests will go hunting, and the woods will resound with gunfire. The guns are paper bags. The first hunter to blow up his bag and burst it with a bang is given a prize.

December brings good things to eat. The guests are asked to form a circle. A sheet of waxed paper is placed before each one. On each sheet of paper is a marshmallow with a string 30 inches long tied to it. The guests place the other ends of the strings in their mouths, and with their hands behind their backs, chew their way to the marshmallow. Anyone dropping the string must start over again. The first to reach his marshmallow has his choice of the paper hats which are to be given as favors. Or the prize may be a box of marshmallows.

Of course, there must be New Year's resolutions. The players form a circle. One of them announces that in 19.. he will not be angry. He may use any adjective beginning with "a." The next player repeats what the first has said, and adds his resolution, using a word beginning with "b." And so the game goes on through the alphabet, leaving out the letters x and z. Anyone who cannot add a resolution or fails to repeat what has gone before drops out of the game. The prize goes to the one who remains in the game the longest.

Valentine Party

A dainty invitation for a valentine party can be made by pasting a small doily, about 4 inches wide, to a 4½-inch square of red drawing, or construction, paper. On another square of the same size write your invitation. Fasten the two squares together at the top with a piece of red or white ribbon. If you prefer lighter colors, you can use pink or peach-colored construction paper. Color the raised parts of the doily lightly with green, blue, and yellow crayolas.

Several days before the party, cut five hearts for each guest from red construction paper. Number each set. After the guests have arrived, you can start them on a heart hunt. Give each guest a number. The object of the game is for each to get a complete set of hearts, with the number given him on each of them. A player might, of course, find all five of his, but this will seldom happen. After several hearts have been found, the players begin to trade. Suppose you have found one of your hearts and your number is 3. You know that another player has a No. 3 heart, but unless you have one of his set, you cannot trade. So the two of you will have to trade with others. The first player to complete a set is given a small heart-shaped box of candy.

An invitation for a Valentine party can be neat and dainty like this one.

While each guest still has his set of numbered hearts, have a heart-toss game. Let each player, in turn, try to toss his five hearts into a wide-necked jar placed some distance away. In case of a tie, those still in the race may toss again to decide the winner.

Your guests may now form a circle and play, "Who has my heart?" This is played like "Button, button," described in "Games for Indoors and Outdoors." But you may use a small paper heart instead of a button.

"Love is Blind" is another good Valentine party game. Set up a blackboard, or pin a large sheet of paper to the wall. Each guest, in turn, is blindfolded and given a piece of red chalk or a red crayon. Then he is turned around once or twice,

and asked to draw on the board, or paper, the outlines of a heart and write his initials in it. The prize goes to the one drawing the best heart.

If your party is held before Valentine's Day, you may give each guest the materials for making paper valentines. Your mother or father can be the judge of which valentine is the prettiest. Give a prize to the guest who made it.

For an extra game, if you have time, play "My Heart's Desire." In this game, the players are divided into two teams. The members of one team then act out, in turn, what they would most like to do to gain their heart's desire. The players of the other team try to guess what it is. This may be something comical, such as digging ditches or riding a bucking bronco. After the players of one team have acted out their heart's desires, those on the other team do the same.

Place cards may be valentines. For food, make sandwiches and cut them with a heart-shaped cooky cutter. Or, perhaps, your mother will help you make cookies which you can cut in the shape of hearts. Sprinkle the tops with red-colored sugar. You can also serve ice cream with a red candy heart on top.

Washington's Birthday Party

February is a good month to have a patriotic party to celebrate Washington's Birthday. You can send red, white, and blue invitations, or you can decorate them with a picture of a cherry tree. The rooms may be decorated with flags and bunting, or with red, white, and blue crepe paper streamers. Small American flags mounted in corks, painted red, may be set at each place at the table. The tablecloth may be of red, white, and blue crepe paper.

At this party you can play the flag relay game suggested for the Calendar Party in January. You might also hide a toy hatchet instead of a thimble for your guests to find. Or you could hide an even number of hatchets and cherries. Those finding the hatchets could make up one team for the relays. Those finding the cherries could be the other team. You could also pass a cherry around the circle as in "Button, button," for "Cherry, cherry, who has the cherry?"

Another jolly game for a party of this kind is "Boston Tea Party." One player, King George, stands in the center of a circle formed by the other players. Announce that tea is being smuggled into the colonies, and that King George is out to catch the smugglers. At that, one of the players in the circle tosses a small bag of tea to another, and King George tries to catch it. If he does so, the one who tosses it plays King George.

Small cherry tarts topped with whipped cream, and chocolate milk shakes, would be good food for your party. The chapter, "Cooking Up Fun," tells how to make milk shakes.

St. Patrick's Day Party

Shamrocks, harps, and tall hats cut out of green construction paper help to carry out your theme for a St. Patrick's Day party. For the invitations, you might paste a paper shamrock on a card. For table decorations, you could scatter paper shamrocks over a white crepe paper cover. Use green candles and make a gumdrop tree for a centerpiece.

A gumdrop tree is easy to make. Take a small branch of any tree that has many stiff twigs. Wild crabapple or hawthorn trees are especially good for this purpose. Place the branch in a small flower-pot covered with green crepe paper. You may have to use soil or crushed rock in the flowerpot to hold the branch up and keep the pot from tipping. Stick a green gumdrop on the end of each twig. Or, if you wish, your gumdrop tree can be of all the gumdrop colors. As favors you could have tiny clay pipes tied with green ribbon, or tiny pots of growing shamrock.

For an active game, you might try a relay race in which potatoes are picked up in a tablespoon. Or the potatoes can be placed in four long rows, for the players to pick up by hand. These are picked up one at a time, and tossed into boxes behind the starting line.

Leprechauns, or "little people," were common in old Irish stories. A leprechaun was supposed to give you a bag of gold if you asked him for it. One of your guests, to be known as Paddy or Kathleen, stands in a circle formed by the others. Those in the circle pass a bag of sawdust "gold" from one to another, behind their backs. If Paddy or Kathleen points to the one who has the bag and

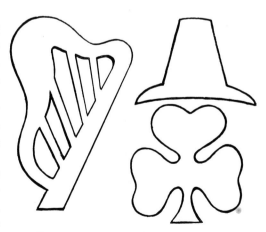

An invitation for St. Patrick's Day

demands the gold, the leprechaun must hand it over, and the two change places.

For a quiet game before supper, ask your guests to see how many words of three or more letters they can make from SAINT PATRICK. They should not use one letter more times in a single word than it appears in Saint Patrick. For example, *tin, sat, pick*.

Mint jelly sandwiches, a cake with green decorations, and mint ice cream may be served for food.

An Easter Party

A party at Easter time is especially interesting, for there are toy baby chicks, rabbits, colored eggs, spring flowers, and bonnets to help carry out your theme.

You can make clever invitations showing a baby chick just popping out of its shell. Draw the outline of the chick at the top of a strip of yellow construction paper about 3 inches long and 1 inch wide. Cut out the top part of the chick from the breast, around the head and back to the tail. But leave the rest of the paper below the chick. On this, write your invitation.

Use purple construction paper to draw the outline of an egg. Make a jagged edge at the top, as if it had been chipped open. This should be 2 inches wide and 2½ inches long. Cut it out. Daub glue around the edges, except at the top, or cracked edge. Paste it on a 4-by-5 inch piece of green construction paper. The purple egg will make a pocket with the cracked edge open. Now slip the yellow chick invitation into the pocket.

Shape paper grass into the form of a nest as a table centerpiece. Fill the nest with colored eggs or candy eggs. You could have a cloth bunny sitting close to the eggs, and a ribbon running from

each egg to the place of each guest at the table. After luncheon, the guests may pull the ribbons and receive the eggs as favors. A fluffy yellow cotton chick could stand beside each place.

For games, you could play "Drop the Bunny" instead of "Drop the Handkerchief" in "A Tisket, A Tasket." You could hide a cotton chick instead of a thimble. And you could use chicks, ducklings, bunnies, Easter eggs, and candy eggs as objects for the Memory Test game described in the chapter, "Games for Indoors and Outdoors." For the egg and spoon race, described in that chapter, use colored Easter eggs.

A different kind of egg relay game can be played with blown eggs and two pieces of thin cardboard, 6 by 9 inches. To blow an egg, use a sharp pin or needle to make a small hole in both ends of a raw egg. Then blow through one of the holes until the liquid is gone. You will have only the light, fragile shell left. Divide the guests into two teams. Place a hollow egg shell on the floor before each team. Each player must fan the egg to the finish line, using the cardboard as a fan. Then he brings the egg back to the starting line and hands it to the next of his team in line. The first team to get all its eggs across the line, wins.

A Bunny Tail game will be great fun to play at your Easter party. Your guests form a circle. One player, the Bunny, is blindfolded. He stands in the center with a handkerchief pinned to the back of his waist with a safety pin. This is his tail. A leader, from outside the circle, signals to a player, who must now try to sneak up to Bunny and pull his tail. If he manages to do so without being caught, he and Bunny change places.

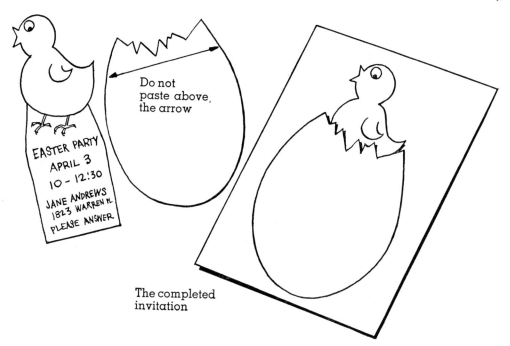

Do not
paste above,
the arrow

EASTER PARTY
APRIL 3
10 - 12:30
JANE ANDREWS
1823 WARREN PL.
PLEASE ANSWER

The completed
invitation

Your invitation to an Easter party might show a baby chick about to hatch.

But if, as he approaches, Bunny points at him, the player returns to the circle. Then another player is chosen to pull Bunny's tail.

To play "Eggs in a Basket," the players, or bunnies, sit in a circle. Each is given a small bag containing ten marbles, for "eggs." The first bunny takes from his bag any number of eggs. Holding them in his closed hand, he asks the bunny at his left to guess how many eggs he has. If this bunny guesses right, he wins the eggs. If he guesses wrong, he must pay the difference with eggs from his own bag. For example, if he guesses five when there are only three, he loses two eggs. But right or wrong, the second player takes his turn as bunny, and draws a handful of marbles. Then he asks the player at his left to guess how many he has. The game continues until each

player has had a turn. Each keeps the marbles he holds when the game ends.

A gelatin egg in a lettuce leaf nest makes a tempting Easter salad. To make gelatin eggs, use egg shells for molds. Chip off the ends of as many eggs as you need, making an opening about the size of a nickel. Then empty the contents of the eggs. Be sure to empty the eggs into a bowl so that your mother can use them for cooking. Rinse out the egg shells carefully with cool water and place them in a muffin tin. Pour liquid gelatin into the shells. If you do not have a small funnel, make one by rolling a stiff piece of paper into a cone. You can hold the edges together with a paper clip. Plan to use gelatin in several different colors. When the shells are filled, place them in the refrigerator, so the gelatin will harden. Just before serving, chip off the shells, as you do on hard-cooked eggs.

You might also serve creamed eggs on toast, cookies cut in the shape of bunnies, and chocolate ice cream. The ice cream could be served in small flower-pots lined with waxed paper. Several gumdrops, placed on the ends of toothpicks, could be stuck into the ice cream just before serving.

May Party

Invitations for a May party can be made by drawing, or tracing, pictures of a Queen of the May on 4-by-10 inch strips of lightweight cardboard. Color the pictures with water colors or crayons. You can decorate them with gummed gold or silver stars, if you wish. Write the invitation below the picture.

Many spring flowers will be in bloom in May. You can use these to decorate the living room. As a centerpiece for the table, use a Maypole with narrow crepe paper streamers. These lead from the top of the pole to the hands of paper dolls that surround it. To make this decoration, anchor a round stick about 2 feet in length in a mound of plasticine. Cover the mound with crepe paper and place it in the center of a round piece of green construction paper.

To make the dolls, cut construction paper into strips 3 inches wide and 12 inches long. Fold the strips in half, lengthwise. Then fold them in half again, and once more in half. You will now have a strip of folded paper 3 inches long and 1½ inches wide.

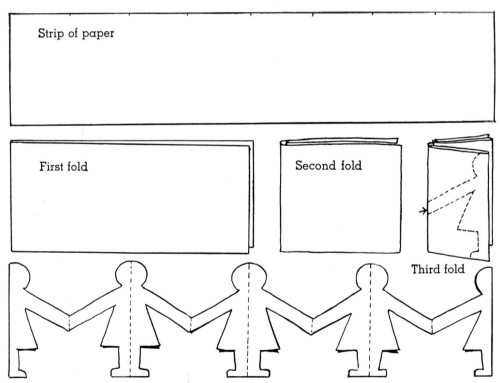

How you can make a chain of paper dolls to attach to a Maypole centerpiece

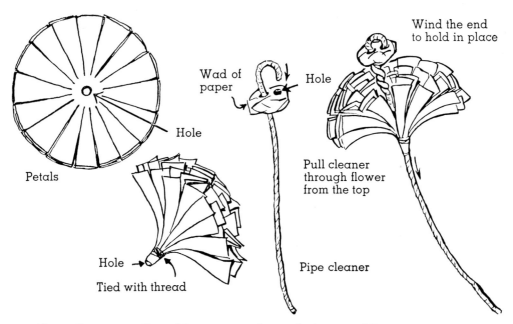

Paper flowers, such as this aster, can be made for your May party baskets.

Draw half a girl's figure on the fold as the center, extending the arm to the outer edge of the paper. Make the skirt long, and have the foot showing. Cut out the figure, except the end of the hand. Now you will have a chain of four little dolls, hand-in-hand. Paste several of these chains together by the hands until you have enough to go around the "village green" on which the Maypole stands. As they are supposed to be facing the pole, you can color the heads brown or yellow, to represent the hair. Decorate the skirts with crayon or with gummed stars. Bend out the feet of the dolls. Where the hands meet, paste the ends of the streamers.

You can make lacy May baskets for favors. Each basket will take a 5-inch paper doily, a large gumdrop, six small gumdrops, six colored toothpicks, and a pipe-stem cleaner. Place the large gumdrop in the center of the doily. Raise two opposite sides of the doily. Stick one end of the pipe cleaner into the gumdrop from the outside, first pushing it through the raised part of the doily. Carry the pipe cleaner across the top of the doily and put the other end into the gumdrop from the opposite side. Now you have a handle for your basket. Stick toothpicks into the small gumdrops, and "plant" your gumdrop flowers in the big one.

Making these things will keep you busy for several days before the party. But there are still more things to make, and you may need help. Your guests will enjoy hunting for paper flowers, which you can make to fill the baskets you make. To make an aster, fold a strip of crepe paper until you have five or six layers. Then cut out a circular disk about 3 inches wide. Slash the disk all the way round, to within ¼ inch from the center. Make these petals about ⅛ inch wide.

Gather them in at the center and bind the point together with Scotch tape or thread. Now punch two holes through a small wad of paper. Run it through one of the holes and loop it. Then run it through the other hole. Wind this end around the other end of the pipe cleaner close to the wad of paper to hold it in place. Run the pipe cleaner through the flower at the center from the top. Dip the pipe cleaner in green ink.

To make a rose, take a strip of yellow or red crepe paper 1½ inches wide and 12 inches long. Fold it into a 1½ inch square. From the top of the open edges, slice the paper to within ¼ inch from the bottom. You will now have a row of square petals. Curl the corners of each petal over the blade of a dull knife or a metal-edged ruler. Then roll the strip around your finger with the edges curling outward. Twist the bottom of the roll together, and hold it in place with scotch tape or paste. Fasten a wad of paper to one end of a pipe cleaner, as you did in making the aster. Run the other end through the center of the rose. Thread a small square of green paper on the pipe cleaner. Cut the paper in the shape of leaves and paste it to the bottom of the rose. Dip the stem in green ink, and fluff up the petals.

These flowers, several for each guest, may be hidden around the house. You can make a basket by cutting and folding a 7-inch square of construction paper, as shown. Fold along the dotted lines. Use a large needle to make holes through which you can run a thread and tie the corners together. Or the corners may be glued together. Paste on a narrow strip of paper for a handle. Or you can cover a flat-bottomed paper drinking cup with crepe paper. Make holes on opposite sides near the top and run a pipe cleaner through them to make a handle.

As the guests arrive, pin a pair of tissue paper wings to the back of each one. Now they can play they are fairies or elves. Give each a May basket, and ask them to find the hidden flowers. The one who finds most will be crowned king or queen of the May. The "elves" and "fairies" will enjoy "statue dancing" in their fluttering tissue wings. Stop the music suddenly, now and then. The dancers must keep the positions they are in when the music stops.

While dancing, the Queen, or King, of the May perhaps lost a shoe. The guests sit in a circle with their hands behind them. The queen stands in the center. A cardboard shoe is passed around the circle, at the players' backs, as they recite:

> What shall we do? What shall we do?
> Our fairy queen has lost her shoe.
> Please look high. Please look low.
> Who has the shoe? Or don't you know?

If a boy is in the center the other players say "king" instead of "queen." The king or queen then tries to guess who has the shoe. If the guess is right, the one who was caught with it changes places with the king or queen.

Of course, everyone wants to be a May king or queen. Before the guests arrive, make their crowns 24 inches long and 6 inches high from sheets of construction paper. Draw a crown on each sheet of paper. If you prefer, the guests can cut out the crowns and decorate them with gold-colored stickers. Fasten the ends together with paper clips. When your guests skip into the dining room, be sure that each one has a crown. Lemon or orange sherbet will seem like royal food for May kings and queens.

June Travel Party

Some of your friends will be going on vacation trips in June. Why not give a travel party in honor of one or more of them before they go? Write your invitation on notepaper decorated with a picture of a train, car, airplane, ship, or a seaside or mountain scene. Announce that Jane Gilbert is leaving soon on a trip to California, and that you are giving a travel party in her honor.

A June party usually may be given out of doors. Toy automobiles, planes, trains, or ships would make the best favors to carry out your party theme. You can start the fun with a "Catching the Train" game. One player is chosen as the traveler, and he is given a suitcase to carry. The others form a line. Each one has his arms around the waist of the one just ahead of him. The ones in line represent the train. The leader, or engine, starts to run. Those in line follow. The train weaves back and forth across the yard. The traveler, weighted down by his suitcase, tries to get aboard the "observation car," by tagging the last player in line. The train, of course, must not break in two.

If you must have the party indoors, play "I packed my suitcase and in it I put . . ." instead of "Catching the Train." "I Packed My Suitcase" is played like "My Uncle Came Home" described in the chapter, "Games for Travel." Each player repeats all that has been named and adds one more object in the suitcase.

Each of your friends would like to send the guest of honor a "happy journey" telegram before he starts. Give each guest a pencil and a telegram blank with the traveler's name printed across the top. Each guest is told to write a

An invitation for a going-away party

message to the traveler. Use ten letters in the traveler's name as first letters of the ten words in the telegram. A letter may be used only as many times as it appears in the name. The telegram may make sense or nonsense. When your guests have finished, collect the messages and read them without giving the names of the writers. Let someone judge which message is the best, or take a vote on it. Then award the winner a prize, such as a box of stationery.

North, South, East, and West, each invites the traveler to explore its wonders. In this game, one player is chosen as the traveler. He stands blindfolded in a circle made by the other players, who stand at least a foot apart. A leader points to one of the players in the circle, who calls out, "Come." As the traveler turns in the direction of the voice, the leader points to three others, in turn, who repeat the invitation. As each says, "Come," the traveler turns in his direction. Then he tries to point to the one who called him first. If he can do so, the two change places. If he cannot, he tries again.

If your party is held outdoors, picnic refreshments served on paper plates will be the most fun. A wiener wrapped in a long bun, with olives for smokestacks, will suggest a ship. A small paper pennant, or flag, glued on the end of a toothpick and stuck in the bun will add to the ship idea. Sliced tomatoes and carrots will go well with wieners. For dessert, you could serve an ice-cream raft with a stick-candy mast in the center.

If your guests are sitting at a table, give them gumdrops of various sizes, and toothpicks. With these they can make trains, boats, cars, or planes. Have an older person be the judge and give a prize to the winner.

As the party breaks up, give the guest of honor post cards stamped and addressed to each of the other guests. Ask him to write messages on the cards during his trip and drop them in a mailbox.

July Beach Party or Picnic

Have your guests meet at your home. Tell them to wear bathing suits and bring towels, if you are going to the beach. Arrange ahead of time for your mother or some of her friends to drive you to the beach or to the picnic grounds. If the party is to be held at the beach, one older person or more should stay with you. In addition to the lunches, take along a first-aid kit and several balls and water toys.

Any of the outdoor games described in the chapter, "Games for Indoors and Outdoors," may be played at a beach

These two are off to the beach to try out the sailboat. The pail will be useful in making sand pies and castles.

party or picnic. Special races are always great fun at one of these outdoor parties.

Instead of toasting marshmallows or wieners, you might toast "angels on horseback." These are made from slices of cream cheese, cut about one inch square, and wrapped in bacon strips. Toast them on long sticks, then slide them into buttered buns. If you prefer a stronger flavor, you could use squares of American cheese instead of cream cheese. Deviled eggs, potato salad, or potato chips will also be tasty for your picnic lunch. Serve peppermint oranges for dessert. Allow one orange and a stick of peppermint candy for each guest. Cut a slice about the size of a nickel from the

Harold M. Lambert

A clever invitation for a circus party

top of each orange. Scoop out a hole at this place in the orange. Use a paring knife and cut into each section. Place a stick of peppermint candy in the hole. As the orange is squeezed, the juice can be sucked up through the candy. A lump of sugar may be used instead of candy, if you wish.

Singing around a campfire is a wonderful ending for a beach party or picnic.

Circus Party

If you could plan a real circus or zoo party, you would have no entertainment to think about. You would need only a way to get to the circus, a lunch, and your mother or father to go with you. But a circus or zoo party at home can be great fun, too, if you plan it carefully.

A gaily colored paper clown holding a hoop can carry your invitation to a circus party. The invitation to the "Big Show" is written in the space inside the hoop. Your invitations might read: "Hurry! Hurry! Have an act ready to perform at my circus party."

Crepe paper streamers running from the center of the ceiling to the walls make the living room into an animal tent. Place as many stuffed animals as you own or can borrow in cardboard cages around the room. The cages may be decorated with crayons or with construction paper. In front of some of them make signs reading, "Do not feed or annoy the animals," or "Keep away from the monkeys' cage."

Make jigsaw puzzles for your guests by pasting pictures of circus animals on cardboard and cutting them into odd-shaped pieces. Give a prize for the guest who can piece his together first.

Announce, then, that one of the animals has escaped from his cage. A reward is offered for its safe return. The guests now hunt for a hidden animal. The first to bring it back is given a box of animal crackers or a big balloon.

After a peanut race, run in relays, announce that the big performance is about to begin. As the guests sit in a circle, each, in turn, enters the ring and performs. One may be a performing seal; another, a tightrope walker; and others, a clown, a lion tamer, an elephant trainer, and so on. Give a prize to the best performer.

By this time, the performers will be ready to pile into the "mess tent." Here a gay balloon floats from each chair, the table is strewn with animal crackers, and a glass of pink lemonade stands at each place. For your main dish, serve stew, a dish which real circus performers often have.

County Fair Party

You can have an August county fair party right in your own back yard. Invitations could be in the form of handbills. These should announce such events as the harness race, and the handwork, sewing, and cooking exhibits. For these, blue ribbons will be awarded. The guests may also be asked to bring their pet stuffed animal for a pet show.

Guests may also bring their stamp albums, butterfly collections, button collection, or model planes for a hobby show. Guests who have raised flowers or vegetables may enter them as exhibits. You can ask your guests to draw or paint a picture for the art show. In this way, your guests will be excited about your party long before they come. An older person may act as judge and award the prizes. No guest should be allowed to go home without at least one prize.

No county fair is complete without a harness race. The guests choose partners for this race. One partner is the horse, the other acts as the driver. A string, for reins, is thrown across the chest and under the shoulders of each horse. The driver holds the reins. The race track may be once or twice around the house. Only three horses should start in each race. The winners of each race then run against each other to decide the final winner.

The guests may now be divided into relay teams for a "dressing up" race. Give the leader of each team a suitcase containing a large dress, a pair of men's shoes, a hat, and a shopping bag. At a signal, the leader of each team runs to a certain spot, opens the suitcase, puts on the clothes, and closes the suitcase. He then runs back to the starting point, takes off the clothes, puts them in the suitcase, and after closing it, hands it to the next in line.

The poultry show is always an attraction at the fair. One guest, the hen, leaves the group. The others sit in a circle, hands over their eyes, heads on their knees. Four are chosen to be chicks. All remain in the same position. The hen returns and says, "Cluck-cluck." The four chicks reply, "Peep-peep." The hen must locate all four chicks. The first to be located plays the hen in the next round.

Instead of setting a table for refreshments, fix a counter or a booth. Decorate it with crepe paper or bunting to carry out your theme. Standing behind the counter, you "bark" your wares. "Hamburgers! Jumbo hamburgers! Come and get them, folks." Or, "Lemonade, ice-cold lemonade!" Or, "Ice cream, made from the double-rich milk of Lake County cows!"

After the guests have visited the lunch counter, give each a balloon to take home as a souvenir.

Harvest Party

A table centerpiece of apples, pears, and grapes, and a big, red apple at each place will help carry out your harvest theme. A farmer carries your invitation neatly folded in his hip pocket. Make the farmer by cutting a yellow straw hat, a green coat, blue trousers, and brown shoes of construction paper. Fit them together and paste on a 4 by 6 inch sheet of heavy brown paper. Cut a ½-inch slit along the farmer's waistline, and tuck the invitation into it.

As the guests arrive, give each girl a sunbonnet and each boy a straw hat. To make a sunbonnet, cut a 6-inch square of crepe paper and a strip of crepe

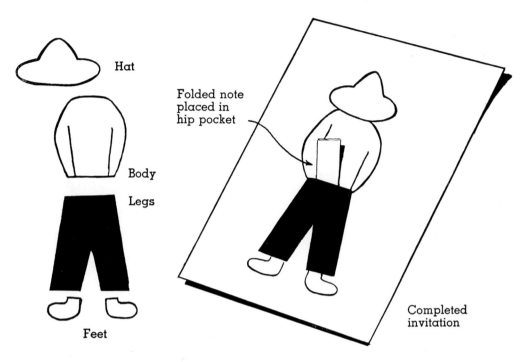

Hat

Folded note placed in hip pocket

Body

Legs

Completed invitation

Feet

An invitation to a Harvest party has a farmer carrying a note in his pocket.

paper 8 inches wide and 18 inches long. Sew the strip around three sides of the square, and attach ribbons to tie under the chin. For the hats, cut round open brims out of cardboard and paste yellow paper over and under them. The hats do not need crowns.

Divide your guests into harvest teams for an apple relay race. The apples, laid on the floor two or three feet apart and in rows, must be picked up and placed in baskets set behind the starting line.

After this race, the guests may enjoy coloring outlined farm pictures, or making vegetable animals. Each group of four should have a small table to work on. You can show them a curious animal which you say you have found in your garden. It has a summer squash body, a small potato head, green tomato feet,

and a long radish or carrot tail, all held together with toothpicks. Give each guest vegetables and toothpicks. Have your mother judge the best animal and give a prize for it.

Call the guests to the dining room with a dinner bell. Seat them at a table spread with a red checkered cloth. Potato salad, wieners, carrots, milk, pumpkin pie, and candy corn would make a good harvester's dinner.

Halloween Party

Send your friends a grinning paper jack-o'-lantern through the mail. They will find out about your Halloween party by pulling the stem of the pumpkin and reading your message. Cut the jack-o'-lantern out of orange-colored construction paper. Make it about 3½ inches

An invitation to a Halloween party which you will find very easy to make

wide and 3 inches from top to bottom. Cut holes for eyes, nose, and mouth. Daub glue around the sides and bottom at the edges, but not across the top. Paste the figure to a 4-by-6 inch piece of black construction paper. Cut out a slip of green paper 2 inches wide and 3 inches long. Cut the top of the green slip into a curved stem about 1 inch long. Have the stem taper from about 1 inch wide at the base to ½ inch at the end.

Write your invitation on the square part of the green paper and slip it into the pocket made by the jack-o'-lantern. Using the point of a red pencil, fill in the eyes, nose, and mouth with red. Write "Pull my stem" on a strip of yellow paper and paste it at the top of the black card.

A lighted jack-o'-lantern beams down on the guests from the mantel. Cut owls, bats, and cats from black construction paper. Pin them to the drapes. Decorate the room with autumn leaves, cornstalks, and orange and black crepe paper streamers if you wish.

Have your guests come to the party in costume. Greet them at the door as a ghost, who talks in a "spooky" voice and gives them a damp handshake. The ghost wears an old pillow slip over his head and a wet rubber glove on his right hand. The pillow slip has holes for eyes and mouth.

Guests are started on a hunt for black cats, bats, and owls to the accompaniment of spooky music played on a piano or a record machine. The master of ceremonies may announce that the future may hold something special for three of the guests. Hidden around the room are a penny, a ring, and a thimble. He predicts that the one who finds the thimble will be the first to own a home. The one who finds the ring will be the first to marry. The one who finds the penny will become rich.

A gypsy ring, an inexpensive bracelet, will bring luck to the one who can win it. The bracelet is hung in a doorway at about eye height of the guests. Each guest in turn is blindfolded, and given a pencil. From a point about ten feet from the ring, he is turned around once or twice. He is then given a chance to put the pencil through the bracelet. The bracelet goes to the one who succeeds in doing this. You might have extra bracelets on hand in case more than one guest is lucky.

Paint a yellow jack-o'-lantern on a large square of heavy cardboard. Cut big holes for eyes, nose, and mouth, and use the board for a beanbag throwing game. A bag thrown into the mouth could count 1 point; into the nose, 3 points; and into either eye, 5 points.

You may announce that the old witch has lost her cat. One player is chosen as the witch. The others sit in a half circle with folded arms and heads bowed. One is chosen as cat, but the witch does not know it. The witch stands a few feet away, facing away from the group. As she calls, "Kitty-kitty-kitty," the "cat" says, "Meow, meow." At this, the witch turns, and tries to locate her cat. If she finds it, the cat becomes the witch.

Halloween is the best time for games

of fortune. Place five bowls on a table. The first contains water; the second, earth; the third, a ring; the fourth, a rag; and the fifth, a penny. Blindfold each guest, in turn, and arrange the bowls differently each time. Lead the blindfolded guest around the table and tell him to put his hand into one of the bowls. If he puts his hand into the water, he will travel. If he puts it into the bowl containing earth, he will be a farmer; the ring is a sign that he will marry happily; the rag, that he will know poverty; the penny means that he will be rich.

From a box of anagrams, turned face

Shume Snow

All ready for Halloween with a witch's tall black hat and a widely grinning jack-o'-lantern ready to be lighted

down, each guest draws three. Each is given a card, at the top of which he copies the letters he has drawn. Under these he writes a first, middle, and last name of some imaginary person, using the letters as initials. For example, if the letters were J, H, and B, they might stand for James Henry Brown or Jane Harriet Black. A girl writes a boy's name; a boy, a girl's. The cards are then passed to the left, and the first question is asked: "What does he (or she) look like?" Each guest now writes three adjectives beginning with the three letters under the name on the card he holds. They could be, "Jolly, handsome, big." The cards are passed again and another question is asked: "What does he like to eat?" Then, "What does he like to wear?" and so on. After four or five questions have been answered, the cards are returned to those who held them first. According to the game, everyone will know something about his future mate.

The "witching hour" arrives as the guests go to the dining room. A big pumpkin sits in the center of the table. It is filled with noisemakers, each attached to a crepe paper streamer extending to each place. The room is lighted by candles. Doughnut hobgoblins hold the place cards.

To make a hobgoblin, push a marshmallow through the hole of a doughnut for the goblin's nose. The eyes and mouth are small gumdrops fastened on with toothpicks. The body is another doughnut fastened to the head with a toothpick. The guests may eat their goblins after being warned to remove the "bones."

As most Halloween parties are held in the evening, the refreshments may be light. Apple juice, sweet cider, or hot chocolate may be served as "witch's brew." Orange sherbet will carry out your Halloween color. As the party comes to an end, each guest pulls his string from the pumpkin, and the party ends in a blare of noisemakers.

Thanksgiving Party

A wide-brimmed, high-crowned Pilgrim's hat carries your invitation to a Thanksgiving party. To make the hat, fold lengthwise a 4 by 10 inch strip of black construction paper in two. On one side draw the outlines of a hat, with the top along the fold. Write the invitation in white pencil or ink on the inner half of the hat so that it can be read by raising the front part by the brim. The back of the hat may be pasted to a sheet of white construction paper.

The living room may be decorated with autumn leaves. If the party is held after school, refreshments may be served as soon as the guests arrive. For refreshments, serve turkey sandwiches, cranberry sauce, sweet cider, and pumpkin pie or orange sherbet. Pile fruit in the center of the table and mark each place with a paper turkey. Double construction paper as you did in making the hat. Then draw, or paste, a picture of a turkey in the upper left-hand corner. See that either the head or tail feathers reaches the fold. Cut out the figure, leaving enough space underneath for the guest's name.

Make lollipop Pilgrims for favors. Take a large spool and paint it blue for a girl's dress. Or paint it black or brown for a boy's jacket. On a sheet of stiff paper, draw a Pilgrim's face, either with a bonnet or a hat on the head. Wrap tissue paper around the lollipop, and paste the face to it. Mount the lollipop

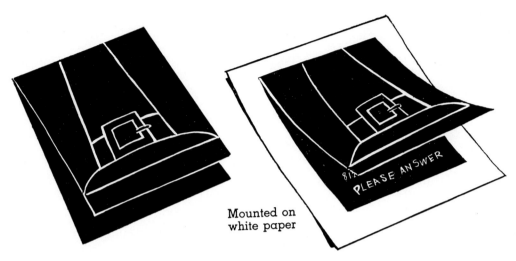

Mounted on
white paper

A high-crowned Pilgrim's hat serves as a fine Thanksgiving Day invitation.

in the spool. For a collar, roll a 3 by 5 inch sheet of stiff white paper into a tube. Slash the lower edge and flare it out to make a ruffle. Fit this under the pilgrim's chin.

After lunch, distribute a cardboard wishbone for every two guests. Then everyone can make a wish and pull. When the "bones" break, the ones who get the larger parts are supposed to have their wishes come true.

"Birds Fly" is a game played much like "Simon Says Thumbs Up," described in "Games for Indoors and Outdoors." The leader flaps his arms and says, "Wrens fly," or "Eagles fly." Each time he names a bird that flies, the others flap their arms. But if he flaps his arms and names some animal, such as a cow, which does not fly, the players must not flap their arms. If they do, they drop out of the game.

Remind your guests that the Pilgrims landed on Plymouth Rock. "But some of them," you add, "may have slipped and fallen into the water." Play "Land-ing on Plymouth Rock" as a variation of the game, "Musical Chairs," described in the chapter, "Games for Indoors and Outdoors." Use magazines placed on the floor for rocks. The guests can march to some old English music. But when the music stops, one guest will not have a magazine to stand on, and will fall in the water.

After harvesting their first crop of Indian corn, the Pilgrims feasted and gave thanks for the successful crop. That was our first Thanksgiving Day. The guests, as Pilgrims, may now harvest their first crop. Ears of corn are laid on the floor to be picked up, one at a time, and placed in baskets by the Pilgrims grouped in relay teams.

Friendly Indians were the guests of the Pilgrims at their first Thanksgiving dinner. Have your guests divide into two groups—Indians and Pilgrims. Line them up, and, at a signal, race across the room and back to the starting line. But instead of running, they must walk in "heel and toe" fashion, taking each step by placing the heel of one foot against the toe of the other. Score ten points for first place, five for second, and one for third, and see whether Pilgrims or Indians win.

Perhaps the Pilgrims taught the Indians some of the old English games, among them, "Thimble in Sight." A thimble is hidden, and each player, as he sees it, goes to another part of the room and calls out, "Rorum, Torum, Corum." The last to find the thimble gets a booby prize.

The Pilgrims could buy many things from the Indians by using beads as money. The Indians strung the beads, and called them wampum. Give each of your guests a paper plate containing glass beads. Also give each a needle and thread on which to string them. Each can make his own wampum to take home. Cranberries or colored macaroni may be used instead of beads.

Christmas Party

Invitations to your Christmas party might be made to look like a door with a wreath on the outside. The door swings open, and the invitation is written inside.

To make this door you need two pieces of construction paper, 4 by 6 inches. Three sides of the door are cut out on one piece, leaving a margin on each side for the door frame. The margin is pasted to the other sheet, on which the invitation is written, behind the door.

Christmas decorations—a glittering tree, and holly wreaths—may already be in place in your home. You can place a tall red candle surrounded by a wreath and an outer ring of red balls in the center of your table. Other Christmas decorations may be found in the chapter, "Adventures in Handwork." A lollipop angel can mark each place.

To make one of these angels, you need only construction paper, a lollipop, a spool to stick it in, a 6-inch paper doily, white paper, crayons, paste, and scissors.

Draw the angel's face on stiff white paper. Make it a little larger than the lollipop. Cut out the face, leaving a square at the bottom for the neck. Fold the doily in half, and lay the fold along the edge of your construction paper. Cut the construction paper into the shape of a half moon, an inch wider than the doily. Roll the construction paper into a cone. Fasten the ends together with a paper clip and leave a small hole at the top.

Cut a small hole in the center of the doily and slip the doily over the cone. Pinch the edges of the doily together so they will stick out like wings. Paste the lower edges of each wing together. Insert the face and paste the neck in place. Place a spool inside the cone and insert the lollipop behind the face. The guest's name may be written at the bottom of the angel's skirt.

After your guests have arrived, tell them that Santa has already come and left toys for them to find. Start them on a toy hunt, but be sure that every guest gets at least one toy. While the hunt is going on, "Jingle Bells" or some other Christmas song may be played.

Pin a large sheet of paper to the wall on which a picture of a fireplace has been drawn. Then recite this verse:

> Hang up the baby's stocking;
> Be sure you don't forget.
> The dear little dimpled darling
> Has never seen Christmas yet.

Door   Message   Completed invitation

This is how one girl invited her friends to come to her Christmas party.

With that, you give each guest a numbered paper stocking to be pinned as near the center of the fireplace as possible. Each player, in turn, is then blindfolded and turned around. The one coming closest to the center may be given a small stocking filled with candy as a prize.

Next, ask the guests to stand in line to play "Jack in the Box." This is a variation of "Simon Says Thumbs Up." The leader calls out, "Jack in the Box," and the players all stoop down. When he says, "Jack out of the box," they all pop up. But if he leaves out the word "Jack," and says only, "in the box," or "out," no one must move. If a player moves, then he drops out of the game.

Now, all warmed up, the guests sit down to play "What I Want for Christmas." Each in turn acts out what he would like to have, while the others try to guess what it is. Each may be given a green paper Christmas tree to decorate with stickers, or a Santa Claus jigsaw puzzle to sort out and put together.

Red and green ribbon sandwiches, and gelatin molds, will add a Christmas touch to the refreshments. To make the gelatin molds, take two large bowls. Mix red gelatin in one, and green in the other. Before the gelatin hardens, whip it with an egg beater. Whip the whites of two eggs in another bowl. Add two tablespoons of powdered sugar to the eggs. Then fold half the mixture in the green gelatin and half into the red. Rinse a larger bowl with cold water. Hold a sheet of wax paper in the center of the bowl, dividing it in half. On one side of the paper pour the red mixture. In the other, pour the green. Remove the paper and let the gelatin harden. In serving, give each guest some of the red and some of the green gelatin.

Make the sandwiches by removing the crusts from an unsliced loaf of bread. Split the loaf into three parts, lengthwise. Mix cream cheese with cream for a soft spread. To half the spread add

Thomas Titcomb, Black Star

A colored hat, made of tissue paper, and noisemakers add to the gaiety of any party.

pure red coloring, and to the other half, add green. Spread the red cheese mixture on the bottom layer of the bread, the green on top of the next layer. Put the loaf together. Wrap it in wax paper, and place it in the refrigerator. The sandwiches should be sliced just before serving.

Singing carols will bring your Christmas party to a joyous end.

Other Theme Parties

In the special parties for every month in the year, you have seen how well-known games can be changed and used as new games to help out the themes of your gayest parties. There may be other parties you will want to have throughout the year. Always choose an idea, or theme, around which to plan your fun.

A Carnival. Colored paper disks pasted on correspondence paper will give your invitations a carnival touch. Crepe-paper streamers, Chinese lanterns, and balloons as decorations will also help to carry out your theme. Set up a "hot dog" or hamburger booth from which to serve refreshments.

If your mother does not mind, you might give each guest a bag of confetti with which to shower the others. Or you could scatter candy kisses and let the guests scramble for them. Each guest may also be given a mask, to cover his eyes. Tissue paper hats and noisemakers will add to the gaiety.

Start the party with a "Merry-go-round," played like "Musical Chairs," but with the chairs placed in a circle.

You can make a cane rack by turning a card table upside down. Connect the legs with ropes. Then stretch strings across from both sides, making squares with the string in which you can stand canes. You can use sticks for canes. Bright ribbons on the heads will make them look like real carnival canes. Rubber rings from glass jars, or curtain rings may be used to throw, or "ring," the canes. Give each player five rings, and a cane, or other prize, if he rings one. Or you can have the guests try their luck at a fish pond, as described in the chapter, "Games for Indoors and Outdoors."

The balloon game provides other lively carnival fun. To an ankle of each player a balloon is attached by a cord two feet long. Each tries to burst another's balloon with his free foot, while protecting his own.

A fortune teller in Gypsy costume may sit at a booth and read hands, or pretend to read them. If you have a bathroom scale or can borrow one, guessing weight will be a good carnival game. You can be the "barker," or your father would be a good one to invite the guests to step up and guess their own weight. Give prizes to those who guess correctly.

A Gypsy Party may be held indoors, or outdoors around a campfire. Each guest can be given a red handkerchief, but earrings must be won. Set up a ring-toss game. Pass out inexpensive bracelets or brass curtain rings. To earn a pair of earrings, a Gypsy must throw two ringers. When won, tie a ribbon to the two rings or bracelets. Fasten the ribbon across the winner's head by clipping it to the hair with tight bobby pins.

Ask the guests to sit in a charmed circle to paint a romantic gypsy word-picture. The first player says, for example, "A pretty girl." The next repeats the phrase and adds, "A silver moon." The others, in turn, repeat what has been said before, and add to it something of their own. Any player failing to do this

drops out of the game. As in the Carnival party, a fortune teller may read palms.

Gypsy music can be played for dancing, if the party is held inside. If you have a portable record machine, you can have gypsy music and dancing around an outdoor campfire. For food, you can toast wieners or marshmallows over the campfire. A Hungarian goulash would make a good main dish. Or serve delicious pocket stew described under "One-Pot Meals" in the chapter, "Making the Most of Your Home."

Mother Goose Party. Jack Horner's Christmas pie, made of construction paper mounted on a square of paper of a different color, has a plum tucked into it, with only the stem showing. Written on the plum is the invitation to your Mother Goose party.

Hidden around the room for the guests to find are sugar plums from Jack Horner's pie; hard cooked eggs laid by your "black hen;" pretty maids, or small dolls, from Mistress Mary's garden; and perhaps tiny pails in which Jack and Jill carried water. Those getting too many of one prize may trade with others.

For your first game, each guest is given a black paper spider—the one that frightened Miss Muffet. Each, in turn, is blindfolded and asked to pin the spider to the center of a big cobweb. The cobweb is drawn on a sheet of wrapping paper pinned to the wall.

For the next game one player, Bo-Peep, is blindfolded. The other players, her sheep, form a circle around her. Bo-Peep calls to one of her sheep. The sheep she calls must enter the center of the circle and answer, "Ba-a-a." The sheep tries to dodge Bo-Peep as she follows the answering "Ba-a-a" and tries to catch that player. When a player is caught, he changes places with Bo-Peep.

Lucy Locket's pocket, a small purse, can be passed around a circle behind the players' backs. "Lucy," standing in the center, tries to find it.

Like Tommy Tucker, have your guests sing for their suppers. Your table could be decorated with a tiny garden, with cockleshells and pretty maids all in a row. The shells can be found at dime or hobby stores, and the maids can be paper dolls. Or you might have a big make-believe pie, with paper blackbirds stuck in the paper crust in the center of your table. The pie could be filled with toys, each tied with a ribbon running to each place. After the dessert is served, the pie is opened, and each guest draws out his gift.

Serve Tommy Tucker's "white bread and butter;" milk from the cow that jumped over the moon; Miss Muffet's "curds and whey," which will be cottage cheese; and tarts made by the Queen of Hearts.

Indian Powwow. A card decorated with zigzag lines, setting suns, arrows, and wigwams will invite your friends to your Indian party. The invitation may be written on birchbark from a fallen tree, or on brown paper. Ask your guests to wear Indian costumes if they have them. Directions for making an Indian costume are in the chapter, "Sewing for Fun."

Greet each guest with a "How." Give him a headband made of a strip of corrugated cardboard with chicken feathers or feathers made of colored paper stuck into it. Clip the band together with a paper clip. Let each guest choose an Indian name, such as "Rain in the Face" or "White Deer." The Indians may then be divided into tribes for relay races.

One of these might be the "heel and toe" race suggested for the Thanksgiving party. Another amusing relay is "Following the Trail." The leader of each team is given two sheets of heavy paper cut in the shape of a footprint, at least 12 to 14 inches long. Call them bears' footprints, if you like. The leader holds one in each hand. At the signal, he places one footprint ahead of him and steps on it with one foot. He places the other footprint ahead of him, steps on it

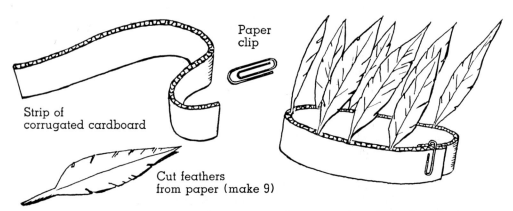

Paper clip

Strip of corrugated cardboard

Cut feathers from paper (make 9)

An Indian headband made from corrugated cardboard and chicken feathers

What boy has not played the part of cowboy and tamed the wildest broncho?

Ewing Galloway

with the other foot, then reaches back for the footprint behind him. In this manner, he makes his way to the finish line and back. He hands the footprints to the next member of his tribe, who does the same. The first team to reach the finish line, wins.

A tom-tom calls the Indians to dinner, at which make-believe "bear meat," "venison," "Indian corn," and similar dishes are served. If the party is held outdoors, you could bake potatoes in a campfire, and toast wieners and marshmallows.

Cowboy Party. A card decorated with a ranch brand, such as 4-X, or Y-O, calls the cowboys, or "waddies," to the big roundup. They should wear cowboy costumes if possible. Each guest is greeted by the Rancher with a hearty, "Hi, pardner," and is given a bandana handkerchief to wear around his neck. Paper cows and horses have been hidden. Divide the cowboys into two teams, and send them to round up and corral the cows and horses in a basket set in a convenient place. One team, the 4-X, for example, will round up the cows. The other will round up the horses. The team bringing in the greater number of animals within a certain time wins.

A bronco-busting contest would be good entertainment. The leader of each team is given a stick horse to ride, but is warned that the horse is still wild and unbroken. He must ride it to the finish line and back, yip-yipping all the way. At the signal, he must turn around three times. Halfway down the course, he must turn around three times in the opposite direction. At the finish line, he must make three complete turns again. He then runs back to the starting point and turns his horse over to the next "wrangler." During the race, the others cry, "Ride him, cowboy."

A dinner bell calls the waddies to the "chuck wagon." The table is spread with a checked cloth, and the food, or "chuck," is served on tin plates.

Before leaving for their home ranches, the cowboys gather around the piano to sing "Home on the Range" and other cowboy songs.

Animal Show or Pet Party. You could ask your friends to bring their pets and have your own animal show. Invitations should announce that the finest animals in the country are to be brought together for this one show. If you have this type of show, be sure to invite only those friends whose pets get along well together. See that each contestant gets a prize, no matter how you have to use your imagination. You could give a prize for the dog with the biggest nose, the cat with the longest tail, the turtle with the saddest look. Perhaps it would be a good idea to have your guests register their entries in advance so you can arrange to care for the pets while you have refreshments.

If some of your friends do not have live pets, suggest that they bring stuffed animals and have special prizes for these too. Blue ribbons are usually given as first prizes at animal shows.

Unusual Parties. There are many other theme parties you could have. A baseball party on Saturday morning with Dad as umpire, would be exciting for boys. A doll party, with a "baby" contest for the dolls, would interest many girls. A hike, a good moving picture, a treasure hunt, or an early morning excursion into the woods to look for birds can all be made into interesting parties.

By using your imagination, you can think up almost any kind of party. Why not a Hobo party, to which your guests come as tramps to get a "handout"? Or a Sailor party, at which you go on a cruise around the world? And you could have no end of fun at a Soap-Bubble party. But when you give a party, be sure that each of your guests receives his share of prizes and gifts. Make sure, too, that everybody has a good time, and goes home happy.

BOOKS TO READ

BREEN, MARY J. *Children's Party Book*. Menus and Favors by Verna Breen. Illus. by Hamilton Greene. Grosset, 1948.

CARLSON, BERNICE WELLS. *Junior Party Book*. Illus. by Magdelena Tolson. rev. ed. Abingdon-Cokesbury, 1948.

Child Study Association of America, Inc. Holiday Storybook. Illus. by Phoebe Erickson. Crowell, 1952. A story appropriate for whatever holiday party you give.

DURLACHER, ED. *Play Party Book; Singing Games for Children*. Illus. by Arnold Edwin Bare. Music arranged by Ken MacDonald. Devin-Adair, 1945.

KEENE, FRANCES W. *Keene Party Book*. Illus. by the author. Seahorse Press, Pelham, New York, 1949.

MULAC, MARGARET ELIZABETH, and HOLMES, M. S. *Party Game Book*. Illus. by George E. Matthews. Harper, 1951.

CHOOSING
A HOBBY

CLARA M. LAMBERT

Gordon Coster, Black Star

A hobby can be almost anything a person likes to do in his spare time. It can develop into something of value.

THERE IS a hobby for everyone and for every age. There are hobbies which you will find interesting indoors on rainy days, or when you are not feeling very well. There are hobbies which will take you out of doors or into the country. And there are hobbies which you can share with your parents. Whether you live in the city or in the country, in the mountains, on the plains, or near the ocean, there is always a special "something" you can do in your spare time which will bring you lasting pleasure. Clara M. Lambert gives us many suggestions for hobbies from which to choose. She is director of teacher education for Play Schools Association, Inc., in New York City.

A HOBBY is something you do just for the fun of it. In choosing one for yourself, you suit your own taste. There is hardly a hobby which will not give you lasting enjoyment, enlarge your circle of friends, and keep you busy in your lei-

sure hours. There are many kinds, or types, of hobbies from which to choose.

"Making" Hobbies

Many boys and girls like to draw or paint, carve things out of soap, or model in clay. Those who are clever with their hands, and like to work with tools, will choose woodworking. What can be more fun than making your own toys and playthings, or some of the furnishings for your own room? One delightful hobby is the making of musical instruments. Your tastes might even run to building model planes, ships, and trains,

Keystone

Building boats is one of the most fascinating of all hobbies.

or to cooking, making candy, and sewing.

Suggestions which will help you in your drawing, painting, and clay modeling will be found in the chapter on "Drawing and Painting." Directions for making toys and playthings are given in the chapter by that name. You can learn to make your own musical instruments from directions in the last chapter. If you are interested in puppets, turn to "Puppets and Marionettes" to find out how to make and operate them. The chapter, "Cooking Up Fun," will give you recipes for all kinds of simple dishes, candies, and confections. Turn to the chapter on "Sewing for Fun," for suggestions on how to sew and what to make.

"Doing" Hobbies

You can make a hobby out of anything you like to do. Even if you have no skill in painting, you could learn to love and to understand famous paintings by visiting art galleries. And you do not have to be a musician to appreciate good music. If you like musical pro-

grams on the air, if you like to play records, or if you like to go to concerts and recitals, you have another "doing" hobby. Music opens to you a new world of melody, harmony, and rhythm. You get to know and love the great composers and their works. In learning to make music, even if only with a drum, you train both hand and mind. Volume 11, MUSIC FOR THE FAMILY, will help you with these hobbies.

Pinney, Monkmeyer

What is more fun than to make dolls from cornhusks and to paint them?

Taking photographs is a hobby which you will find not only interesting but entertaining.

Elizabeth Hibbs

Photography, especially color photography, is another hobby of this type. Color photography has been made easy, and beautiful results may be obtained, but camera work of any kind takes skill.

Have you ever thought of raising butterflies and moths as an interesting hobby? The chapter, "Insects and Spiders," in Volume 7 explains how you can do this. Perhaps you will like to photograph these insects in their different stages, or draw crayon pictures of them.

Harold M. Lambert

That is a hobby that has interested many boys and girls. Or if you like birds especially, you might try raising canaries. Many boys and girls have made a hobby out of raising and training their pets.

Any hobby which will take you out of doors and help you to build a strong body is especially worthwhile. Most boys and girls like to go for long hikes and ride bicycles. In many parts of the world, there are trails and rest camps for those who make hiking and bicycling their hobbies.

Perhaps you belong to a Cub Scout or a Brownie troop, and even go on overnight camping trips. If you are a Scout, you have a wonderful opportunity to develop many outdoor hobbies. The boys and girls in 4-H clubs also have the opportunity of taking part in many outdoor activities, including the raising of farm animals as a hobby.

To make a hobby of an outdoor sport is to do your best in it. Tennis, swimming, diving, speed or figure skating, and horseback riding are hobbies which

Anyone who takes up music as a hobby will have a new world of melody, harmony, and rhythm open up for him.

will hold your interest for a long time. Or you can choose an indoor activity, such as gymnastics or dancing.

"Studying" Hobbies

If you are really interested in some subject, and are studying it for fun, it never seems like work. Nature study— the study of plants, birds, animals, and insects—is one of the most interesting of all hobbies. Young explorers in science will also find that chemistry or astronomy will unlock to them many secrets of nature.

Would you like to travel and see foreign lands? Then why not take up the study of geography as a hobby? Maps can be especially interesting, and some people like to take imaginary trips just by studying maps. Perhaps some day, you will visit some of the countries you have studied. Your visit will be more enjoyable if you have learned to speak one or more foreign languages. This can be done out of school, if you care to make it a hobby.

Reading will add to your friendships not only the great authors, but also the many delightful characters they have created. You will feel as if Tom Sawyer, Huckleberry Finn, Little Nell, Tiny Tim, and Louisa Alcott's "Little Women" and "Jo's Boys" were your personal friends. And books in themselves are silent companions.

There are many other studies you can take up as a hobby, such as costumes, folklore and legends, rugs, fine china, jades, and precious stones. Whatever study you choose, you can't go wrong.

Collecting as a Hobby

Collecting is fun because it is a never-ending game. If begun when you are young, the game may last a lifetime. A collection grows with you. It leads you on to new discoveries. It sharpens your curiosity and increases your powers of observation. When you begin a new collection, you are off on an adventure— on a treasure hunt.

Once started with this hobby, you meet boys and girls who are collecting the same things that you are. Your best friends are usually those whose interests are the same as yours. Often you write to others in distant cities or in foreign lands. You may exchange duplicates with them or make trades.

The collector is a kind of historian. His collection, if properly arranged, may, after a time, become a miniature historical museum.

Have you ever explored the attic of an old home? There, stored away in trunks, may be letters written during pioneer days—or a lavender-scented wedding gown of long ago. Many things prized by collectors were once loved and cherished—the doll that awaited some child under a Christmas tree a hundred years ago . . . . tin soldiers . . . . a music box . . . . or a kicking mule bank.

But whatever your collection, you will be surprised at the interest your parents and your friends, young and old, will take in it. They will think of you on their vacation trips, and will often send you the very thing you need for your collection. Collecting is a game which the whole family can play. The hobby also is one that often solves the problem for parents, uncles, and aunts, as to what to give you for Christmas or on your birthday.

There is hardly anything you can collect that will not give you some new interest. Nature exploration may begin in

You need scissors and paste if you are keeping a scrapbook.

Elizabeth Hibbs

your back yard with the bird's nest you found under a tree. The snail shell or the curious pebble you picked up and put in your pocket may be the beginning of a life interest.

The hobby of collecting need not be an expensive one. But now and then you may find yourself in possession of a prize. It was a nine-year-old schoolboy who found the one-penny British Guiana stamp—the rarest stamp in all the world, and valued at $50,000. Even the youngest collector often has the thrill of owning something that none of his fellow collectors has. It may be a Columbian half dollar, a triangular Cape of Good Hope stamp, an Indian relic, or a button from the uniform of a soldier in an early war. If an article is rare and in demand, it becomes a collector's item and is highly valued.

Collecting is more fun when you can share it with others. If you and one of your schoolmates begin a stamp collection, you can start a club. Invite others to join. Soon you will have a group which will meet regularly and exchange stamps and ideas. As your collections grow, you may want to subscribe to a collectors' magazine, or share the costs

to buy the latest catalog. Perhaps you can arrange an exhibition and award prizes for the most attractive displays. Friendly competition is always exciting, and it often makes you try harder.

Collecting is fun. But it is more than fun. It is a worth-while game and one which, once begun, you will never tire of playing.

Collections for Beginners

Picture Cards are easy to collect. Almost every city or town in the world has post cards showing its public buildings, museums, parks, and monuments. It would be impossible to collect them all. You would do well to limit your selections to a single subject, such as American cities. An interesting album could be made of city views from each of the states in the United States, and from each of the provinces in Canada.

Another post-card collection might include views of vacation resorts or scenic wonders, such as Niagara Falls, Grand Canyon, Carlsbad Caverns, Mammoth Cave, or Yellowstone National Park. A collection of this kind could be entitled "America the Beautiful." You may have visited some of

Newell

The hobby of these three girls is collecting pictures of birds. Similar picture collections can be made of flowers, butterflies, trees, or wild animals.

these spots, or you may do so in the future. But even if you have to do your traveling at home, your picture post-card album will make a colorful and interesting hobby. Steamships, trains, planes, hotels, and restaurants also are represented on picture post cards. A collection of these could be labeled "By Land, Sea, and Air."

Picture cards may be obtained from packaged foods. These are usually numbered and issued in a series. The subjects may include famous athletes, movie stars, or comics. If you are unable to obtain a complete series, some of your friends may have the missing pictures.

Nature Pictures. Magazines and rotogravure sections of newspapers offer a variety of nature pictures. These can be cut out, classified, and mounted in albums. In this way, you can make a travel album of American or foreign scenes, arranged according to states or countries. Your collection might include

views of the Swiss Alps, a Mexican market, or the Pyramids of Egypt. A series of such views would take you on an imaginary trip around the world. Or you could collect pictures of people of foreign lands in their colorful costumes. Another attractive picture collection could be made up of wild animals, birds, butterflies, or trees. Can you think of any easier way of studying geography or zoology than by making picture stories of this kind?

Have you ever thought of making a collection of flag pictures? The United States alone has had many historic flags. Each state and territory and each Federal department has its special flag. Pictures of these and flags of other nations would not be difficult to get. Some persons have made large collections of actual flags, but the pictures would be easier to get and keep.

Playing Cards are always a popular collectors' item. The pictures on the backs may be works of art. Some of them are reproductions of famous paintings. Other subjects include birds, flowers, and landscapes. Collectors try to obtain one card of each set. Perhaps some day you could add miniature and European cards to the collection. The building of a playing-card collection offers many opportunities for trading, and an album is soon filled.

Greeting Cards and Valentines. Greeting cards are used more and more for sending good wishes and congratulations, or for expressing sympathy. There are cards for almost every occasion—birthdays, wedding anniversaries, graduations, Christmas, New Year's, and Valentine Day. There are cards for father and mother, uncle and aunt, husband and wife, and other relatives.

Christmas cards and valentines may be especially interesting to the collector. Cards of long ago were often very pretty. Christmas cards sparkled with artificial snow, and valentines sometimes had frames of paper lace through which one could see Cupids with their darts, forget-me-nots, and hearts. These old cards will add greatly to the interest of a card collection. Both Christmas cards and valentines have reflected, year by year, the changing thoughts, hopes, manners and customs, and costumes of peoples. During wars, cards and valentines have been patriotic. Many of them were decorated with pictures of the Flag.

You may not be able to get many Christmas cards or valentines that are more than a year old. People do not always save them. But you can start a collection now, and within a few years it will begin to be historic. Christmas cards might be grouped according to the subjects pictured on them. Suppose you select winter scenes to begin with, or churches, stained glass windows, Santa Claus, or pictures of the Christ Child. Save only the pictures and when you have enough of one kind, mount them on the pages of a loose-leaf scrapbook by inserting the corners in slits.

Monograms. An attractive collection can be made of monograms, crests, and engraved letterheads. These souvenirs cost nothing. They can be obtained through friends or by exchange, if some of your schoolmates happen to have the same hobby. There is no limit to the number and kinds of materials for such a collection. Many persons have specially designed letterheads for their writing paper. Sometimes these are in the form of interwoven initials or of a coat of arms. Many business firms have their letterheads engraved. Hotels, ships, trains, clubs, and colleges can supply interesting letterheads. A prize item might be a White House letterhead.

Programs. Theater, opera, and circus programs may recall pleasant times. But even if they have no personal associations, they will have real value some day. In some collections will be found programs from famous theaters in New York, London, and Paris. Actors and opera stars of today will retire from the stage in time and leave only memories. If you are interested in the theater, ask your friends to save their programs for you. Before long, you can have a good collection of programs with the names of famous actors, actresses, and movie stars.

Menu Cards. Menu cards of famous restaurants, hotels, steamships, and railroad dining cars may appeal to you for a collection if you have friends who like to travel.

Recipes. If cooking is your favorite hobby, why not collect and file recipes? Many famous persons have their own recipes for salad dressings, cakes, spaghetti, and other dishes. Other recipes, such as Philadelphia pepper pot and scrapple, New Orleans pralines, Boston baked beans and brown bread, and Cape Cod clam chowder, are associated with towns and places. Many recipes have been handed down in families for generations, and come from other countries. Recipes for Scotch haggis, an English veal and ham potpie, or plum pudding are examples. To this group could be added recipes for klopse and rouladen, tortillas and enchiladas, Turkish pilaff, and many Chinese and other Oriental dishes.

Buttons were once thrown together in boxes or perhaps strung in chains to make necklaces. They were not regarded as something to collect. But now they have become collectors' items. Young and old alike are saving them, antique shops are selling them, and button clubs have been formed in many cities.

Buttons, thousands of years old, have been found in Egyptian tombs. While you will hardly have to go so far in search of buttons for your collection, your search may lead you on exciting treasure hunts. Old dresses with buttons running from neck to hemline, or old uniforms are often stored in attics and forgotten. Perhaps you can persuade the owners to let you have a few buttons for your collection.

Buttons are made of various materials. Many are made from metals, such as gold, silver, pewter, and brass. They are also made of mother of pearl, glass, vegetable ivory, bone, and wood. Among many other kinds, there are plastic buttons of many pretty colors, made in shapes of flowers, bows, animal heads, and stars.

Buttons may be mounted on heavy cardboard. You can sew them to the cardboard with stout thread. They can be grouped in any way you wish—by size, color, age, or material. But each group should be arranged to be attractive.

You may have an opportunity to collect political campaign buttons and badges. A Hoover, Roosevelt, or Eisenhower campaign button would now stand out in any such collection. Many like to pin campaign buttons and other button pins on caps they keep for this purpose. Later, the buttons may be pinned to sheets of cardboard.

Convention badges also make interesting collections. A badge worn by a delegate to a national Republican or Democratic convention, especially a convention at which a future President is nominated, is a prize.

Marbles. A permanent marble collection can be interesting and colorful. Your collection could perhaps include the small, plain marbles as well as the beautiful agates and large glass "shooters."

Match-Book Covers. Match-book covers are an especially good collection to make if you have never before made a collection. For you can find match-book covers almost anywhere and in any number and variety. Always be sure, however, that there are no matches left in the book.

This is one collection that will cost you almost nothing. You can buy inexpensive mounting cards at stationery stores, or you can make your own. Cut two parallel slits in a sheet of cardboard about an inch apart and as wide as the covers you are planning to mount. Tuck the match book between the slits so that it folds over and fastens. If your covers are mounted in this way, you can read any verses, jokes or recipes on the inside simply by opening them. When you have collected fifty or a hundred different kinds, you will want to classify them. When you classify the items of your collection, you are adopting scientific principles. Your match-book covers can be grouped according to color and design, by states and cities, or in many other ways. Perhaps you will want to classify them as business firms, clubs, hotels, restaurants, trains, ships, and persons. A collection of this sort not only can be very attractive, but also it can tell a story of present-day America and its match-cover advertising.

A somewhat similar collection may be made of pencils, many of which are stamped with the names of banks, business houses, and individuals.

Autographs and Autographed Books. The autograph of a famous person gives you a personal touch with someone in whom you may be particularly interested. If you see a movie in which one of your favorite actors has a leading role, you may enjoy it more by knowing that you have his autograph in your collection. A good way to get autographs is to write to these famous persons. Be sure to enclose a stamped return envelope for a reply. Or you can buy a photograph of your hero and send it to him for his autograph.

Authors, explorers, scientists, artists, musicians, and public officials are others whose autographs you may wish to add to your collection.

A worth-while autograph collection

should contain the signatures of famous persons in all walks of life. If such a person answers your letter, you may want to keep the entire letter. Many autographs may be obtained from your friends who may have duplicates.

Autograph collecting may lead to a study of handwriting, or *graphology.* This in itself is an interesting hobby, and there are some who even make a profession of it. The handwriting expert is often called on, for example, to detect forgeries. Books on the subject may be found at the public library. From them, you may learn how to amuse your friends by reading their characters from their handwriting.

You have probably made a start on collecting a library. A library is something that will grow with you and provide you with silent friends all your life. As a book lover, you will be interested in having a bookplate. This may be pasted to the end sheet, the first sheet inside the cover of the book. A set of bookplates makes a fine Christmas or birthday gift. The design may suggest the activities or interests of the owner. Owning a set of bookplates may lead you on to another collection, beginning with the plates of some of your friends. Others may often be picked up at second-hand bookstores. Now and then you may find one designed for a famous person.

The books you prize most highly will be those signed, or autographed, by the author. Many bookstores sell autographed copies of new books. If you own a recent book which you would like to have autographed, you might send a letter to the author. Send it in care of the publisher or at his home address, with a request for his signature to paste on the flyleaf. Be sure to enclose a stamped return envelope. Most authors will be pleased to send you their autographs. The children's bookshops in cities near you also announce when authors will be in their shops especially to autograph books.

If you are fortunate, you may have an opportunity to add to your book collection some of the children's books of bygone years. The Kate Greenaway books of years ago are now considered collectors' items. An early edition of Edward Lear's Nonsense Book, or a Horatio Alger book are among others that would make interesting collections.

Have you ever thought of writing to some of the artists of favorite comic strips and picture books? Perhaps you could tell them how much you like their work, and request an autograph. Your letter can be sent in care of the publisher, or to the syndicate which distributes their drawings. The editor of your newspaper will usually give you the name and address of the syndicate. If not, someone at your public library can supply the information.

Silhouettes. An attractive collection can be made of silhouettes or shadow pictures of your friends. You can make these yourself, even if you are not much of an artist. Pin a sheet of paper to the wall and ask your friend to stand beside it in such a way as to cast the shadow of his head on it. You will want only a side view, of course. Draw the outline of the head with a pencil. Cut along the line. Now you have a silhouette pattern which you can place on a sheet of black paper. Trace around the edges. Then cut and mount the silhouette. Your friend can autograph it as a finishing touch.

Headlines. A collection of important newspaper headlines, begun at any time, will record history in the making. The boy or girl interested in current events will find such a collection well worth while. The clippings can be protected by covering them with cellophane.

Dolls and Stuffed Animals. A doll collection will have a special appeal for girls. Children of all nations love dolls. Some of the earliest dolls were made of wood, cornhusks, and stuffed cloth. We still have rag dolls. And there are yarn and stocking dolls with painted faces, and rubber and celluloid dolls in many shapes and sizes. Back in the 1880's, girls played with china dolls with cloth bodies stuffed with sawdust. For as little as a penny, small china dolls could be bought in those days. Today these dolls are collectors' items. Wax dolls and bisque dolls with weighted eyes that opened and shut were highly prized at one time. The most expensive of these dolls, if squeezed, could say "Papa" and "Mama." Today we have lifelike "character" dolls, which look like real babies. Some of them have imitation skin.

An interesting collection could be made of dolls of all nations in their colorful native costumes. Sometimes these can be bought in the foreign quarters of large cities. If not, you can make your own costumes for a set of dolls. You can find colored pictures of foreign costumes in many of your CHILDCRAFT books and at the public library. If you prefer, you can dress your dolls in period costumes, dating back as far as you care to go. You might also like to dress them like such storybook characters as Little Red Riding Hood, Cinderella, or Hansel and Gretel.

Sometimes a doll's clothes are as in-

Collecting dolls from many lands is one of the most exciting of hobbies. This little girl is enjoying herself playing music for a make-believe wedding of one of her many pretty dolls.

Harold M. Lambert

teresting as the doll itself. If so, the garments can be sewed to cardboard and placed in a box beside the doll.

Each doll in your collection should be placed in an open box covered with cellophane.

If you find a doll collection too expensive, you might collect paper dolls. These can be clipped, wardrobe and all, from magazines or from special paper-doll books. They can be bought also in packages. If you are a good paper-doll dressmaker, you can add many clothes of your own design. Dress the dolls for spring, summer, fall, and winter—or for such sports as swimming, hiking, skiing, and skating. Paper dolls can be mounted in a scrapbook, one on each page. Or they can be pasted to cardboard with a stand at the back, and set in boxes or on shelves.

Stamps. A stamp collection, once begun, may start you on a hobby which will last the rest of your life. There are stamp collections which are worth many thousands of dollars. And collectors, or "philatelists," as they are called, include many famous persons who live in all parts of the world.

Many postage stamps are miniature works of art. The true collector is interested in classifying his stamps and arranging them in proper order in his album. He is also interested, for example, in watermarks. These are letters or designs which you can see by holding the stamp against the light. These watermarks are pressed into the wet paper

pulp before it is flattened into sheets. An occasional error makes stamps especially interesting for collectors. For example, the plane in the center of one of the early United States air-mail stamps was upside down. Stamps with small mistakes are especially valuable because they are so rare.

Stamp collectors note the perforations, or small holes for tearing the stamps apart, especially the kind and number of perforations. It is also interesting to watch for embossing. This is a process by which the design is made to stand out from the paper, as in the case of a stamped envelope. Many collectors save the entire envelopes, or "covers," to which the canceled stamps are pasted. Air-mail stamps on covers carried by planes which started new services are especially valuable. When the first clipper plane hopped off for Honolulu, it carried letters written by scores of collectors to friends across the sea.

A general collection, one representing all the nations, is perhaps the best for a beginner. He often starts by buying

119

Pinney, Black Star

And who has not, at one time or another, spent many profitable hours in collecting stamps!

from a stamp dealer a packet of 100 kinds, or 1,000 assorted stamps. In the larger packet some of the stamps will be the same. But these can be traded with friends.

The next step is to clean the stamps by steaming off any paper that may be stuck to the backs. In cutting stamps from envelopes, care should be taken not to slice off the perforations. The stamps are then dried. Place them, face down, on white blotting paper and weight them down with books or irons. The stamps should then be mounted in an album. A collector soon learns from what countries his stamps come.

The stamp album will have sections for mounting stamps of every civilized country in the world. Pictures of the different stamps will be found on every page, with squares in which to mount stamps of the same kind but of different values. An album for the beginner need not be large.

The stamps are mounted on gummed paper hinges folded at about one-fourth of their length, with the small end stuck to the back of the stamp near the top. These hinges may be purchased, or you can make them yourself. A pair of tweezers will help you to handle the stamps.

You may want to collect only one kind of stamps, as many collectors do. If so, you may choose only stamps of a certain color or design. These might include stamps with pictures of animals, famous men, trains, or planes. Or you can limit your collection to the stamps of a single country or a group of countries such as those of Latin America. A collection of United States stamps alone will contain hundreds of kinds. Many of them are beautiful, and all are historic.

There are some stamps, such as Christmas seals, sold to raise funds for charitable causes. These do not take the place of postage stamps.

Postmarks are also collected as a hobby. If you should start to collect postmarks from different cities, you might soon have some curiosities. There are many towns with odd names, such as Santa Claus, Indiana, and Tombstone, Arizona, and other towns with names you may never have heard. Some postmarks contain slogans reminding us to "mail early for Christmas" or to con-

Coin collecting is a hobby that will teach you many things of this country and other lands.

Harold M. Lambert

tribute to the American Red Cross.

Coins. Coins also are miniature works of art. The rare coins are the most valuable, but collectors also value coins for their beauty. Many coins bear likenesses of national heroes and presidents. They are decorated with various designs such as shields, swords, plants, birds, and animals. The oldest coins were issued several hundred years before the birth of Christ. But even some of these may not be too rare for boys and girls to obtain in starting a coin collection. The earliest known Greek coin, for example, is worth only about $5.00 today.

There are coin collections worth thousands of dollars. But this should not discourage the beginner. The easiest and least expensive way of starting a collection is to limit yourself to coins of small values. These may include copper coins of various nations; or United States or Canadian dimes, quarters, and fifty-cent pieces. United States two-cent and three-cent pieces, although no longer in common use, turn up now and then.

A copper coin collection might be arranged by dates, by countries, or by designs. United States Indian-head pennies for every year up to 1909, and Lincoln pennies for every year since 1909, make interesting collections. On some of these you will find a small letter "S" or "D." The "S" means that the penny was made, or coined, at the San Francisco mint. The ones with the "D" were made at the Denver mint. Pennies without initials came from the Philadelphia mint. So, you could have three kinds of pennies for each year. A similar collection might be made of streetcar or bus tokens of different cities.

Coins may be mounted on sheets of heavy cardboard with holes cut into it to fit each coin. If cellophane is pasted on the back of the cardboard, both sides of the coin can be seen.

As your collection grows, you may want to visit museums and see larger collections. The public library or a dealer will have price lists of United States and early Colonial coins, and of rare coins of every kind.

Nature Collections

Feathers make one of the prettiest and least expensive collections. All birds molt or shed their feathers at least once a year, usually early in summer. Cast-off feathers may be found under trees, in

121

Newell

If you have sharp eyes, you can get together a colorful collection of feathers at no cost. These are pretty, and you will learn about birds from them.

the woods, or along country lanes. Boys and girls living near a zoo will have a wonderful opportunity to collect feathers of many kinds of water fowl and tropical birds, especially if they make friends with one of the keepers.

Each variety of bird has its own special kind of feathers. Your collection might include a bright green feather from a parrot; a golden one from a canary; an orange feather from a Baltimore oriole; a cardinal's red feather; or a blue one from a jay. To these might be added a red or bronze-green feather of a hummingbird, a peacock's showy feather, or a pheasant's brown one.

As you work on your collection, you will notice the tiny hooks at the edges of the feathers. These hold them together and protect the bird from rain and from the cold. You will notice how

the patterns on some of the feathers help the bird to hide from its enemies. These blend with a background of dry leaves, meadow grass, or twigs. If you will turn to the chapter on birds in Volume 7, you will learn many important things about birds which will help you with your feather collection.

The Mexican Indians make pictures out of feathers. Perhaps you, too, will become interested in this art.

The feathers you collect may be mounted on cardboard. Leave a space at the side for a picture of the bird itself in color. You can cut these pictures from old magazines. Underneath, you can describe the bird's habits; its song, if any; and its nest and eggs.

Birds' Nests. Birds seldom come back to the same nest after they have once used it. So there can be no harm in collecting old nests. There are almost as many different kinds of nests as there are birds. The nest of the Baltimore oriole, for example, is shaped like a purse and hangs from the limb of a tree so the baby birds are rocked in a treetop cradle. The meadowlark makes its nest in tall grasses. The grasshopper sparrow builds a tunnel leading into its snug little home. The nest of the cliff swallow looks like a tiny pot of clay. Marsh birds make their nests on rafts anchored to reeds.

Flowers. A collection of wild flowers will appeal to every young nature lover. There are some wild flowers which are protected and should not be picked. But you can find others for your collection in the woods and fields and marshes. Or you can collect many flowering weeds and grasses, as well as garden flowers. Many boys and girls have started a collection with a four-leaved clover.

Blossoms should be pressed between sheets of blotting paper or the pages of a book, and mounted on heavy paper. They may be fastened with narrow strips of Scotch tape. The flowers can be classified either according to the families to which they belong or the places where they grow. One group could be made up of meadow flowers. Others could be made up of woodland, marsh, mountain, or desert flowers.

You might even be able to gather some of the unusual flowers, such as the Venus's-flytrap and others that eat insects. Or you might try to make a collection of the state flowers or of those of the Canadian provinces. You will find the chapter on wild flowers in CHILD-CRAFT, Volume 7, a guide in making any kind of flower collection. In the chapter, "Trees and How They Grow,"

also in that volume, will be found instructions for collecting and arranging tree leaves.

Another interesting collection could be made of artificial flowers. Materials such as silk, linen, satin, velvet, gauze, paper, metal, shells, and glass are used to make artificial flowers. Most of them are inexpensive and easy to find. Shallow boxes are the best places to keep them. The flowers may be sewed to the bottom of the box or held in place with gummed paper. Sheets of cellophane over the tops of the boxes will protect the flowers.

Butterflies and Moths. Even the brightest flowers will fade when pressed and mounted, but butterflies and moths will keep their colors when preserved. There are butterflies and moths in your own neighborhood to provide you with a good collection. "Things to Do" in Chapter 7 of Volume 7 explains how to preserve butterflies for mounting.

Moths and butterflies, and larger insects such as dragonflies, wasps, grasshoppers, and crickets are best mounted on pins run through the center of the three parts making up the insect's body. The pins are then driven into the bottom of a shallow box and the exhibit is covered with cellophane. A drop of rubber cement may be placed on the under side of smaller insects to fasten them to the bottom of a cardboard box. If you tire of chasing butterflies with a long-handled net, try raising them from caterpillars or even from eggs, which are usually found on the under side of leaves.

With more than half a million known kinds of insects in the world, you will have no difficulty in starting and continuing a collection of these creatures. There are insects that can easily be mistaken for twigs or leaves, and the curious shapes of others will amuse you. After mounting them, you will probably want to know more about them—which insects are our friends, and which are pests.

Rocks, Ores, and Crystals. Rocks and stones may not seem very interesting at first. But if you could trace them back to their beginnings, as geologists do, you would read in them wonderful stories. These would give you a better understanding of the earth we live on.

If you live near the mountains, near hills and cliffs, or near the seashore, you will have an opportunity to make a collection of many kinds of stones. A collection of rocks, stones, and crystals will be of little value if it is merely a jumble. You will have to learn the names of the different materials, how they were formed, and from where they came. You should also learn something about their uses. It may be that you can add to your collection some of the semiprecious stones—agate, turquoise, opal, and amethyst.

The smaller specimens can be glued to heavy cardboard or thin slabs of wood. A cabinet with shallow drawers or trays would be the best place for filing a collection of this kind.

Shell Collections. Boys and girls living near the sea can find hundreds of pretty shells along the beach at low tide. But you do not have to live near the sea to discover shells. You can find them in ponds and brooks, under old logs or loose bark, or clinging to water plants. Although shells are no longer used for

These young nature lovers are proud of the beautiful butterflies which they have caught, mounted, and carefully arranged in special boxes with glass covers.

Newell

These school children have collected and mounted all kinds of attractive colorful leaves.

Madison (Wis.) Public Schools

money, as they once were by some people, they are prized for their coloring and shape. There are more than 50,000 different kinds of shells. They range in color from the most delicate pearl gray and pink to purple. The smallest shells are hardly larger than a pinhead. Among the largest are those of the sea snail, which are about 2 feet long. Those of the giant clam measure about 4 feet across. Some shells are spindle-shaped, like little conical spires. Others are shaped like trumpets. Still others have the shape of fans.

Among the most beautiful is the rose-branch murex shell, which looks like a flower with rosy petals. Other beautiful kinds include the golden jingle shells; the chambered nautilus, a "ship of pearl;" and the cockle shells, such as Mistress Mary had in her garden.

Save only the perfect shells, clean them, and sort them according to size and kind. The smaller shells can be kept in boxes cushioned with cotton batting. The larger specimens can be displayed on shelves. If starfish and sea urchins are added to the collection, they should first be soaked in fresh water. Then dry and place them in shallow trays or box covers on clean sand. Labels on your boxes and shells should give the name of each specimen and tell when and where it was found.

Collecting Wood. If you are interested in collecting tree leaves, you may also want to collect samples of wood. You would not have to go far to find such specimens. You could obtain samples from dead trees or from fallen branches. Your collection in time might include wood from such trees as the pine, elm, oak, poplar, linden, maple, willow, hickory, black walnut, horse chestnut, and sycamore. You could also have samples of fruit trees, such as apple, peach, pear, cherry, orange, lemon, and grapefruit. The samples, sawed into small squares or oblongs, and polished, would make an attractive exhibit. They should be mounted on cardboard with a picture of the tree itself at the side of each sample. The label should give the name of the tree and other interesting information.

Other Collections

Bottles and Glassware. Many boys and girls eye their mothers' perfume bottles enviously, and can hardly wait until they are emptied. These and other small bottles, even when made by machinery, have attractive shapes and colors. Some of these are made to imitate hand-blown bottles. Early American glass blowers made bottles in the shapes of hands, fish, violins, and other shapes. The collector will be lucky if he can obtain one of these. Also prized are the glass bowls, vases, mugs, and dishes etched with delicate designs or decorated with designs in gold. If you begin a glass collection you may some day want specimens of the famous Venetian and red Bohemian glassware. They are usually rare and costly, but can often be found in curio or antique shops. Glass animals, which are not expensive, appeal to many collectors of all ages.

Small bottles can be mounted in square shallow boxes and held in place with Scotch tape. The larger bottles can be displayed on shelves.

Plates and Pitchers. Most children's and dolls' dinner sets are now made of aluminum or plastic instead of porcelain, which is easily broken. Small plates from these sets, especially if decorated with storybook characters, make interesting collections. Porcelain plates of American make, decorated with historic scenes, birds, or flowers, are also favored by collectors. Those of European make are often rare and expensive. Many beautiful articles, such as Sevres vases and Dresden china shepherdesses, were once made in Europe, and are highly prized. Cream pitchers of odd shapes and pretty colors, however, are inexpensive. An attractive collection could be made of these.

A holder for small plates can be made by using a strip of cardboard as the false bottom of a box. Place the cardboard in the box about two inches above the bottom. Cut slits in it the width of the plates, and insert the plates.

Miniatures. Such a collection can be started with those you find in some packaged foods. A visit to the trinket counter of stores might offer suggestions. Such items as toy dishes, miniature airplanes, automobiles, street cars, doll furniture, miniature vases, and animals are interesting to collect. You can mount your miniatures either by running a string through them or by crossing it over them and tying the string to the back of stiff cardboard. A few miniature etchings might even be included in the collection. With enough of these small articles, you could furnish a dollhouse of your own.

Models. If you have made a model plane, you will want to keep it. This first success may lead you to make other models and to collect them. Model sets of planes, automobiles, railroad cars, and ships, ready to be put together, may be bought in many stores. Some of these sets, made only of wood or paper, are simple and inexpensive. Metal sets cost more.

A collection of plane models could show a complete history of aviation from the first plane to the latest rocket plane. Other collections could tell the story of automobiles and trains. As your skill improves and your collection grows, you may become interested in models of furniture, bridges, or buildings.

The boy or girl who chooses models for a hobby soon becomes one of a large circle of friends, all eager to learn more about the subject. If you are among this number, you may have an opportunity

Some boys and girls like to play records of music and stories.

Leavitt, Frederic Lewis

to visit one of the well-known museums. Among these are the Museum of Science and Industry in Chicago, or the famous Smithsonian Institution in Washington, D. C. In these museums, you can study the life-sized models on display.

Records. You may already have some good phonograph records. Why not start a library or collection of your favorite records? By looking through the catalogs which you can get at any record store, you can find many albums from which to choose. There are stories told with sound effects or with musical backgrounds. There are albums of cowboy songs, folk songs, and Christmas carols. On your tastes may run to violin, piano, or orchestra music.

With so many records available, you will do well to limit your collection at first to records of a certain kind. But be sure to select the kind you like. Your collection will grow as your parents and your uncles and aunts take an interest in it, or as you earn money yourself to spend on records.

Records should be numbered and arranged in compartments according to type. The name and number of each should then be written on cards filed in a narrow drawer.

You would not want to collect records as a miser would hoard money. They will be of little value unless you use them. By playing them often, for your own satisfaction or for your friends, you will learn to appreciate and understand good music, and to take an interest in the composers. For suggestions, see list of recordings in CHILDCRAFT, Volume 11.

Figurines. Statuettes of painted clay, plastic, or metal, sold at dime stores and gift shops, make excellent collectors' items. Your collection might include dancing girls, musicians, and storybook and comic strip characters. Such souvenirs cost little, and can be attractively displayed on shelves or in small cabinets. You might collect, also, small flower containers made in the shapes of dogs, rabbits, cows, and other animals.

Beads. Brightly colored beads appeal especially to girls. There are many kinds of beads, some made of coral, amber, and ivory; others of stone, glass, metal, wood, shells, beans, and plastic. Some are exquisitely carved. Many kinds cost little to buy. Beads, like shells, have

127

Charles Town Train Club

Members of this electric-train club in Charles Town, West Va., build their own train tunnels, do all the wiring, and whatever repairs may be necessary from time to time.

been used for money. Prayer beads, such as those in rosaries, may date from ancient times.

Indian Curios. An Indian arrowhead made of chipped flint may be the beginning of a home museum or collection of Indian curios. Indians, especially those of the Southwest and Mexico, are natural artists. As you travel around the country, you will stop at places where the Indians have their wares on sale. Their pottery, baskets, blankets, and beadwork are colorful and not too expensive. If you visit Mexico, you will see in the markets the lacquered plaques, feather pictures, painted tiles, and clay kitchen utensils which you can buy for very little. You will also see gay serapes used as shawls and blankets. The women use them to carry their babies on their backs. The handwork of Indians south of the Rio Grande River is especially colorful.

Among other items that might go into an Indian collection are stone axes, arrows, pipes, dolls, beaded moccasins, miniature birch-bark canoes, and perhaps war bonnets and masks. Baskets and pottery alone will make an attractive showing.

Fan Collections may prove more expensive than others, because decorative fans are becoming more rare in the United States. The folded or pleated fan, which is said to have originated in Japan, is still used there. These fans were introduced in Europe during the sixteenth century. They were most popular in Spain and France. Even men at that time carried fans, as they still do in Japan and China. Folding fans are made of silk, lace, or ostrich and peacock feathers, and are often hand-painted. They are mounted on sticks of ivory, tortoise shell, sandalwood, or bone.

Old-Fashioned Things. Antiques, as very old things are generally called, are treasured not only for their associations but also for their fine workmanship. A collection of old-fashioned things may be started from some interesting old object you might find in an attic.

Once a person starts to collect antiques, he is usually interested in this hobby for the rest of his life. He may attend auction sales and antique shows. As he travels, he looks for pieces to buy.

It is possible that some of your older relatives can supply you with some old brass candlesticks, a copper kettle, pieces of china, and an old sporting print or other pictures. Glass paperweights, snuffboxes, castors, and even coffee grinders are collectors' items. Many people have such treasures handed down from parents or grandparents.

If you like old-fashioned things, you will enjoy visits to museums, where such relics of colonial days as spinning wheels and warming pans are usually preserved.

Selecting a Hobby

In choosing a hobby, select one that will take your mind off your regular schoolwork or your chores. Your hobby should be PLAY. If it teaches you something or adds to your skill, so much the better. It will be the answer to the question: "What shall I do now?" If you become interested in a hobby, you will never have dull moments. Every hour of your time will be happily occupied. Once you have chosen a hobby, you are on the road to an adventure.

BOOKS TO READ

CORMACK, MARIBELLE. *First Book of Stones*. Illus. by M. K. Scott. F. Watts, 1950.

GABA, LESTER. *Soap Carving; Cinderella of Sculpture*. Crowell, 1940.

GILMORE, HORACE HERMAN. *Model Planes for Beginners*. Illus by the author. rev. ed. Harper, 1947. (Young America's Aviation Library series.)

LEEMING, JOSEPH. *Fun for Young Collectors*. Lippincott, 1953. *Fun with Puzzles*. 1946. *Fun with Paper*. 1939. *Fun with String*. 1940.

LEWIS, ROGER (pseud. for ZARCHY, HARRY). *Stamp Collecting*. Knopf, 1952.

MASTERS, ROBERT V. (pseud. for BOEHM, DAVID ALFRED), and REINFELD, FRED. *Coinometry; an Instructive Historical Introduction*. Illus. by H. Simon. Sterling, 1952.

PETERSHAM, MAUD FULLER and MISKA. *America's Stamps; The Story of One Hundred Years of U. S. Postage Stamps*. Illus. by the authors. Macmillan, 1947.

PETTIT, TED S. *The Book of Nature Hobbies*. Illus. by Don Ross. Didier Pubs., 1947.

SCHNEIDER, HERMAN and NINA. *Rocks, Rivers and the Changing Earth*. Illus. by E. Herron. W. R. Scott, 1952. *Let's Find Out; a Picture Science Book*. 1946.

VAN RENSSELAER, ALEXANDER. *Magic*. Illus. by John N. Barron. Knopf, 1952.

WOOLLEY, CATHERINE. *Schoolroom Zoo*. Illus. by Iris Beatty Johnson. Morrow, 1950.

YATES, RAYMOND F. *Boy's Book of Model Railroading*. Illus. by author. Harper, 1951.

PLAYMAKING
AND
PLAY ACTING

MOYNE RICE SMITH

Harold M. Lambert

MAKE-BELIEVE is an important part of most play. Our toy airplanes take us on imaginary trips above the clouds. Our dolls are almost like real persons who live and talk and play with us. The magic words, "Let's play that . . ." lead us into all sorts of interesting adventures. Moyne Rice Smith opens doors for us into an exciting new world as she describes the art of playmaking and play acting. This author is a dramatics teacher, and the director of the Junior Community Players of Princeton, N. J.

The land of "make-believe" makes it possible for us to give full play to our imaginations. This boy and girl are enjoying themselves playing store.

"LET'S pretend" fun starts long before we can say any words. When a baby puts his hands in front of his face and someone says, "Where is Baby?," the game of let's pretend has started even though Baby is not a year old. You began to play other games of make-believe at an early age. Perhaps, you pretended that your toes were little pigs. Or, when you were just learning to walk, you may have hidden behind the door and scared Daddy by popping out

at him and making your best bear noises. In doing this, you discovered the secret of make-believe.

You can be anyone—an elf this minute and a witch the next. You can be a king or the beggar at his gate. You can go anywhere—to Grandma's house, the North Pole, an Enchanted Island, or the Moon. You can do any of these make-believe things at any time because of your imagination. Imagination is the magic power of your own thoughts to make pictures. It can make your bed a ship and you the captain. It can make your room a cave and you a cave boy of long ago. And who has not played "cops and robbers" and "cowboys and Indians?"

The Fun of Make-Believe

Playing House. Perhaps you have spent many happy hours playing house. You took a stick and marked out the rooms under a big tree. One of your playmates acted the part of the mother. Another was the father. The dolls, of course, were the children. You pretended to get them ready for school. Perhaps your doll had trouble with her first tooth. Or she might have had the measles, and you gave her a make-believe pill.

After packing the children off to school, you may have gone to market to get supplies for the week end. One of your playmates was the grocer. "Prices are SO high!" you may have said, as you gave him little paper squares for money. You came home with a market basket filled with make-believe oranges, bananas, candy bars, cabbages, and jam. Then you had a tea party with make-believe tea and sandwiches, and conversation about make-believe things.

Playing Train. After your first train ride, you probably played train as soon as you got home. You went to the station, bought your ticket, and got on the train. Perhaps the dining-room chairs were the train cars. "All aboard," the conductor called. "Ding-dong," went the engine bell and you were off.

A young couple drop in for a make-believe cup of tea with their hosts.

Kaufmann, Fabry

Harold M. Lambert

Here Mr. and Mrs. are coming home from a visit to the store with little Miss.

pretending that you are somebody else, you are really play acting. For, in make-believe, you play characters, or "parts," just as actors in the real theater do. You make up your words and your action as you play. You go from one room to another, or to all parts of the back yard, or park, or neighborhood. An actor has to stay where his stage is. He is acting for an audience to see and hear him. But you are acting just for your own fun. Sometimes you play house or soldier for days or perhaps for weeks. A real play, however, must begin, tell its story, and end within an hour or two.

In your outdoor games, the action is more important to the story than the

Dressing Up. Every girl knows what fun it is to "dress up" in her mother's old dresses. Boys, too, like to put on one of their dad's hats and play "grownup." A scarf around your shoulders can help you look like an old lady. Put on a red cape, and you are Red Ridinghood. Put on a big hat and a wide belt, and you are a cowboy. And with a feather in your hair, you can be Hiawatha.

Start your own dress-up box. Ribbons, scarves, rags, old clothes, hats, masks, string, and lace are things that are likely to come in handy in your make-believe play. The more different materials and colors you collect, the more dress-up fun you can have.

Play Acting

In playing games of make-believe, or

Dressing up in mother's old clothes provides all kinds of fun for a girl.

Newman-Schmidt, Frederic Lewis

Girls like to play house and do such work as washing, ironing, and cooking.

Loder

words are. This is true, also, if you give a real play out of doors. Your make-believe games have plots just as real plays do. Real actors do what you do in your make-believe games. They use their imaginations to make themselves into characters who tell a story in words and deeds.

Playmaking

Perhaps you and your friends would like to form a theater group and give a play. You can have a meeting and decide some important questions. What play do you want to give, and when and where will you produce it? Do you want to give it more than once? Will it be outdoors, at somebody's home, in a classroom, or in the school assembly room on a real stage? Before what kind of an audience are you going to present it? Will your parents be invited, your schoolmates, or the other boys and girls in your neighborhood? Are you going to charge admission and sell tickets or will you send invitations?

One of the best things about play-making is that there is always something for everyone to do. Most of you will probably want to take an acting part. But if you all do this, you will each have to find time when you are not acting to fix scenery and to make costumes. Some of you will want to design and build scenery. Some of you can be the stage crew who move the scenery and set up the "props." Some may want to experiment with simple lighting. Still others may want to design and make costumes. You can trade jobs, too, so that everyone gets a chance to do different things.

Selecting a Play. You can, if you wish, use a play that is already written. But it is more interesting to write your own play. There are many ways to start writing a play. Start with a situation. For instance: You are in your living room after supper, when the doorbell rings and a stranger comes in. You go on from there, and make your own play.

"Let's pretend we're all cowboys, or fairies, or Chinese children, or Indians, or pioneers, or kings and queens, or animals in a zoo." This is starting with characters. You must then decide what these characters are doing and what will happen to each.

Another way to start a play from characters is for each of you to choose a favorite character. If one of you wants to be Cinderella, another Alice in Wonderland, Snow White, Robinson Crusoe, Tom Sawyer, or Simple Simon, you will have to figure out how you can all be in the same story.

Another way to make a play is to

133

build it from a story which you know well. You have all done this. You have acted out stories like "The Three Bears," and "The Three Billy Goats Gruff." You can choose a story which has many characters in it. A story like the "Expotition to the North Pole" from "Winnie the Pooh" can use many boys and girls for Rabbit's friends and relations. "In the Great Walled Country" uses many actors because it is about a kingdom of children who live next door to Grandfather Christmas. The story of "The Tailor of Gloucester" can have as many mice as you have boys and girls.

Perhaps you will choose "The Three Wishes" as a story to make into a play. If so, read the complete story in Volume 3. In this story there are only three leading parts—the woodcutter, his wife, and the fairy. But you can make up other parts. There could be as many fairies

and elves as you wish. You could also have neighbors who drop in at the woodcutter's cottage at the most embarrassing times.

Selecting the Actors. Every boy or girl who would like to play one of the parts can try playing it. Even after you choose your players, you can plan on trading parts. If the play is to be given more than once, a different set of characters can be chosen each time. There should also be an understudy for each part. The understudy should know the lines and action so well that he can step in and play the part at any time. Let everyone try out. You should not overlook the shy members of the group. The boy who never has much to say, or who mumbles his words when he talks, may be just the one for the role of the woodcutter if he imagines himself to be that character. The shy girl who holds back may make

Playing grocery store in school is fun and an interesting way to learn.

Chicago Public Schools

In putting on a play, it is important to pick the right person for the part.

Elizabeth Hibbs

a charming fairy or a modest violet.

Music makes a play more interesting and pleasant. It helps the actors in their movements. It helps to explain the play and the characters. It helps the play become faster or slower or more exciting or quiet, as the action and story indicate. There are many ways to use music. Your story may have good places for singing and dancing. Perhaps you will want to use music as a background for the entire play. Music has been written for some stories. There are books of music and records for the Hums of Pooh, which fit well with a play, or dramatization, of stories from "Winnie the Pooh" and "The House at Pooh Corner."

Sometimes you will find it interesting to play certain music for each character. In "The Three Bears," Goldilocks would have light music to which she moves and speaks. But it would change when the porridge is too hot, too cold, and just right. When she tries out the chairs and breaks one down, you would want a "crash bang!" You would play a lullaby when she finds the little bed is just right. Each bear would have his own music— big, middle-sized, and little.

You can present some of the play by a number of players saying lines together to chords of music. This is called choral reading. It is good to use when you do not want your play to depend on a few people saying most of the lines. One person can do the action while the chorus group says the words together.

Any music you use in a play, and any singing, or dancing, must add to the story and meaning of the play. Otherwise, no matter how good it is by itself, it is bad for the play. The boys and girls who furnish the music should have it ready for the early practice, or rehearsals. They should help with the music during rehearsals and production.

The Play Director is the general manager of everyone who is working to produce the play. He makes sure that all the actors understand the play. He also makes sure that everyone who is helping with the play knows what he is to do and when. The producing of a play is a group activity. It needs as much teamwork as a football game. Every member of the entire group must have the same idea of what you are trying to do. The play director helps the actors work out the meaning of each scene, the meaning of each character, and the meaning of the lines. He helps the actors decide on their stage movements. This is called working out the "business." The director must see the play as the audience will see it. He works with everyone who is helping with the play. He is the captain of your team.

135

Some boys and girls enjoy making and painting the scenery.

Acme

The Scenery. If you like to make things and paint, you will enjoy designing and making the scenery. The first thing the audience sees when the curtain rises on a play is the scenery or stage setting. This tells them something about the time and the place of the action. Scenery can be what is called realistic. That is, it can look like a room or a garden. Or scenery can just suggest these.

Drapes are good to use for walls, or for sky or any kind of background. If you make drapes you will need to get an older person to help you. Any kind of cloth which hangs well can be used. It can be dyed any color you wish. Cotton flannel and unbleached muslin are good to use for this purpose. And you can make all sorts of curtains from worn sheets that your mother has discarded. Ask her to save these for you. You can loop drapes to make doorways and entrances. Screens, also, are especially handy for making scenery. They can be used in front of drapes or alone against a plain wall. You can cover them by sticking paper, cardboard, canvas, or cloth on them with Scotch tape. The chapter, "Making Toys and Playthings," shows you how to make a good screen, which you can decorate in any way you wish. You can suggest the scene of your play by tacking paper or cloth across the back wall of your stage. You can paint a big picture, or mural, as a background for the action.

The right kind of doorway can suggest an entire building. The right kind of wall can suggest a whole courtyard. Keep your outlines big and easy to see and understand. Powdered paint, which can be bought in boxes, is easily mixed with water. It can be put on quickly by brushing, spraying, or spattering. Try different effects in your painting to see what interesting colors you can get. Be sure everybody has the same idea of the stage picture you want before you begin work.

The scenery usually tells the feeling, or mood, of the play. Suppose the curtains open on a garden wall with giant sunflowers propped against it, a bright blue bench, a big red water can, and sunlight flooding the scene. The audience will smile and get ready to enjoy a gay comedy. If they see dark drapes with a single big window of blue light, they are ready for mystery. If they see a background of orange toadstools and funny trees and purple rabbits playing leapfrog, they will hope to find an elf on the stage any minute. You should try to create not only a place but also a mood of make-believe.

When the play director is ready for your scenery to be used, the stage manager sees that the scenery is properly placed on the stage before he starts the rehearsal. If you do not have a separate stage manager, the boy or girl in charge of your scenery can do this job. Those who have made the scenery can be the stage workers, or stage crew. At the first rehearsals, the scenery workers will mark where the scenery is to be put on the stage, and where the entrances and windows are. Change the scenery if there is more than one scene. For this, you will need rehearsals of the stage crew, so that each person knows exactly what he is to do. You must learn to change scenery quickly, quietly, and safely. The stage manager gives the signals to start each scene of the play, and pulls the curtain. He is in general charge of the stage, so the play director can be out front—where the audience sits.

Costumes. "Dress-up" for your play is the work of the costume director and his helpers. This group is responsible for the way each actor looks, and for the way all the actors look when they are on the stage together. The first costuming job is to study and understand the play. Then discuss with the cast and the director the kind of costumes that will be best.

Costumes should be a blended part of the whole stage picture. Like the scenery, they should tell the audience many things. If the actors are dressed in evening dresses, the audience knows the time of day. Costumes help to tell in what country the play is laid. They also tell the period of history, and whether the actors are rich or poor, young or old, funny or serious. A court magician may have golden owls pasted on a long, blue robe. The court mathematician may have big white numbers pasted on his black suit and four long pencils stuck in his wig. The audience knows who these people are from their costumes. And the audience knows that they will be funny characters. The only good costume is one which is right for the character and the play. Otherwise it is wrong, no matter how beautiful it is.

See how many of the costumes you can make by yourselves. Many of the things you need can be borrowed from your homes. All sorts of things are useful in making costumes: oilcloth, card-

Costumes are an important part of the play. They should be carefully studied.

Acme

board, cheesecloth, metal papers, muslin, old scraps of material, ribbons, and laces. Cloth can be dyed to get the right colors. Sewing can be done with big needles, coarse thread, and big stitches. You can also decorate cloth with paint and crayons. Costumes are the greatest help to the actors. But actors must feel as if their costumes really belong to them. They must wear them often and learn to handle them easily and naturally. Everyone in your playmaking group should help to get suitable costumes. The costumes should be put away carefully after each play. In this way you can gradually build up a costume supply. You will find that the same costumes can be used again and again.

If you make a play of "The Three Wishes," you will require little costuming. For the woodcutter and his wife, use a leather jacket, an old pair of trousers, an old felt hat, and a gingham dress. For the fairy's costume you will need only a pretty white dress, and a gold cardboard crown.

Make-up. If you are dressing up for your play, it will be fun to "make up" too. Make-up helps to bring out a character's face. Without it, the players' faces may look like a blur from the back rows. The bright lights seem to deaden the faces of the players and make them appear pale. For dim lights, also, make-up helps to bring out a character's face. Touch up your cheeks with rouge. Eyes can be made up with an eyebrow pencil. The brows can be made darker.

Even the shape of the eyes can be changed by making lines around them. The lines of the eye can be sloped up or down, depending on the kind of character you represent. If you are playing a Chinese part, you can make lines, sloping up, at the outside corners of your eyes. Then your eyes will appear as though they actually slope up. If you make lines sloping down at the corners, your eyes will appear to have drooping lids. Eyes will also stand out more behind lights if eye shadow is put on beneath them. Frown lines and wrinkles can be made with an eyebrow pencil or with charcoal. By the time you have put on a wig and a mustache, and drawn a few wrinkles around your mouth, you will hardly know yourself. Like costumes, make-up helps the actors themselves by making them feel they are really the characters they are pretending to be.

Properties are of two kinds. Stage "props" are the big pieces of furniture with which you set your stage. In a kitchen, the stage props might be a cupboard, table, and chairs. Hand props are smaller things, such as the bowls on the table, spoons, kettles, and so on. Personal props are hand properties which belong to the actors. These include such things as the sword of a soldier, the wand of a fairy, or the fan of a lady. Be sure that the properties are right for the time and place of the play. Also, see that the properties are suitable to the scenery.

It is the work of the boys and girls who have charge of the properties to borrow or make the props needed. Many properties are easy to build. Even they can be make-believe. Always use what you already have when possible, such as cardboard, wallboard, paper, plywood, canvas, wire, plaster, papier-mâché, crayons, and paint. First, make a list of the properties you will need. Then study your list with the idea of getting the effect you want most easily, cheaply, and

The properties for this play, "The Three Little Pigs," were cleverly made by the children who staged this old favorite.

Madison (Wis.) Public Schools

quickly. There are many good short cuts.

Properties should be used in all the rehearsals. Before you have final props ready, you should provide substitute props to be used in rehearsals, or practice. All off-stage noises, such as bells, thunder, door slams, and so on, are also the responsibility of the properties group.

Tickets and Programs. If you are charging admission, the tickets should be made and sold ahead of time. If any member of your theater group has a small printing press, he can print your tickets. Or tickets could be made on a typewriter. Several tickets could be typed at one time by using carbon paper. You may want to give free tickets to your teacher, the pastor of your church, or friends who have helped in producing your play. Anyone who has lent costumes or properties should not be forgotten. And you might also send tickets to the editor of your local newspaper, or to any merchants who may have displayed your homemade posters in their windows.

Your program should be headed with the name of the play and that of its author, or the author of the story, if the play is based on one. It should list the characters and the names of the boys and girls who act the parts, in the order of their appearance. A program also lists the scenes of the action, and the members of the staff.

Everyone can help to make tickets and programs. This work is usually directed by the publicity group. If you are planning to sell tickets, you will want everyone to know about your play. Some of you may want to make posters to advertise your play. Others may want to write stories about it for your local newspaper. Announcements may also be posted on bulletin boards. Everyone who works on a play is equally important to the fun and success of the production.

Producing a Play

Suppose you have decided to give a free play. You want to make a play from a story which has action, little scenery, and easy costuming. First read the story you are considering before all the boys and girls who are going to help with the play. How many scenes will you need? Can the action take place without change of scenery? Can one of the scenes be used twice? Can you add characters to the play that are not in the story?

Sometimes, much of the conversation, or dialog, can be used from the story. But often in making a story into a play it is necessary to make up the conversation. This is called writing the script. *"The Three Wishes"* is a good example of a story that has only three characters. But you can add as many characters as you wish, and you can easily imagine the words for the play. The characters are: Jan, a woodcutter; Joan, his scolding wife; and the Fairy Queen. But if you have more boys and girls to take part in the play, you might add a chorus of fairies and elves. They could dance to music in the forest early in the morning. When the woodcutter comes, they could scurry away. You could also introduce curious neighbors, an innkeeper, a town gossip, and others. These could drop in at the woodcutter's hut after the sausage had been fastened to his nose. The sausage is called a "black pudding" in this story written long ago.

The action of the story could be in three scenes:

  Scene I: Kitchen of Jan's hut.
  Scene II: Forest in early morning.
  Scene III: Same as Scene I.

As the curtain rises, Joan, in a shabby gingham apron and a gray wig, is busying herself about the kitchen. A black pot hangs from a crane over the open fireplace. Pans hang from the walls on both sides. A large ax stands in one corner. A window at one side of the fireplace is open. A colored curtain is blowing in the wind. From outdoors a bird calls, or a rooster crows. Joan, mumbling to herself, sets the table with a plate, a large knife, a loaf of dark bread, and a hunk of cheese.

JOAN (calling): "Jan! Wake up! Are you ever coming to breakfast? Here it is sun-up already, and you are still snoring like a pig. High time you were up and taking your ax and getting out into the woods. . . . Jan!"

JAN (from wings, in sleepy voice):

"Coming, my good dame! Coming!"

JOAN: "Well, come then. Your breakfast is waiting. (To herself) Working my poor hands to the bone for a bare living. If Jan weren't such a lazybones. . . ."

(Jan enters, yawns, and rubs his eyes. He is dressed in a leather jacket. His red hair is mussed.)

JAN: "And what's that you were saying?"

JOAN: "I said if you weren't such a lazybones we'd be riding in a gold coach —a coach with four horses. And I'd be dressed in silk and satin. Sometimes I wish . . . ."

JAN: "So it's WISHING you are, again. If wishes were horses, beggars could ride. I wish you'd have done with your nagging and complaining. I'm tired of it."

(Jan pulls out a chair and sits down to the table.)

JAN: "Black bread and cheese again! Ho, hum!"

JOAN: "And what did you expect? Cake, perhaps, or a fine black pudding?"

JAN: "A fine black pudding! Now, that would be to my liking, indeed."

JOAN: "Take your ax then, and out into the woods with you, or we'll be eating nothing tonight."

This is only an outline of Act I. But it shows how you might build a play from a story. To supply more conversation, or dialog, you could have the woodcutter tell his wife about the big tree he saw yesterday in the forest. Perhaps it looked enchanted to him. He wondered if a fairy prince were imprisoned in it. And his wife might recall the fairy music she heard in her dreams last night. As she mentions music, it could be heard faintly in the distance. The two could argue about whether or not Jan should cut the tree. The curtain falls on Act I as Jan takes his ax and leaves the hut.

Act II could open with fairies and elves dancing around the big tree. Why must this tree be spared? Should the Fairy Queen explain before the wood-cutter comes on the scene? As the wood-cutter arrives, the fairies could disappear. Or perhaps Jan could find the dancing elves and fairies and talk to the Fairy Queen, who might ask him not to cut the tree.

Perhaps, after the sausage has grown on Jan's nose, you would like to have the Fairy Queen come peeping into the window. And, for the closing line, Jan might say, as he takes up his ax, "I'm going to cut down that tree."

Your stage and properties can be imaginative if you wish. A table and chair, several pans, an ax, and a loaf of bread would be all the necessary properties. The pudding, or sausage, to be used in a later scene, could be made out of a rubber balloon and fastened on with a small piece of Scotch tape. Imagine the fun and laughter when this happens in your play!

"The Golden Goose," from *Grimms' Fairy Tales*, is another good story to make into a play.

It is a story of a man who had three sons. The first two were selfish. In the forest they met a little old gray man who was hungry and thirsty. They would not share their wine and cake with him. But Jack, the youngest son, fed him. The old man told Jack to cut down a tree. Among its roots Jack found a golden goose. Everyone Jack met—the three daughters of the innkeeper, the parson, and the sexton—wanted to pick

a golden feather from the goose. But when the first girl reached for a feather, her hands stuck fast. The next person stuck fast to her. Jack went through the countryside with a line of people follow-ing him stuck together. He reached the town where the King lived. The Princess was so solemn that nobody could make her laugh. The King had said that who-ever could make her laugh could marry her. When the Princess saw Jack with all the people stuck to him, she laughed. Jack, of course, married the Princess.

The first scene could be in the home of the three brothers, the second in the forest, the third in the country, and the last scene in the castle of the King. Or the entire play could happen in the forest. All the characters could come there, including the King and Princess. The entire play could also take place in the palace courtyard.

Your play could start by having some court ladies and some of the King's sol-diers discussing the Princess, who is so sad. At the sound of trumpets, the King's guards enter with the King and the sad Princess. The King proclaims that anyone who makes the Princess laugh can marry her. A herald is sent to carry the news through the countryside. Each of the soldiers and guards then tries to make the Princess laugh, by do-ing some special stunt. But the Princess only sighs and shakes her head. Sud-denly, there is a great commotion. Jack with his golden goose enters, with the people who are stuck to him yelling and trying to pull loose. They look so silly that the Princess laughs.

The King tells Jack about the Procla-mation. But Jack is still stuck to the other people. So how can he claim his reward, and marry the Princess? Jack

Harold Lambert

Boys and girls in the orchestra furnish music for a school play.

tells the King how he got the goose. Then the little old gray man from the forest appears. He throws off his gray cloak. He says that Jack is the most unselfish and kindly person in the kingdom, for he shared his food with a poor, hungry man. He deserves to marry a Princess. He touches Jack with his wand, and the people fall back, one on top of another, in a pile. Jack kneels before the King. The King invites everyone to come inside the palace to the wedding celebration.

There can be action, color, and fun in this play. Musical accompaniment can be worked out for the entire play from nursery-rhyme music.

First, the people in the courtyard might be moving about in a simple dance to the tune of "On the Bridge of Avignon." This music continues while they tell the story of the sad Princess. At a trumpet call, or chords played on the piano, the soldiers stand at attention and the ladies bow. The King, his guards, and the Princess enter to the

tune of "The King of France." The King and Princess take positions in the center of the stage as the guards and soldiers do a military drill for them. The trumpet call, or chords on the piano, are again played and the King proclaims his new law. A herald goes off calling the news of the Proclamation.

Then each soldier and guard takes a turn at making the Princess laugh. One sings "Old King Cole." A second person does acrobatic stunts to the tune of "Jack and Jill." A third person does a funny dance to "Here We Go Round the Mulberry Bush." A fourth does juggling tricks to the tune of "I Had a Little Nut Tree." After each performance, the court ladies laugh and clap, but the Princess only sighs and turns away. The music changes to "Pop Goes the Weasel." In come Jack and his followers doing a chain dance, trying to pull away from each other every time the music goes "Pop." They circle around the courtyard and everyone, including the Princess, laughs. This music continues softly while the King and Jack speak to each other.

Then the old gray man enters to the tune of "There Was a Crooked Man." This continues while he talks with the King and waves his wand. It changes to "Pop Goes the Weasel" as all the people fall when they are freed from Jack. Then, as the music plays softly "Lavender's Blue," Jack kneels before the King and the Princess. Those present go off in couples to the wedding festival. They dance to the gay tune of "The King of France."

All the action in the play is in large groups, so you must keep your stage open and free for movement. The courtyard needs only a big wall with, perhaps, some cutouts of bushes and trees against it. The play needs bright, sunny lighting. A garden bench is the only stage property needed. Hand props are: swords for the soldiers, spears for the guards, a trumpet for the herald, a scepter for the King, golden balls for the juggler, a golden goose, and a wand for the old gray man. The costumes are the biggest job in this play. You could use robes for the King and Princess, but all the costumes should be colorful. They must be ready to wear in early practices so that the actors can get used to them.

The characters include: the King, the Princess, Jack, the Old Gray Man, the Three Daughters of the Innkeeper, the Parson, and the Sexton. That makes a total of nine. You can have as many Court Ladies, Soldiers, Guards, and Heralds as you wish. After the actors have had a good chance at trying each of the parts, you can agree on who will start playing each part. Change around until everyone is sure who is best for each of the parts.

Playing Your Part. When you are in a play, you should learn all you can about your character. You think about what he looks like, how old he is, and where he lives. He must become so real in your own mind that you know his whole story, not just the part of it you are acting. Study the whole play and know what your character's relation is to the other persons in the play. You must know how he feels and thinks about them.

When you put on a play you ask the audience to pretend with you that what they are seeing is the courtyard of a palace, and that you are a Prince or a

Eriss, Monkmeyer

When you are acting in a play, you should learn all about the character you are playing.

soldier. Whenever any person on the stage stops pretending for one second, then the audience stops pretending too, and you have spoiled the magic of make-believe. Even if something goes wrong in a play, you must stay in character. Anything you do that is out of character, such as looking in the wrong direction, or fidgeting with your costume, draws the attention of the audience and the play is spoiled at that point.

Listening is one of the most important things an actor has to do. It is much simpler to strut across the stage with a sword and say funny lines than to stand quietly as a guard or a court lady. What you must do is listen to what is being said as if you were hearing it for the first time. A play must always seem to the audience as if it is happening just this minute.

The most important thing is to make the audience understand what is happening. Your words must be distinct and loud enough to be easily heard. At the beginning of a play, the audience is looking at the scenery and the costumes and trying to learn what the play is about. Then it is especially important for the actors to talk clearly and slowly. Give the audience a chance to understand everything. No matter how clever you are in your acting or how good the story is, no one can enjoy it if he has to strain to hear what you are saying.

Think of the meaning of your lines. What are the important words in each sentence? Which speeches should be said fast and which slowly? Don't get the bad habit of starting a speech clearly and slowly and then letting it run down so that it can't be heard.

The secret of all good acting is freedom of body and voice. This comes from knowing your character thoroughly. You must know what you are to do and say so that you can forget everything else and just have fun acting. Then you will be relaxed and your movements and voice will be free and well controlled. Everything that your body does should result from your thinking what your particular character would do in a particular situation. There should be no movement or gestures without meaning.

Rehearsals of a play should always be fun. You will talk about the meanings of the lines, and work out the action of the play and the positions of each actor at every moment of the play in the first rehearsals. You will not memorize your lines until you have rehearsed several times. If you memorize lines before you rehearse, you will not fit your words to the action, and you will have a hard time trying to change lines wrongly learned.

Dress rehearsal is always a time of great excitement in any theater. It means that the play is to be rehearsed as nearly as possible like the finished performance. Many things may go wrong the first time costumes, scenery, lights, and props are used. Costumes may come unfastened. Wigs may fall off. Scenery may wobble or even fall. The King may trip over his robe. The curtain may get jammed or not be pulled at the right time. The lights may accidentally go off. Any number of sad and funny things can happen. Everyone will be excited.

The Performance. When the day of the play finally comes, the wall and bushes and trees are in place on the stage. The lights are fixed so that all the action can be clearly seen. The bench is standing in front of the wall. The hand props are on a table near the stage en-

Princeton University Photo Service

Before the play is performed, the actors take part in several full-dress rehearsals to make sure that costumes, properties, and lights are perfect.

trance. The costumes are ready in the dressing rooms. Those taking care of publicity and programs have arranged chairs for the audience. They are waiting at the door to give out programs and to help seat the guests.

You come to your theater early, so that you can take plenty of time getting ready. You will know the play so well that you will be able to go ahead with the idea of the play even though some lines may go wrong. You will be able to stay in character and make up lines until the play gets back to the right place again. "Places," says the stage manager, before he takes his place at the curtain ropes. Now the soldiers and court ladies are on stage, the other actors are waiting at their entrances with their hand props ready. The music begins. The audience

lights go out. The stage lights go on. The curtain opens!

Now you are having the big thrill of acting before an audience. Something happens when you have an audience that never happens in rehearsals. There is a kind of magic which makes the people out there in the dark a part of the whole exciting experience. You are playing make-believe and they are playing make-believe, which makes both you and your audience a part of the play.

Pageants and Festivals

From the earliest times, people have come together to sing, dance, and act out stories. In the spring, the festivals were celebrated to welcome the return of the birds and flowers. In the fall, when crops were stored away, festivals

145

were held to celebrate the harvest. There were also many religious ceremonies of this kind and there were pageants in honor of national heroes. Our Easter, Christmas, and Thanksgiving were first celebrated with pageants and festivals. At first, the story part of the celebration was not so important as the dancing, singing, and parading. But gradually, the early festivals began to take on a story form. As a storyteller recited, the chorus acted out the story as it sang and danced.

Historical Pageants are exciting and colorful. They might include the story of the first white men in America, their meeting with the Indians, their learning to be friends with the Indians, the planting of the first crops, and the celebration of the first harvests. From these events, you could make the story of our first Thanksgiving. You could also make a pageant about the people who were the first leaders in America, the men who signed the Declaration of Independence. This might be a Fourth of July Pageant. An outdoor pageant could be centered around the movement of the early settlers to the West. The pioneers with their scouts and wagon trains, their songs and their costumes, and their meetings with the Indians, could be made into an exciting show. The history of early voyages to Canada furnishes wonderful background material for such pageants.

Community Pageant. The story of your own community would also be of interest as a local pageant. Find out how your own community grew. Have a pageant showing the important events from the earliest days of its settlement and history to the present time. The story of transportation or the story of agricul-

ture would also be interesting to present.

In a pageant, you must be sure that the events you select are clear and colorful. Your story should be simple and direct, and your costumes should be like those worn during the times you show. Pick out only the most important events. Put them together so that you can use processions and music. If you use speakers, or narrators, to tell the story, be sure that they have good voices. Keep the speeches simple and easy to understand. The action, or movement, and the pictures presented in a pageant are the important parts.

May Festival. May Day is a good time for a Spring Festival. This should be presented outdoors. Decide first on the main idea you wish to follow. Then figure out the order of events, and begin work on your costumes. A good way to start a festival is to have a parade, or procession, with music. Have different costume groups. Then the groups can be seated and become part of the audience while the individual groups perform. A May Day Festival could show springtime folk dances and songs of different countries. You might end with the May Pole dances and the crowning of the May Queen. The story of Sleeping Beauty makes an interesting outline to follow for a spring festival. Think of the story as if the fairy, Winter, put the court and all the birds and flowers to sleep. A Prince, as the Spring Sun, could awaken the court to new life and beauty. There are many other stories of long ago and other lands which could be adapted for pageants.

"The Pied Piper," a story told in Volume 2, would be especially colorful as a pageant. The pageant could open with the Mayor of Hamelin and his council-

Loder

Many Junior Community Players put on pageants and festivals out of doors.

men talking about the rat problem. As the storyteller reads the poem, the mayor and councilmen break in with conversation:

"If there were only some way of ridding this town of rats! They are frightening everyone. They are devouring our grain. They are even eating the food right off our tables!"

At this point in the story, the Pied Piper enters. He is dressed in a ragged suit of many colors.

MAYOR: "Well, sir?"
PIPER: "So! You have been troubled by rats."
MAYOR: "TROUBLED is no name for it. We have tried everything, but we can't get rid of them. Are you a rat catcher?"
PIPER: "I'll make a bargain with you. For a thousand guilders I will rid this town of rats."
MAYOR: "A thousand guilders! You are asking plenty, my man. But if the councilmen agree. . . ."

The councilmen murmur, but finally agree, and the reading goes on. The colored pictures with the story of "The Pied Piper" in Volume 2 will give you many suggestions for striking costumes.

A Peace Pageant. Life today is just as exciting and important as at any time in history. Perhaps you would like to make a pageant of stressing world peace. Your theme could be "The Children of the World Want Peace." A good way to start would be to have your best readers tell simply and clearly that we want the world in which we live to be a neighborhood of understanding and friendliness. The boys and girls could be divided into groups dressed in the costumes of different nations. They might march in these groups in a parade, or procession. Then each group could do a folk song and dance of the country it represents. The group could also act out a scene showing what its country can offer. At the end of the pageant, all the actors could do a simple circle dance together, and march out with children in costumes from different countries.

A pageant or festival is a big job.

147

Many actors and helpers are needed to give a successful one. A pageant should always be started in plenty of time, so that everyone working on it can enjoy it from the first idea to the final production. Then everyone taking part will understand the pleasure and value of a large group working together.

BOOKS TO READ

ABESON, MARION. *Playtime with Music; for Anyone Who Is or Ever Was a Child.* Music and arrangements by Charity Bailey. Illus. by Sally Michel. Liveright, 1952.

BROWN, HELEN ADA, and HELTMAN, HARRY JOSEPH, eds. *Let's-Read-Together Poems; An Anthology of Verse for Choral Reading.* Row, 1949–50. First book of the 5 volume set covers kindergarten and grades one and two.

COLEMAN, SATIS N. *Dancing Time: Music for Rhythmic Activities of Children.* Illus. by Vana Earl. Day, 1952.

DURLAND, FRANCES CALDWELL. *Creative Dramatics for Children; a Practical Manual for Teachers and Leaders.* Antioch Press, 1952.

KISSEN, FAN. *The Crowded House and Other Tales; Radio Plays.* Houghton, 1950. (Tales from the Four Winds series.) How to put on a radio program. Scripts, and directions for sound effects.

LEASE, RUTH and SIKS, G. B. *Creative Dramatics in Home, School, and Community.* Harper, 1952.

WARD, WINIFRED LOUISE. *Playmaking with Children, from Kindergarten to High School.* Appleton, 1947. *Theatre For Children.* Illus. by Charles Vance. rev. ed. Children's Theatre Press, 1950. *Stories To Dramatize.* 1952.

Plays, the Drama Magazine for Young People is published monthly from October through May, by Plays, Inc., at 8 Arlington Street, Boston 16, Mass.

DRAWING AND PAINTING

CAROLYN S. HOWLETT
AND
ISABEL SMITH

Elizabeth Hibbs

THE THRILL of working with pencil, brush, or crayons and creating your own pictures is one which anyone, old or young, can enjoy. Picture subjects are everywhere around us, above and underfoot, and even in our hearts. Carolyn Howlett, head of the Junior School of The Art Institute of Chicago, and Isabel Smith, her associate, tell us how to find these subjects, and how to express our thoughts about them in pictures. Others may then share our thoughts and see the things we paint or draw as we have seen them.

Just as some boys and girls like to write stories and compose poems, so, too, others like to draw and paint.

SOMETIMES you feel like painting just as you feel like running or jumping, or eating an ice cream cone. Painting and drawing pictures can be just as much fun as playing games, singing, or dancing. For many, it is more fun to make pictures than to do anything else. Often, when you are thinking about something, you feel that you must draw a picture about it! One idea after another pops into your head.

You think about the things you like to do, the funny things that other persons do, and how they look while doing them. Sometimes you just imagine things. You could not photograph such things as fairies or dragons. But you could draw or paint them. That is why it is so much fun to express your thoughts in pictures. You can let others see things as you see them. You can even let them read your thoughts.

Some persons have the idea that only artists can draw or paint pictures. As a matter of fact, all boys and girls can draw or paint pictures if they will observe carefully what they see. They may

149

Before you begin with your art work, be sure you have all the paper, crayon, pencils, and paints you need. Place your table near a window so you can get the best light possible for your work.

Watson, Monkmeyer

see things that others overlook. There is no reason why you, too, cannot make pictures of these things. You can draw and paint what you think and remember, and the things you see and do.

Where to Work and What to Use

First of all, for your adventures in painting and drawing, you will need a place in which to work. Look around your home for a good place. It is best to have plenty of space so that you can move around while painting. Plan to work near a window, for you will always need good light for drawing and painting. On pleasant days, even in winter, you can take your drawing materials outdoors, on the porch, on the lawn, or in the park. If you are working in the park, it is a good plan to take only a tablet or a notebook, and pencils. Then you can make small sketches of the things you see. Later, you can use these small sketches to make bigger pictures at home.

It is best to have a low table and chair, with room to reach all around your picture. But you may want to stand while you make pictures. Then you can easily cover all the corners of your paper. If you like to draw while standing, you will want an easel, a small blackboard, or a wallboard to which you can attach a sheet of paper. Be sure that the board is larger than the picture you want to make. The center of the board, or paper, should be at the height of your eyes.

Most artists, when using pen and ink

or water colors, like to sit at a table. But, when you use paints and big brushes, it is easier to see what you are painting if you tack your paper to the wall or to a board resting on an easel. A piece of wallboard can be fastened to the wall, and on this you can tack your drawing paper. If you are working at a table, the paper can be tacked to a drawing board, which rests on the table. Place a book under the back of the board so that the board is lower in front. Thumbtacks, pins, or drawing-board clips may be used to attach your drawing paper to the board.

You will need, also, at least two glass jars, a small tray for mixing paints, or a palette with compartments. If you are using chalk or ink, you should have an apron or a smock.

Dry Materials, such as pencils, colored chalk, crayons, and charcoal, are easier to use than brushes. Also, you can work faster with them. You can probably find several kinds of pencils around the house. Some will have hard leads, with which you can make fine, light marks. Others will be soft, and will make black, smudgy marks. But many prefer bright-colored crayons. When you press down hard with them, they make a bright, shiny color. When you press lightly, the color is pale and dull.

If you want to make big pictures in a hurry, you can use big, fat, colored chalks. Chalks are softer than crayons, and spread more easily over the paper. And you can make the marks as wide as you like by drawing with the long side of the chalk. Charcoal is much like chalk. It spreads and smears in the same way, but it is black. You can make bigger pictures with it than with pencils.

Wet Materials. Inks and paints are known as wet materials. You need more space to work with wet materials than you need with dry materials. You can use your fingers to draw with dry materials. But to put paint and ink on your paper, you usually need a brush or a pen. In fact, you will need two brushes. Use a big, fat one to paint all the large things in your picture. Use a small, fine brush for the small things. Long-handled

camel's-hair brushes are excellent to use.

When using wet materials, you will probably get better results if you work at a table or some other flat surface, for these materials will run. First, you may need a little practice in holding a brush or a pen. If you bear down too hard, the ink will spatter, and the paint will smear all over the paper. The brush or pen should be held lightly between the first and second fingers and the thumb.

Ink is wet, like paints, but thinner. It is used mostly for line drawings, and to make fine lines, such as those with which you draw hair, eyelashes, or stitches on dresses. It takes practice to hold a pen just right. Younger boys and girls should use ink with a brush. You can use any kind of pen to make pictures. But to make your lines dark or black, you will find India ink much better for your work than ordinary writing ink.

Spread your paints, or water colors, on the paper with a wet brush. You can also mix them with a wet brush. The more water you have on your brush, the lighter and thinner the color will be. You will need a jar or pan of water handy. Besides water to make your paints lighter and thinner, you will need water to clean the brush. After you have used your brush with one color, be sure to wash and dry it before wetting it again and using another color. When you have finished your painting, clean and dry the brushes, and place them, brush side up, in a jar.

If you are like most boys or girls, you

Harold M. Lambert

This homemade double easel makes it possible for these two boys to paint original pictures on large paper sheets.

Pinney, Monkmeyer

When you are finger painting, put newspapers under a large sheet of paper on the floor.

will like to paint or draw in bright colors —red, yellow, blue, and green. But you can get almost any color you wish by mixing your paints. You can do this either on your picture, while the paint is still wet, or in the little trays of your paint box. It is interesting to experiment and see how many different colors you can make. Red and yellow will make orange; blue and yellow, green; red and blue, purple; black and white, gray; red and white, pink.

Finger Painting. Instead of using brushes, you may even like to smear the paint on with your fingers. Jars of finger paints can be bought at art supply stores. But perhaps your mother or father will help you make some finger paints. Have jars with tight lids ready to put the mixture in when it is done. Then you will have it ready to use whenever you wish.

To make finger paint, you will need ⅓ cup of glossy laundry starch, 2 cups of boiling water, and ½ cup of soap flakes. Dissolve the starch in a small amount of cold water, to make a paste. Then add the boiling water. Cook the mixture until it becomes clear, and stir constantly. Then remove the pan from the stove and add the soap flakes. Stir until the flakes are dissolved. Pour some of the mixture into as many jars as you want colors. Pour only a small amount if you are going to use only a little of some color. Add vegetable or calcimine coloring to the mixture in each jar to make the colors you want.

When you are using finger paints, spread newspapers on the table and floor where you are working. A large pan of water in which to dip your paper before starting will be needed. But when you are ready, you can smear, splash, and pat the colors, and push them to the places on the paper where you want to use them.

Papers to Use. You do not need to buy special kinds of paper on which to draw and paint. You will find it is fun to paint on wrapping papers, cans, paper cartons, and even bottles and jars. If you ever happened to color the faces in newspapers with chalk, you will find that it is just as easy to cover all the printing. Then you can not even see that it is newspaper. Many boys and girls use paints on newspapers. The paint, also, covers the printing. So you can paint and paint, with no fear of running out of paper.

If you want to take the creases or wrinkles out of wrapping paper, you should press it flat with a warm iron. White paper will make your picture look dainty and light if the paint is spread in even strokes. Coarse, rough paper will make your picture look rough. Many beautiful paintings are made on china and cloth. And a blackboard is handy for drawing because it can be used over and over.

Clay is another good material to use in your art work. When it is wet, you can make pictures on it by using a pencil or sharp-pointed stick. You can rub out the lines, or the whole picture, as if on a blackboard. Then you can start the drawing again if you want to do so. When the clay is dry and hard, you can carve your picture on it with a nail. Pictures drawn on clay may also be painted.

What to Draw or Paint

Sooner or later, you will want to draw pictures of the things you see, or touch, or think about, or imagine. But now,

suppose you have received a box of crayons as a birthday gift. You will want to see what you can do with them. Perhaps you feel that you could learn to draw by copying the pictures in a book. But you will not have as much fun in doing this. The pictures you copy are not your own. Even if your own pictures are not so good, at least they have something of you in them. They stand for what you see and feel.

Boys and girls live in a world all their own. Every day brings new adventure. Life is gay. It is filled with balloon men, lollipops, ice-cream cones, parties, circuses, toylands, birds, trees, and flowers. Wherever you look, around you, at your feet, or overhead, you see something interesting.

Things You See. You see houses and people and dogs. You see children skipping rope or racing back and forth on the playground. You see children on bicycles or roller skates. At your feet, ants are scurrying along, or caterpillars are crawling. Up in the blue sky, cloud castles of every shape and color are in the making.

Everywhere, on every side, there are always pictures. Whatever you see, whatever you think or imagine, is a sub-

Loder

There are interesting pictures all around you which you may want to draw or paint on paper.

ject for your pictures. The mail carrier comes down the street, bringing good news to some, bad news to others. The milk wagon draws up at the curb. Dad comes home from work. You can make pictures of everything that happens.

Look out the window. Does it frame a beautiful landscape? The grass and trees are green. The sky is blue, the clouds white and fleecy, like a flock of sheep. The distant hills are purple in the haze. Buildings, too, are beautiful. Some are red, others white, brown, or blue. A boy in his play suit makes a bright spot of color.

The things you see are not always standing still. Trees bend and sway in the wind. Squirrels scamper up the trunks of trees and peep out at you. Shadows fall on houses. Clouds scud before the wind. Trains sweep around curves. Airplanes dive and zoom. Most boys and girls like to picture things in motion. But to do this, you may want to use only a few swift brush strokes. Action pictures you may want to draw or paint include bareback riders in the circus leaping on their horses; a tight-rope walker keeping his balance; your playmates skating on the pond, or roller-skating on the sidewalk. A dog chasing an automobile runs so fast that only a speed camera could picture him in motion. No matter how fast you worked with your pencil, you could never do it. So, if you want to make a picture of a dog running, watch him carefully. Does he have all four feet off the ground at once? Is his body humped up, and is his neck stretched out as he runs? Or, perhaps, he looks like a black streak to you. In any case, make your picture come to life as you yourself see the dog.

The next time you go to the zoo,

watch the animals carefully. The big lion appears sleepy as he gazes at you from behind the bars. Now he opens his mouth and yawns. The tigers walk back and forth restlessly in their cages. How lightly that big tiger leaps up to his shelf! The monkeys swing by their tails. Here is a bear seated on the ground, holding out his paws for peanuts. After you get home, see if you can draw these animals. Can you make the animal seem friendly, savage, happy, sad, or lonesome?

When you go into a garden you see bees and butterflies hovering around the flowers. A bird is taking a bath in the spray of the lawn sprinkler. All these make gay and colorful pictures.

Suppose you look for pictures in the city. The street cars, buses, taxicabs, and automobiles are all of different colors. Some are red, some are yellow, some are green. Notice the gay colors of the magazines on the corner stand. In the toy department of the big store you will see all kinds of dolls and games, bicycles, scooters, wagons, and mechanical toys that spin and whirl. You could spend days painting some of these pictures.

Perhaps you would like to paint a big picture, one in which you put together many ideas about trees, houses, animals, persons, and sky. Some boys and girls like to draw pictures of hills and mountains, or of lakes and beaches. A bathing beach in summer makes a gay picture. The yellow sand, the blue water, the beach umbrellas, the bathing suits make bright colors for a picture. Did you ever try to paint an island? Did the island look to you as if it were floating in the sky? Would you have liked to have a picnic there?

You do not have to paint the things

LET'S DRAW

Grown-up artists draw the things that they know best. You can do the same. Playthings, surroundings, trips—all are good subjects for your drawings. Jane, Van, Walter, and Carole did that in making these unusual pictures.

A bicycle is a cherished possession. Jane, age eight, liked hers so well that she took the time to draw it.

A boat means adventure to boys. Van, age seven, captures the memories of his boat trip in this drawing.

Drawing real persons can be fun. Walter, age ten, used a model in picturing a stroll in the park.

Art Institute of Chicago

Our homes mean much to us all. Carole, age six, has provided a large sunny yard for play and games.

you see as they really are. It is much better to paint them as they look to you. Or you can put only the things that interest you in a picture and leave out others. Suppose a group of boys and girls all painted a picture that might be called "Sue's Birthday Party." Each picture would be different. One might show only the birthday cake with the candles on it. Another might show Sue with her arms full of gifts. Perhaps another would tell about a game of "Drop the Handkerchief" or "Blindman's Buff."

Each picture would tell about the party in a different way, for every artist sees his subjects differently. To one, tall buildings may look crooked. To another, they might look like boxes. The shadows on the snow might look yellow to one artist, and purple to another. How would you paint a tall building or shadows on the snow?

If you were to paint a birthday party picture, or a picture suggested by your visit to the zoo, you would not have space enough to crowd in everything you saw. You would have to leave out some things and put in only what interested you most or seemed most important. In the zoo picture, it might be only a baby monkey or the zebras. If you wish, you can also paint into your picture things that you did not see.

You can put in things that you know are there. You may, if you like, make a picture of the outside and the inside of a house at once. You can arrange things to suit yourself. If you are painting a landscape, you can place the trees anywhere you want them. You can move the houses around too.

Sometimes you may paint things as you would like them to be. You might put blue and yellow spots on a dog be-cause you would like to see a dog with blue and yellow spots. A house in your picture can be pink because pink is your favorite color. It is just as much fun to paint things according to your own fancy as to paint them exactly as they are. So you may paint a robin bigger than a house, because the robin is more important to you.

Things You Touch. There are things you like to touch, and other things which you would rather not touch. Rose petals feel cool and smooth. The bark of an oak tree feels rough. A chestnut burr feels prickly. Jam feels sticky. Seaweed feels wet and slimy. Down feels soft and fluffy.

If you experiment with different materials, you may be able to get into your picture the way things feel to the touch. Paint thinned with water and brushed on with smooth, even strokes, will make a surface look as smooth as satin. Short jabs with pen and ink will give a prickly appearance. Or you could make something look sticky by thickening your paint. Try using charcoal, ink, and chalk the next time you are painting a picture of a tree. See which makes the bark look rough. With yellow paint or crayons, draw a picture of an orange on rough paper to see what result you get.

Things You Hear, Smell, or Taste. Often the things you hear, smell, or taste may suggest pictures. You hear the raindrops pattering on the roof or the snowflakes splashing against the windowpane. Do these sounds make pictures come to your mind? Paint what you think about when you hear:

Church bells on a quiet Sunday morning.
A locomotive whistle echoing among the hills.
The roar and crash of the surf.
The splash of a canoe paddle.
Bird calls in the woods.

Cowbells in the distance.
The rustling of leaves in the wind.
The chirp of crickets in the grass.
The tinkle of ice in a glass of lemonade.
The band playing in a parade.
The squeak of chalk on the blackboard.
The ticking of a clock.
The crackle of burning logs in a fireplace.
The screech of automobile brakes.

How often, too, smells bring pictures to your mind! For example, the smell of Dad's pipe might suggest a picture of Dad in his easy chair. He may be reading his newspaper with a cat purring at his feet. The smell of wet fur might remind you of the day at the beach when you tossed sticks into the water for your dog to bring back. Do you remember how he shook water out of his coat, giving you an unexpected shower? When you smell gasoline, does a picture come to you of an automobile trip, and Dad pulling up at a filling station? Do the following smells make you think of pictures?

Tangy pine needles.
Cookies baking.
The steaming earth after a rain on a hot summer's day.
Burning leaves in autumn.
New shoes.

Tastes, too, may inspire you to make interesting pictures. For example, a sour green apple, a salty cracker, a strawberry soda, or currant jam may give you ideas for any number of pictures. Such tastes might make you think of a boy doubled up with stomach-ache, a bakery shop, boys and girls at a soda fountain, and your mother in the kitchen, making currant jam.

You need never be at a loss for ideas.

While on a trip to New York, this young girl went to see the Statue of Liberty. She is painting a picture of it.

For you can pull them out of the air almost as a magician pulls rabbits out of a hat.

Things You Do. Sometimes you may feel like making pictures about the things you and your friends do. For example, you may want to make a picture of boys and girls on slides and teeter-totters or playing other outdoor games. You may want to make a picture of someone riding a bicycle, dressing up, tap dancing, or even painting pictures. Perhaps girls are playing hopscotch on the sidewalk. Dad is working on his car. Ellen is washing the dishes. You can get many ideas for pictures by watching others as they work or play.

Things You Remember. Some pictures you will like best to paint are the ones you will paint from memory. These may tell little stories. They may bring back to mind good times you have had and tell others about them. Do you remember the day your baby brother tried to

Pinney, Monkmeyer

Art work does not have to be real to be interesting. It can be something you have imagined.

Acme

eat his first ice-cream cone, and how he got most of it on his clothes? Do you remember how you tried to teach your pet kitten to drink milk from a saucer, and how she got her paws in the saucer, and milk all over her face?

What good pictures some of your memories would make! Among these might be memories of your ride on the merry-go-round, the school picnic, the snowball battle, the day at the circus, or rowing in the park lagoon. Memories of the summer camp in the woods, of going shopping with your mother, and of that wonderful automobile trip might make you think of more and more pictures to paint.

Storybook Subjects. Poems and stories also suggest pictures. Almost everyone likes to hear about things that happened "once upon a time," or long ago. Boys like to draw pictures of cowboys and Indians and soldiers. Girls often like to draw princesses, and pictures of Cinderella, Alice, and Snow White—heroines of their favorite storybooks. How do you think Aladdin would look? What would an angel look like? What do you think Cinderella's pumpkin looked like as it was being changed into a coach? As you hear more stories and

read more yourself, they will suggest many pictures for you to draw and paint.

Things You Imagine. At times, you probably like to be alone and dream. Sometimes there is no end to the things you can imagine. In your thoughts you can travel to strange lands—to Cloudland, or to Fairyland, or even to the moon. Perhaps you can imagine all kinds of persons, animals, and trees. Why not try to draw or paint some of them? What would men from Mars look like? Would they have big heads and tiny bodies?

How would you like to paint a fierce, fire-breathing dragon, a pretty mermaid, or fairies and elves? And wouldn't it be fun to paint a sugar-plum tree, a lollipop tree, or even a tree with umbrellas for leaves? Or you could paint a picture of a happy dream which you enjoyed after a picnic in the park. In pictures you can imagine and paint anything you wish.

Moods and Feelings. When it is spring, you may feel like dancing. Or you may feel lazy and sleepy. On rainy days perhaps you feel like curling up on the sofa with a storybook. Sometimes you may feel sad and lonely, and now and then you may even feel cross. Perhaps you would like to paint a picture of

158

these feelings or what you would like most to do at the moment. How would you make pictures of yourself when you are especially happy or when you are cross? Even when you are painting something else, your picture often will tell others your feelings while you are painting it.

Your pictures will show, also, how you feel about others. Perhaps you are sorry for the street musician who is blind. The cross gardener may frighten you a little. Sometimes we also wonder about persons, and our thoughts show in our pictures of them. Do the balloon man's children have balloons to play with? What are circus people like, and what do they do when they are not performing? Does the mailman wish that people didn't get so many letters?

Animals and even objects seem to have their moods and feelings. Perhaps your puppy is mischievous and playful. Your cat may seem haughty and "stuck up." Cows look peaceful and contented. We may imagine that a big, yellow pumpkin is jolly, and that flowers are gay. An old, neglected house looks as if it were haunted. A dead tree might seem like an old witch. A downtown street looks busy and excited.

Have you noticed that some houses, with their doors and windows, look very much like people—sometimes happy, sometimes sad? Our pictures of these things can show others how we think they seem to feel.

The world of nature, too, seems to have moods—smiling, laughing, sparkling, frowning, weeping. We have crisp, frosty days, sunny days, gray days, golden days, and stormy days. We can paint these moods into our pictures. We can paint a restful landscape or a stormy

day. Appearances of other things change with different moods of nature. After a rain the streets look black and shiny. The trees and grass look greener. On a misty day things look mysterious. In the moonlight even the common, everyday things look romantic.

The sky and water are always changing, too. The sky is blue, or gray. At sunset it is pink or red. At night it is black and mysterious. The sea has many shades of blue and green. Did you ever notice the silvery path the moonbeams make as they are reflected in the water? Where does this shimmering path of silver lead? If you could follow it, what would you find at the other end?

The world is so full of so many wonderful things to draw and paint that you could make a different picture every day. You should never waste your time drawing the same thing over and over, or copying the work of others.

How to Make Better Pictures

Sometimes your pictures may not turn out just as you had planned. But if you keep on painting and drawing, and trying to learn something new each time, your pictures will get better and better. First of all, you should learn more about your materials.

Use of Your Materials. There are many ways in which to use your paints, brushes, and crayons. You can save time and make better pictures by choosing the best materials for each subject. Often you can use more than one kind of material in the same picture.

Clouds against a painted sky will look white and fluffy if drawn with chalk. Use a sharp pencil, or pen and ink to make fine, delicate lines. You might try mixing wet and dry materials, or use white paint on colored paper, just to see what happens. Try using your brush in different ways, first with a fine point, then when it is rough and shaggy. You might even try using the handle. Sometimes you can get an idea for a picture just by playing with your materials. For example, you might try spreading the paint on wet paper. Here are a few pointers which may help you:

To keep wet materials from spreading, wait until one color is dry before putting another color next to it. Don't wet your brush too much. If the paint is too wet after you have put it on, soak it up with a dry brush, a bit of blotting paper, or a cloth.

To blend your colors, apply one color next to another while they are both wet. They will then run together. Or, if you wish, you can add another color over the first while it is still wet. Brush the second color on lightly at first. Use only a little at a time. Colors made by chalk or crayon can be blended by rubbing them at the same time on the paper. Or you can rub one color gently over the other.

To make big pictures fast, use big brushes full of paint, or large pieces of flat chalk. Rub the side of the chalk, not the point, on the paper. To make things look rough, use rough paper. Dab on the paint with short, jerky strokes, with very little water on your brush.

Remember to wash your brushes clean each time you finish painting. If you should happen to forget sometime and let your brushes stand, they will become stiff. If this happens, first soak the brushes in water. Then wash them clean with soap and water.

Studying Your Subjects. As you learn more about your subjects, you will be surprised at how quickly and how much your paintings improve. Notice especially the shapes and parts of your subjects. What do they remind you of? Do the houses look like boxes? Does an automobile look like a long box on wheels? Is that big elm tree shaped like a vase? Does a long train remind you of a snake?

Colors may be light, or bright and vivid. Sometimes they are deep and dark, or dim and dull. Have you ever thought about how things would look if they were only black and white?

As you learn more about your subjects, you may notice that the same thing looks different at different times and from different points of view. Houses and trees and people look different from above. Imagine that you are in an airplane. How would these things look to you? Or suppose you were sitting on the ground peeking through a fence. Perhaps a dandelion is right in

Ellis O. Hinsey

If you want to make large pictures, use a big brush full of paint, or use the long side of your chalk or crayon.

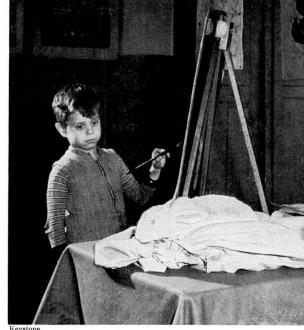

Keystone

To get a good drawing, study your subject very carefully. Then arrange it to make one thing the center of interest.

front of your nose. But what is behind the dandelion and behind the fence? Can you see one thing beyond another, and something more beyond that?

As you stand at a corner, looking at a tall building, the sides seem to meet at an angle. Look down a long street. The automobiles seem to get smaller and smaller as they get farther away. The buildings, even the big ones, seem to get smaller too. And the street seems to get narrower until both sides meet in a point. But if you think that the street should get wider towards the end, and the buildings bigger, you can have fun painting them that way. Some artists do, and get some interesting effects.

Cartoonists usually draw long things longer, and big things bigger than they really are. They make wide mouths wider, big chins bigger, funny noses funnier. To a cartoonist a happy boy would be mostly smile. Cartoonists make every line count, and use as few lines as possible. Often they leave out lines altogether. Whatever makes a subject different, is the important thing in any picture, but especially in a cartoon.

Planning Your Picture. If you are trying to make your pictures better, you should learn how to arrange your subjects. In painting a picture in which there are several objects, you can move these objects and arrange them to suit you. But you may want your picture to tell only one thing. If so, you must make one part stand out from the rest. You can do this by making its shape different from other shapes in your picture. For example, a boy alone in a forest of trees

would stand out as an important part.

Another way to make one part of your picture stand out from the rest is to make the color different from other colors in your picture. Perhaps you are painting a group of boys and girls, but want one to stand out. You could paint a pink or yellow suit or dress on that one and have the others dressed in blue. Still another way to make a part of your picture stand out is to make that part much larger or smaller than the other things. Usually, you will place the part you want to stand out from the rest in the center of your picture. Plan your picture so that the person looking at it will see the most important thing first.

How to Judge Your Pictures

Every artist is an adventurer when he makes a picture. When he starts to paint an idea, he is never sure what will happen, or exactly what the picture will look like when it is finished.

How can you tell when you have painted a good picture? If the idea is your own, and if you have chosen your colors and arranged the subject to fit the

161

idea, you will feel satisfied. The picture may look real, or it may look fanciful, but it must somehow make others see the subject through your eyes. It must bring out your idea.

No two artists see the same thing in the same way. Each uses his materials differently. You, too, feel and paint differently at different times. It is these differences that make an artist's style.

Perhaps you would like to save some of your best pictures and frame them. They should be hung so that their center is about the height of your eyes. You can use pictures, too, to make party invitations and place cards. But you may wish only to draw and paint for the joy of expressing your own ideas.

BOOKS TO READ

BANNON, LAURA MAY. *Patty Paints a Picture*. A. Whitman, Chicago, Ill., 1946.

BERKLEY, ETHEL S. (pseud. for BERKOWITZ, ETHEL STRACHSTEIN). *The Size of It; a First Book About Sizes*. Illus. by Kathleen Elgin. W. R. Scott, 1950.

BROMHALL, WINIFRED. *Mary Ann's First Picture*. Illus. by the author. Knopf, 1948.

ELLSWORTH, MAUD, and ANDREWS, MICHAEL F. *Growing with Art*. Sanborn, 1950–51. 8 books. I–VI—Fun to Begin; Learning to Talk a New Way; Seeing and Doing; Discovering Surprises; Exploring and Making; Art Where We Live—deal with practical art for young children.

HOGEBOOM, AMY. *Trains and How to Draw Them*. Vanguard, 1953. *Familiar Animals and How to Draw Them*. 1946. *Wild Animals and How to Draw Them*. 1947.

KESSLER, LEONARD P. *What's in a Line? A First Book of Graphic Expression*. W. R. Scott, 1951.

LATTIN, ANNE. *Peter Liked to Draw*. Illus. by Richard M. Powers. Wilcox and Follett, 1953.

SCHLEIN, MIRIAM. *Shapes*. Illus. by Sam Berman. W. R. Scott, 1952.

WEBBER, IRMA ELEANOR SCHMIDT. *It Looks Like This; a Point-of-View Book*. W. R. Scott, 1949.

WHITE, PETER. *Easy Drawing Book*. Sterling, 1953.

WRITING OUR THOUGHTS

PAUL ENGLE

O. V. Gordon, Century

THERE IS magic in words! When put together skillfully, they can convey your thoughts, ideas, and feelings to others. Writing about your experiences in prose or poetry is one of the most pleasurable of all activities. Paul Engle, Professor of English at the State University of Iowa, describes how you can develop this gift for creative expression. He is the author of *West of Midnight*, *The American Child*, *Always the Land*, and other books, as well as articles on writing.

MUCH as an artist can share his thoughts by making pictures, you can share your thoughts by making word pictures. You do this when you tell your friends about something you have seen or done. You do the same thing when you put your thoughts in writing. You can share the experiences you enjoyed at a birthday party or at the circus. You can make others see the children dancing to the organ grinder's music, just as you saw them. Or you can write about the adventures of a snowball battle, a picnic at the beach, or walking home in the rain.

Learning to express your own thoughts about everyday things will bring you and your many friends real pleasure.

What to Write

You do not have to look in books to find something about which to write. You have only to look around you. Think of the things that happen every day—your happy and amusing experiences, and even your disappointments. For writing should be about all your life, not just a part of it.

Anything you see or feel or think makes a good subject about which to write. Perhaps you were scared when a train rumbled or whizzed by you at a station, but when you were on the train its swift motion soothed you. You may have watched a robin patiently listening with one ear to the ground to hear a worm crawling. And later, you may have seen the robin pull the worm out. When

163

you turn on a radio you hear a low hum before that first faint sound of music comes into the room. You think a child is generous and then, one day, you find that he will not share his toys with his playmates. What a shock to you this is! But when you are seeing and feeling and thinking about the things that happen every day, remember that this is a wonderful world to live in even when it is sad.

Think of a simple thing like light. Suppose the world were always dark and you live forever the way you do now at nighttime. Suppose someone said that in twelve hours something called "light" would come to the earth. You did not even have a word for light because there had never been any. So you waited in wonder. Then gradually, far away in the east, you saw a thin, gray line. The gray color turned into blue and climbed up the sky. Then you looked around, seeing the world for the first time in all its daytime beauty. Imagine seeing the grass, the trees, the flowers, your friends, your doll, and your toy fire engine for the first time! Soon the whole sky would be full of light and seem to blaze at you as

if it were on fire and, suddenly, you would know what daylight was. How surprised and excited you would be! And yet this happens every day, and you are not surprised or excited simply because it comes every day and you do not think about it.

Many things in our lives are as wonderful, as strange, as exciting as daylight. When you are writing, you should try to share with other people that wonder and excitement which you yourself feel. To do this, you should try to see all the things in life as if you were seeing them for the first time.

When you talk to another person, you share what is in your mind. That is what you do when you write. You use words in talking to describe what has happened or how you feel about a new book or a new neighbor. Your voice rises and falls as you say certain things louder or more gently than others. Perhaps you use your hands or your head to gesture and emphasize what you are saying.

Word Magic. In writing, you don't have gestures or special voices, so you have to make the words do what your voice and your gestures might otherwise

Gendreau

Working on an invitation to a party. It is important for you to use the exact words to express your message correctly.

The more words you collect and master, the easier it will be for you to write interestingly.

Elizabeth Hibbs

do. Writing is not just putting on paper the same things you say aloud. You must think how to put the words together so that they will excite the person who reads them. Make the words rise and fall. Choose the most exact and interesting words. You will find after a while that you will get the word which describes the thing you are writing about in such an exciting way that anyone can see it.

Beginning to Write

Every boy or girl who talks is, in a way, a writer, for he is choosing words and is trying to make someone else understand what is in his mind. Therefore, the simplest way to begin writing is to think about what you say aloud and try to make your spoken words better. Think of all the different words you might use for what you are saying.

Collecting Words. You can collect words just as some persons collect butterflies or stamps. Learn all the words you can. Use all the words you can. And listen to the sounds of words when other persons are talking. You can get to like words so much that you can even taste them when you say them. Repeat words

quietly to yourself and you will find that you can get the sound of them on your tongue. Only if you love to have words in your mind and in your ears can you ever put them together so that you can express yourself well.

Long before you can even write a word on paper, you can be collecting words. And you can have the sound of words singing in your mind. Many persons have good things to say. But unless they have a feeling for the sound of words they can never put them together in an interesting and appealing way.

As you say words over to yourself, notice what different feelings they have. "Doll" is a gentle and friendly word. "Bulge" is a word which seems to swell out when you say it. "Purple," with its full sound, describes the full rich color. "Hawk" has the sharp and quick feeling of the bird itself. "Grab" is blunt and solid, as is the act of grabbing. "Hog" seems to be as round and stocky as the animal.

Repeat every new word you learn. Then you will fix its sound in your mind, for you should know the sound of a word as well as its meaning. After you have fixed the sound of a word in your mind, try using it with another word. Then use those two words with others, until you have built up a whole sentence. There are boys and girls who have such a good feeling for the sound of words that they can use them more interestingly than many grown persons.

First Writing Experiences. If you already know the sounds and tastes of words, you will enjoy your first writing experiences. As soon as you can form letters on paper you can, perhaps, begin to write some words. You will find that you can use words to put sounds on paper much as a musician puts notes on paper to stand for certain sounds. Help your mother make shopping lists, writing the easier words first. If you have a party, write your own invitations. When Grandma sends you a toy you especially like, learn to write: "Thank you."

Writing Letters. Letters, too, are a good way for you to begin writing. You probably will not even remember the first letter you write to Santa Claus. But you can write letters just to tell something. Almost every boy or girl has someone to whom he or she would like to tell something. Perhaps you want to tell about the way the first snow looked when it fell on the oak trees that still had their leaves. You may want to describe a new puppy the neighbors have. Or you may want to tell how funny you looked when you had the mumps. In these letters, try to use every word you have learned. Try to think that even the stories you read in books are just letters addressed by the author to anybody who wants to read them.

How Stories Are Made

Anyone who likes to listen to stories or to read them for himself will want to make up a story of his own. This means not simply describing something. You have to decide what is the most exciting way to tell it. Think about the best kind of ending, and what the persons in the story would look like and what kinds of voices they would have. Decide about their voices in order to make them talk naturally. Then you can begin to put down the words that sound best.

Take, for example, a story like "Cinderella." The reason it is such a good story and has lasted so many years is that it is written in an exciting and dramatic way. Cinderella was, of course, a fine person. But a good story takes more than that. The purpose of stories is to tell what they are about in as moving a way as possible.

Real Persons. Remember when you write your own stories to tell about real things and real persons. Use the words they might use just as you would say them when talking to a friend. Only if you make your own stories as exciting and real as your own life will you be able to get people to read them. The way to make stories like that is shown by the story of Cinderella.

A Problem. First of all, notice that there is a problem at the beginning of the story. What will happen to the poor girl Cinderella, so cruelly treated by her stepmother's daughters? The rest of the story shows just what happens. In your own story, then, be sure you have something at the beginning which will make the reader wonder what is going to happen.

Perhaps your story will be about a boy who goes boating with older friends. As they row along, one of them says, "Here is the place where my friend Jim hooked a big fish last summer. He had

Writing letters will keep you in touch with your friends and relatives, wherever they are.

Press Syndicate

to fight it ten minutes before he landed it." At once the reader feels, just as the person telling the story feels, a little thrill of excitement as he thinks that maybe he, too, could hook and land such a fish. When you read the story of Cinderella, you wanted to know how her life would turn out. So, too, the reader of your story will want to know whether or not the boy really had the chance to land a big one.

Suspense. In the end we find that Cinderella is rewarded for being an honest and good human being. For she meets the Prince and he marries her. But this is not as important as the fact that before the end we follow several incidents which keep us from finding this out. These incidents are necessary in order to make the story attractive to us. Cinderella leaves the dance three times before the story ends. In this way the reader is kept in suspense, wondering how it will end. This makes the end all the more dramatic when it comes.

Notice that the story is not all sweetness and sentiment. No effort is made to soften the nastiness of the two sisters and their mother. Remember, when you are writing, that the best stories do not hide things just because they are ugly. They try to keep close to life as it actually is. Was Cinderella different from other girls? Perhaps not, but she was very pretty. What did she want? Only what most of us want, some delight in life. Think of yourself in her place and ask what you would have done. Would you have been as patient? Probably not, for Cinderella was a person of enormous patience. And yet you would surely have refused to act as selfishly as the other girls in the story. When telling about your characters, make them like ordinary persons. Don't hide their bad qualities, if they have any.

For example, if you are telling the story about the boys in the rowboat, you may have a boy who thinks he knows all about boats because he has been at the lakes before. Let him tell what he knows about fishing and boats. Let him show off his knowledge so that he lets a big fish get off his hook while he is talking, and misses catching it.

"Cinderella," like all good stories, has suspense and the excitement of things happening and the real sound of char-

Eva Luoma, Monkmeyer

acters talking. In your own story you should try to have these same qualities. Perhaps there will be three times when the younger boy has a chance to catch a fish. The first time he may lose his bait. The second time his hook may get caught on a sunken log. But the third time, he may enjoy the thrill of catching a big bass.

Writing Your Story

When you write your story, be sure that you understand what each person, or animal, in it is really like. Do not make any person so good that he could never have lived. Do not describe things happening, but show them happening. Tell what everyone says, and make voices sound like the voices of persons you know. Let them use slang words, if necessary, and let their voices rise and fall the way real voices do. A voice will get loud as it says something important, and it will get soft as a person tries to sound close to someone. Listen, also, for the sounds which the words make

when you write groups of them together.

A Meaning. You must know what your story is going to mean before you write it. Stories aren't plain accounts of things that happened. Even a simple fairy story, such as "Cinderella," has meaning. In the story of the boat, your meaning could be to keep trying. And don't brag. If you know what your story is going to mean, you can make everything that happens in it emphasize that meaning. But do not write out the meaning in the story, because then you would have no reason to write the story.

The "what if" story is a favorite one. You can begin by thinking what would happen if you could know what was in books simply by placing them, opened, on your face for a few minutes. How much you could learn and how quickly! You can show in your story how much our lives depend on chance and on decisions that could easily have been different. What if you had not cancelled your reservation on an airplane? Then you might have arrived early enough at your destination to see a colorful parade. Remember that every day is crammed with all kinds of exciting events, as well as events that could easily not have happened at all.

Poetry

Poetry is about everything in your life. It can be about all the things you do and say and feel. It puts those things into words which have rhythm. (Rhythm is simply the way the voice rises and falls in talking.) Those things are written in poetry to emphasize them. Poems often have the same sound at the ends of lines. This rhyme, as it is called, is there for emphasis, too, and to make the poem sound better. The following poem was written by a boy:

A pale yellow jelly on a pale blue dish,
Plump, jazzy jelly, shimmering like a fish,
Fat, jolly jelly, bedecked with orange jewels,
Gleaming like the moonlight on deep dark pools,
Mad yellow jelly, rocking with glee,
Rolling fat, laughing at me.
JEROLD W.

Notice how the rhymes make the poem more musical. Notice, too, how the words are well chosen to emphasize what they are describing. The jelly could have been described as "Thick, quivering jelly," but that would have been much duller than "Plump, jazzy jelly." The "plump" is exactly the right word, for have you not seen jelly looking fat and sleek on a dish? And the jazzy is wonderful, for it suggests so many kinds of things, not merely the way jelly shakes, but the special, jumpy, jouncing way it moves.

"Shimmering like a fish," tells us that jelly has the same wet gleam which fish have. It is a good example of comparing one thing to another. Comparison makes you SEE an object in a way which other description could not. It was not best to use an outworn word such as "bedecked." Avoid using such words in your own poems. Do not use words which you have not heard people say.

This is what you must do in your own poem—find the really right word, the one which sounds like what you are describing. This poem makes the jelly come alive as a real thing laughing back at the author. Its words even describe the live way jelly slips over a dish.

Poems about things that happen to you are easy to write, for everyone has interesting events happening almost every day. Maybe it could be going to a farm and being chased by a hissing goose. One small boy wrote the following poem about the way he felt cold whenever he went into the shadow of tall trees at his grandmother's house.

At my grandmother's house
There are two tall trees
On each side of the road.
They close up their branches
At the top.

When I go underneath
I shut up my coat
Because I always think
It's colder there.
ARTHUR R.

Your poem should make the person who reads it feel your idea. Perhaps you have heard music that has seemed to sway in your ears, just the way something you could see might sway. The music may have seemed to hit you as if it were a musical hammer. If so, you might be able to tell the reader about the experience so that he could hear music sway and feel it himself. The following poem was written by a boy who listened to music and wanted to tell about it in just the way it came to him.

When I go to hear music
I hear the sway of it
In my mind.
It strikes my heart like a hammer
And makes my world a happy one.
URICK K.

What a good, solid, simple poem that is! There is nothing fancy about it. There is not any talk about fairies. It is just a real experience. Make your own poems that way.

Your Own Poems

First, read poetry so you know what

it looks like and how many different ways there are in which it can be written. Listen for the sound of words. Try to put all kinds of words together in your mind. Then write them down on paper, even if they do not make real sentences. Try putting your words together in shapes like the poems you have read, but do not bother about rhyme at first. Do this as you would play at drawing, or painting, or sewing, or making something out of wood.

You can even write some poems with your friends, each of you writing one line. Or you could have a friend fill in words you especially want. Perhaps you could read a Mother Goose poem and a group of you might write your own Mother Goose poem. Remember that anything can go into your poem. What matters is that you should make the sound of the poem beautiful. You can put into your poems such things as a hurt dog, the sudden scare a storm might give you, the exact way a flower looks, the sadness of a monkey in a cage, or the things that you think a doll might think about. You can pretend that there are fairies in some new machine like an automobile or a vacuum cleaner. You can even put in your verses some little animal such as a crab, a worm, or a butterfly. And your feelings —happy, hopeful, unhappy, or hurt— can always be put in your poems.

After you have written a poem, read it aloud. This is the way all poems should be read, for words are really sounds. Does your poem sound like something that has actually happened? Are the words exciting? Instead of writing about the "sound" of a bell, perhaps you wrote "clang," which is more like the real sound of the bell. Did you say

one thing was like another? This is called using *imagery*. Instead of writing that a small girl walked "carefully and delicately" it seemed better to write: "She walks like a grave kitten on a fence." * Don't you think that the picture of the cat on the narrow fence describes the little girl's way of walking much better than dull words such as carefully and delicately?

Another time this same girl thought that happenings in books were more real than those she found in the world around her. They were more real because she felt safer with them when they just lived inside books. Following is the poem which expressed these thoughts:

Books were the actual world she touched and knew
Where trolls were real and friendly goblins hid
Under the bed, and gentle dragons blew
Smoke from their mouth and talked the way she
    did.
Wolves between the covers of a book
Wandered all day their safe, familiar land,
Brown squirrels came down from colored trees and
    took
Imaginary acorns from her hand.*

You, too, may have felt the same way when reading a book. Authors work hard on lines like these. Some of these lines were perhaps written over, and over, as many as ten times. And many other lines may have been thrown away. Write your poem over and over until, when you read it aloud, you feel that it expresses your own thoughts and feelings. While you are reading your poems be sure to listen for the sound the words make together.

Improving Your Writing

After you have written a story, a letter, or a poem, read it and ask yourself

* Courtesy of Random House, Publishers. Copyright 1945 by Paul Engle.

these questions: Is it interesting to me? If not, it will not interest anyone else. Is it written simply and naturally? Does it make people SEE what I am writing about? Are the words used in a new and exciting way? Do the words have a good sound when read aloud, or are they hard to read?

Be Hard-boiled about your own writing. If it doesn't suit you, do it over, again and again, if necessary. Maybe you have seen a bug trying to climb over a wall. Time and again, it almost reaches the top, and then either falls back or finds that the wall is too smooth for its feet. But the bug keeps trying, and, in the end, over it goes. Sometimes, like the bug, you may have to try many times. Make a game of writing. When you write something that really suits you, you win.

Make Things Happen. If you write a story, be sure that things happen in it. Have people do and say things just as they do in life. What matters most in a story is the people in it. Make them talk to each other. Make them do things so that the reader knows what kind of people they are. Begin your story with something happening. Action is the important thing.

Write several beginnings and endings, until you have found the best words and the most exciting actions. As you put down each word, ask yourself if it is the one word that sounds most like the thing about which you are writing. If you are writing about a boy skating, don't say that he came sailing, or speeding, or striding. Say that he whizzed, or zoomed, because these words sound more like the speed with which the boy was going. Write that a creek splashed, or crept, or slid, but not that it ran, or laughed, or flowed. Always choose the most active word.

Compare Things. When the wind blows leaves that are lighter colored on one side than on the other, you might say that they look like small faces peering quickly at you. When you describe a quick-moving person, say that he popped into the room, not that he came in. Watch a dredge at work. Doesn't it look like a giant burying his long neck and his head in the water to catch something to eat? Would heavy snow melting from bushes look like ice cream?

Don't use comparisons that have been used too many times before. Don't say "gentle as a lamb." Say, perhaps, "gentle as a child's hand." Don't say "packed in like sardines." Say something new such as, "Packed in like kids in a school bus." Don't say "spreading like wildfire." Say "spreading like people caught in sudden rain." Don't say "cross as a bear." Say, perhaps, "cross as a baby with its first tooth."

Always remember that, in a poem or in a story or in a plain description, it is the word that is most like the thing you are writing about which is the best word, not the word that is fanciest or biggest. One five-year-old girl wrote:

> I love to walk on the grass
> In the morning
> When it's—juicy.

Keep Writing. Write to your friends. Write your own cards, don't buy them with verses other people have written. Start a little magazine or paper of your own. It will be fun to have all your friends write for it. Write poems and stories, and little two-line descriptions of something funny, or new, or queer that happened. For example, "I saw a

The more you write, the better writer you will become. Plan a weekly paper or magazine and have your friends write for it.

Madison (Wis.) Public Schools

brown squirrel in a tree. He had his tail wrapped around him like a muff." Keep all your writings that you like. You can write them in a booklet, paste them in a notebook, or staple them together, and add pictures. Then you can read them months later and think of all the ways in which you can make them better.

Writing is the simplest thing in the world to do. You only need a pencil and some paper. Remember, you need to listen to the sounds of words, either spoken by someone or read from a book. Before you write any word, say it to yourself so that you know how it will sound as well as look on the page. Learn to like words and the music and magic they can make. Even make up silly phrases and new words without real meanings, if they have good sounds.

Soon you will be writing interesting new phrases and sentences every day. You can write them for your friends in notes, for your own collection, for relatives on holidays, and for the things you do at school. You will find that you can write for fun and that it is as easy as playing or talking to a cat or a bug on the grass or the boy or girl next door. For writing is words put together excitingly. And putting them together is exciting.

Poems by Children

The following poems were written by boys and girls to express their own thoughts and feelings about everyday things. They may not be the best poetry, but each poem gave the writer the pleasure of creating a word picture.

MY LITTLE ROSE

I have a little rose,
And it has a rosy nose,
And every time I look at it,
It's dancing on its toes.
MARGARET K.

I HAVE

I have a house
Made of grass and twigs.
I go there when I can.
I find a chair
To sit upon.
It is nice in there.
No one says, "No!"
BRUCE M.

A SNOWFLAKE

I saw a flake come floating,
Come floating toward the land;
I watched it till it came so close,
Until it touched my hand.

It was so soft and pretty,
So weak and faint for strife,
That when I gave it one warm breath,
I took away its life.
HOWARD C.

172

FEET

I am a little boy.
When I go walking with my mother,
    all I see is feet.

I get tired of seeing feet, feet, feet.
They make me dizzy.
When anybody speaks to me, I have to look
    to see who it is.

Then my neck gets tired.
But some day I will grow up and see
    faces.

                HARRY

THREE CATS . . . IF

We have three cats
If Thomas Aquinas comes back.
There's Jane Sullivan
And Baby Baker,
But Thomas Aquinas went away.
He may come back—
We don't know yet—
But we have three cats
If Thomas Aquinas comes back.

                JOHN

WHAT NANCY LIKES

I don't like faces that are crossish,
I don't like people that are rushy,
I like
Medium-quick ones,
Half-slow.

                NANCY

MY SHOES

Oh! little shoes
Why do you quarrel
All the time
Just over the one
That gets laced up first?
You naughty little shoes.

                JACK E.

WORMS

Some worms don't have any feet—
They pull themselves out
And they pull themselves in
They pull themselves out—
And that's the way they get along
Because they don't have any feet.

                DICKIE

BOOKS TO READ

COURTIS, STUART A., and WATTERS, GARNETTE. *Illustrated Golden Dictionary for Young Readers.* Illus. by Beth and Jo Krush. Simon & Schuster, 1951. This simple dictionary, copiously illustrated, may be useful to the young writer in his choice of words.

"Creative Writing in The Elementary Grades." Curriculum Department, Madison (Wis.) Public Schools, 1951.

KRAMER, ANNE. *It's Fun to Make a Book.* Illus. by Carlyle Leech. Dutton, 1946. Two stories arranged so that space is left for the child to supply his own endings and pictures, though the real endings are included. Also space for the child to write a story of his own.

KRAUSS, RUTH. *A Hole Is to Dig; a First Book of First Definitions.* Illus. by Maurice Sendak. Harper, 1952.

SMITH, EUNICE YOUNG. *Denny's Story.* Illus. by the author. A. Whitman, Chicago, Ill., 1952. In his own words, a seven-year-old boy writes stories about his seven sisters and brothers and their future plans, giving a short but effective account of his own plans at the end.

WRIGHT, WENDELL WILLIAM, and LAIRD, HELENE. *Rainbow Dictionary.* Illus. by Joseph Low. World Pub. Co., 1947.

The Horn Book Magazine is published bimonthly by The Horn Book, Inc., 585 Boylston Street, Boston 16, Mass. *The Horn Book League* is a department for children's and young people's own writing and drawing. Rules for membership and the submission of contributions will be sent upon request.

MAKING TOYS AND PLAYTHINGS

LAWRY TURPIN

Wolff & Tritschler, Black Star

WHAT A THRILL it is to make your own toys and playthings! You can even make a workbench and a place to store your tools. Bookshelves, a teeter-totter, chairs, and tables are among the useful things you will want to make after you learn to use tools. Besides the fun of making your own things, there is a chance to make something for everyone in the family. Father, mother, and even the youngest can join in helping with workshop projects. Lawry Turpin, teacher, and author of *Toys You Can Make of Wood*, shows us how to make many especially interesting playthings.

A TOYSHOP, with its cans of paint and its curly shavings littering the floor, is one of the most exciting places. Often when we think of toyshops, we think of Santa Claus and his elves getting ready for the Christmas rush. What could be more fun than to be your own

Making your own toys and playthings gives a great feeling of accomplishment.

toy tinker with a workshop all your own? There, amid the tangy pine boards and turpentine, you can spend many happy hours making toys and playthings for yourself or as gifts for friends.

What You Will Need

All you need is wood, a few tools, and a place in which to work. In order to simplify the directions in this chapter, the following symbols will be used: ′ for foot or feet; ″ for inch or inches; and x for "by." For example, 4″ x 2″ x 1″ means 4 inches long by 2 inches wide by 1 inch thick.

174

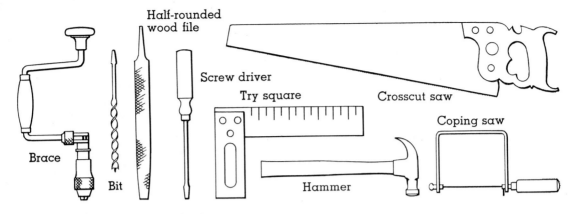

For making toys and playthings, you will need the tools which are pictured here.

Wood. You can buy plywood, planks, or wallboard at any lumberyard. Handcraft shops also sell wood in small quantities. But a less expensive way for you to obtain material is to use orange crates and apple boxes. To make separate pieces of them, saw them apart, as close to each end and partition as possible. Pull out all the nails, and you will have good material, both thick and thin. Avoid knocking or prying the boards apart, for this will splinter the boards and make them useless.

Boxes vary in size, but usually the ends are 11½″ square, and about ¾″ thick. The sides of orange crates are thin, and those of apple boxes are a little thicker. With this material, you can make many things without having to buy any wood. Ask the grocer to save these boxes for you, as well as empty cheeseboxes of all sizes. Ask the hardware dealer to save you some empty nail kegs to use in making a table.

Tools. You will need these few tools: a crosscut saw, a coping saw with an adjustable frame, a brace with ³⁄₁₆″, ⅜″, and ½″ bits; a half-round wood file, a screw driver, a hammer, a try square, and a clamp vise. If you have a plane or jig saw, you will save both time and energy, but they are not necessary.

Crosscut Sawing. It is easy to get a clean start when using a crosscut saw.

First, place the teeth of the saw near the handle at the saw line. Then "knuckle" the first finger of your left hand and hold it against the flat side of the blade. Pull up on the saw once, and you have a neat start without any nicks.

Coping Saw. In using this tool, remember that for all inside cuts, such as the centers of rings, a hole must first be bored. Then insert the saw blade, and refasten it to the frame. After completing the sawing, remove the blade from the frame first, then from the wood. Always watch the blade to keep it going straight through the wood.

Brace and Bit. Drill all holes needed before any parts are sawed out. In this way splitting is avoided.

Try Square. If the handle of the square is kept tight against the side of the wood, the line drawn across the wood will be squared with the edge.

Where to Work. If you have a closet large enough for a box to be kept in it, then you can make a workbench your-

How you should use a crosscut saw.

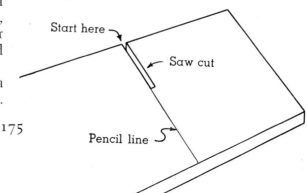

175

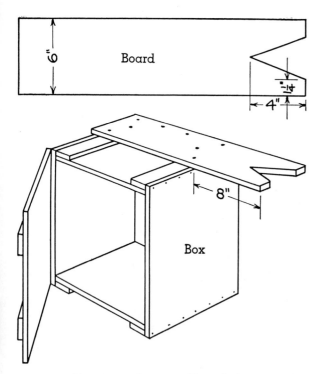

How to make a workbench from a spare box which you can store in a closet.

belts to the wall to form loops for the tool parts to slip into. Nails driven in on a slant will keep saw handles in place. Old felt or carpeting, glued to the bottom of the box, will keep the floor from being scratched when the box is moved.

Helps. To use a drawing that is on squares in a book, redraw the same number of squares on a sheet of wrapping paper. Draw the corresponding lines in each square until the picture is completed. Cut out the figure with scissors, and trace the outline on the wood. Be careful that the grain runs the long way of the design.

If the article you are sawing has long narrow parts, such as beaks and tails, always start your coping saw at the tip end and saw from there. Start again on the other line of the tip and saw away from it. If you are careful in doing this, the wood will not split.

Nailing. It is wise to start all nails in place in each piece before joining. Have the point of the nail barely showing on the underside. Two nails slanted slightly towards each other make a stronger joint than if both nails are straight down. This is called *toenailing*. In nailing two flat pieces together, it is

self, and have a good place to work. A basement, closed back porch, or garage are good places for a workbench.

Buy a packing box from a storage company. A box about 17″ x 17″ x 29″ will do. The boards for nailing it shut should come with it. With these you can make a door to be attached with metal strap hinges. A screw hook and screw eye will hold the door when closed. Stand the box on end. Across the top at the back, nail on a piece of wood extending 8″ at one side. Saw a V notch at this end, as in the drawing. This piece is for all coping saw work, the saw to go up and down in the notch.

Hang the tools inside the box. Whenever possible, screw strips of old leather

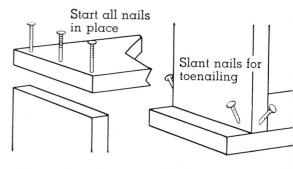

Start all nails in place as shown on the left before driving them in. Toenailing will strengthen all joints.

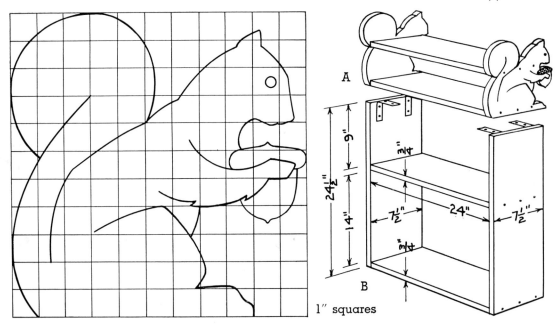

1" squares

A plan for building a bookcase decorated with squirrels on top of a two-shelf base

sometimes best to have the nails go through on the underside. The nail points can then be bent over with the hammer flush with the wood. This is called *clenching*.

Painting. Have all surfaces sanded and clean before painting. Sand again lightly between coats with fine sandpaper. If parts are to be of different colors, paint them separately before putting them together.

Toys. You can make most of these toys yourself, if you know how to use a ruler and a saw. In making larger toys, such as a teeter-totter, you may need help. Sometimes the whole family may want to work as a team. It is fun to work together, for things grow much faster, and there is usually something for each one to do. Even the youngest can be taught to sandpaper edges. Whenever possible, make it a family workshop.

Bookshelves

Materials: Apple box; plywood or pine board ¾″ thick; paper and pencil; paintbrush; 2″ nails; glue; paint; metal angles.

If you love books you will want to take good care of them, and keep them on a shelf where you can always find them. The two squirrels, which are made of box ends, plywood, or any wood ¾″ thick, will help to keep the books in place.

1. Draw the patterns on wood ¾″ thick. Cut them out with a coping or jig saw. Then file the edges smooth. All edges, except those at the bottom, should be rounded with a file.

2. Cut the shelves of ¾″ wood also, 7½″ wide and 24″ long. They can be longer or shorter according to your need.

3. Start 2″ nails in place while the squirrel pieces are flat on the workbench.

Smear glue on the ends of the shelves, and nail the squirrel pieces to them.

4. Paint if desired. Gray squirrels with black lines go well with bright red shelves. So do brown or black squirrels with tan lines. You decide.

If you need more space than the shelves shown in Figure A supply, build a base, as in Figure B, of ¾″ wood, 7½″ wide. Glue and nail a side to one end of each shelf. Turn it over, and nail on the other side piece. To attach the squirrel unit, use metal angles at each end as shown.

It might make the squirrels stand out more if you reversed your color scheme and made the new shelves gray with red sides. But you should use the colors you want.

Bulletin Board

Materials: Pencil and paper; wallboard 2′ square; paintbrush; orange, red or brown, and green paint; nails.

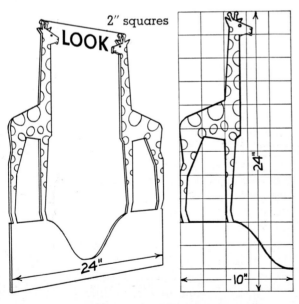

A plan for a giraffe Bulletin Board

These tall giraffes would like to know what is going on too, and they are saying LOOK in letters 2″ high. The bulletin board is easy to make, for it requires only one piece of wallboard 2′ square.

1. Paint the entire board tan, white, or light blue.

2. Draw a giraffe on 2″ squared paper and cut it out. When the paint is dry, copy the design on the wallboard so that the giraffes face each other. Have their horns just touch the top, and their tails the edges. Draw a slightly sloping line for the grass.

3. Saw only the outer edges, from the horn to the grass, with a coping saw.

4. Paint the animals bright orange, with red or brown spots. Paint the grass and letters green.

5. Hang the bulletin board on the wall.

Teeter-Totter

This is really a family project, for there are big pieces and small pieces to saw, file, and sandpaper.

Materials: Wood plank, 10′ x 8″ x 1″; orange crate or pine board 1″ thick; plywood ½″ thick; hardwood dowel 8″ x ½″; 2″ x 4″ beam, 54″ long; glue; nails; paintbrush; red, yellow, and white paint; pencil and paper.

1. Trace the curves for the saddles at both ends of the plank. These will form the seats of the teeter-totter. Saw the curves out. Then thoroughly file and sandpaper all edges.

2. Someone else could be sawing out the duck heads from orange crate ends or any wood about 1″ thick. Drill a hole ½″ in diameter in each head. Glue in a hardwood dowel 8″ long and of the same diameter. This will give the rider something to hold.

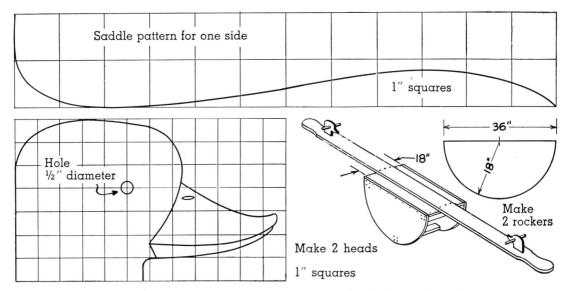

Saddle pattern for one side

1" squares

Hole ½" diameter

36"

18"

18"

Make 2 rockers

Make 2 heads

1" squares

How you can make your own teeter-totter with attractive duck-head handles.

3. Another member of the team could be making the two rockers from ½" plywood. The connecting top piece is also made out of plywood. The rockers are half circles on an 18" radius. The top piece is 18" wide and 36" long.

Saw three lengths of 2x4's each 18" long. Use one for additional strength at the bottom of the rockers. The corners should be flush with the curve. Use the other two at each end at the top. Toe-nail in place with 2" nails.

4. Balance the plank exactly. Drill holes through the plank, top, and 2x4's for bolts, two for each end.

5. Now paint in gay colors. Why not use a red plank, yellow ducks, and blue rockers with white scallops on them, perhaps with a star in the middle? But always let your own taste rule.

You will have no trouble in making a practical teeter-totter like this one.

Percy H. Prior, Jr.

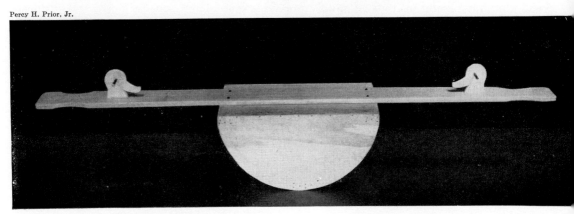

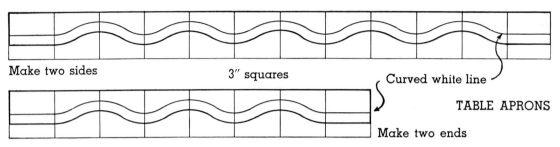

Make two sides   3″ squares   Curved white line

TABLE APRONS

Make two ends

This plan shows you can make and paint aprons for the sides and ends of your table.

Small Table

Materials: Two nail kegs; pine board; plywood; nails; paintbrush; red, blue, and white paint; pencil and paper.

Two nail kegs of equal size will serve as the supports of a playroom table around which four or six can gather.

1. Place the kegs, open ends down, on the floor. Fill in the other ends with pieces of wood the proper thickness to be even with the keg edge. Nail in place and clench nails from the inside.

2. Place the kegs 5½″ apart at their tops. Nail to them a piece of ½″ plywood 23″ wide and 36″ long. Use 2″ nails and clench.

3. Make a paper pattern for the aprons. Trace these on plywood and saw out. Nail the side on first, then the ends.

4. Paint the kegs red, the top and aprons medium blue. Paint a curved white line on the aprons. This will make a popular color scheme. Make sure that

the colors do not clash with the color scheme of the playroom.

Small Chair

Materials: Three orange crates; sandpaper; nails; putty or plastic wood; brush and paint; pencil and paper.

This chair requires five endpieces of orange crates. Use one piece for the front legs, one for the back legs, one for the seat, and one for the chair back. The fifth is used as a brace.

1. Draw the patterns on 1″ squared paper. Then transfer to the pieces of wood. Be careful to keep the grain running up and down in each case. The brace is 4″ wide and 9″ long.

2. Saw out all the parts. Then file and sandpaper the edges until smooth.

3. Bore a hole inside the heart outlines to admit the blade of your coping saw. Then saw out the heart-shaped piece, **and** round off the edges smoothly.

4. The back leg must be sloped or

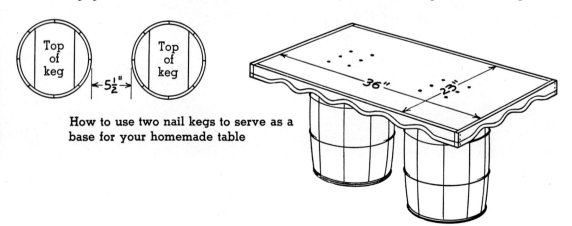

How to use two nail kegs to serve as a base for your homemade table

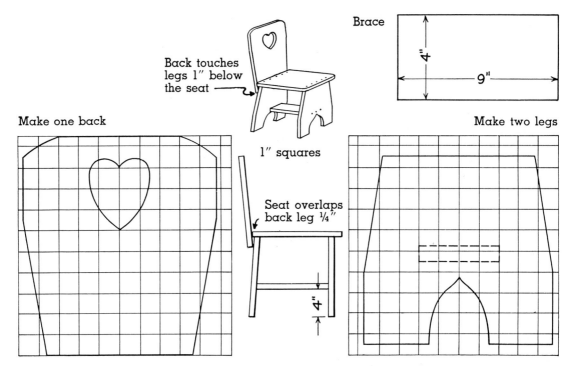

Back touches legs 1" below the seat →

Brace

4"

9"

Make one back

1" squares

Seat overlaps back leg ¼"

4"

Make two legs

By using three orange crates you will be able to build a very useful chair.

slanted off at the top ¼" so that the chair will not tip over backwards. Shape one end of the brace in the same way.

5. Put together by nailing the front and back legs to the brace. The brace should be 4" from the floor. Use 2" nails.

6. Check to see that the chair stands evenly on the floor. Then nail seat to legs so that it overlaps ¼" at the back.

7. Nail on the chair back (which touches rear legs 1" below the seat). Use five nails in seat and four in leg.

8. Fill the nail holes with plastic wood. Finish with either a stain and wax, or with bright-colored paint.

Sandboxes

Two types of sandboxes are shown. One is for the yard. If your mother and father will permit, a sandbox may also be made for the playroom or porch.

Materials: Pine board, 1" thick; plywood or tongue-and-groove material; nails; metal angles; sandpaper; brush; red or yellow paint; chicken wire (for outdoors).

The Sandbox for the Playroom should be made of four pieces of wood about 48" long, 12" wide, and 1" thick.

1. Nail together and strengthen with metal angles at each corner. A tight floor of either plywood or tongue-and-groove material will keep the sand from sifting through the bottom.

2. Make two seats at diagonally opposite corners. Use the same material as for the sides. Cut in quarter circles on a 12" radius.

3. Use gay paints for the large, simple designs of hearts, stars, or funny ani-

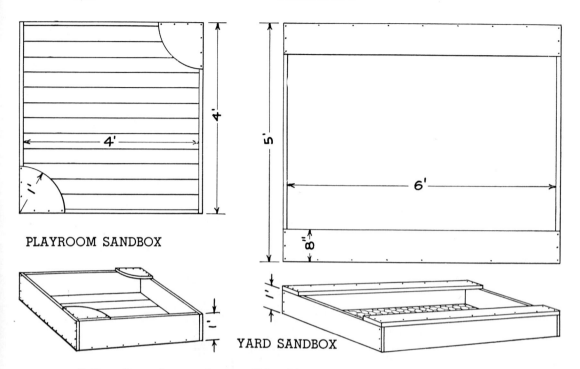

PLAYROOM SANDBOX

YARD SANDBOX

Follow these plans, and you will be able to make a fine playroom or yard sandbox.

mals. A rickrack, or zigzag, line also is attractive, or a series of triangles.

A Sandbox for the Yard should be larger, with the sides at least 6′ long, 1′ wide, and 1″ thick, and with the ends 5′ long. Nail at the corners and strengthen with metal angles. A floor of chicken wire will keep the soil from mixing with the sand. Use planks 8″ wide down the length of each side to make good seats and provide a surface for mud pies, or sand figures. The seats also help to keep more sand in the box and less on the grass. Plane the seats, and sandpaper them before painting.

Avoid painting the box green as your friends may not see it. They may trip over it and skin their legs. Use red or yellow paint.

A Screen-Playhouse

This interesting screen will serve either as a screen or as a playhouse for your room. There can be as many panels as you wish.

Materials: Pine wood; canvas or wallboard; double-action hinges; metal angles; screws; thumb tacks; brush and paint; paper flowers.

1. Make the frames of 1¾″ x 1⅛″ wood. Glue, nail, and strengthen each corner with metal angles.

2. Cover both sides of the frames, or only one, with canvas or wallboard.

The material used should be tacked on even with each edge. If you cover the frame on only one side, be sure to tack the cover on the outside, covering the frame as in picture B. Make the over-all measurements 2′ 4″ wide and 4′

long. This will make the screen stand 4′ high.

3. Screw one side of double-action hinges 8″ from the top and bottom of the center panel. Then screw the hinges to each of the other panels to make a three-panel screen as shown in picture B. Follow the same method for a four-panel screen.

4. Paint to look well with the color scheme in your room. To make the windowpane sections look more like glass, paint a gray color. Then wipe off most of the paint with a cloth.

5. Make the window frame and box by sticking on wide bands of colored adhesive tape. You can also use adhesive tape to make the window appear to be divided into smaller panes.

Change the paper flowers in the window boxes often. Make spring, summer,

and fall flowers, and even little Christmas trees brightly decorated. Attach with thumb tacks.

Blocks

Blocks require careful and accurate sawing. They make a wonderful present for a younger brother or sister, and at almost no cost.

Materials: Orange crate or 2″ x 4″ white pine; pencil and paper; ruler; stain and wax.

Two ends of an orange crate, A and B, will make a set of 50 small blocks. When not in use, they may be kept in a brightly painted potato-chip can. It is even fun to put them away, for they make a delightful noise as they are dropped in the can.

1. On piece A, draw vertical lines running with the grain, 1″ apart. Starting

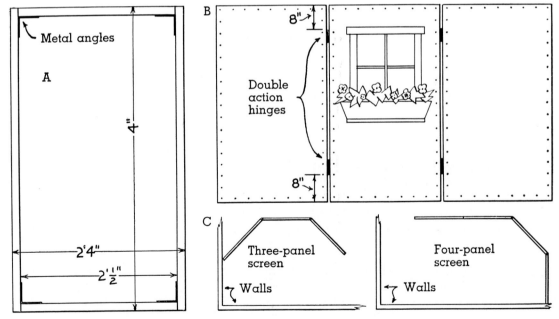

You will find it a pleasant experience to make screens for use in your back yard.

with the fifth block from the left, divide the remaining lines in half horizontally. From the ninth row, again divide each section. Saw apart to give you 1″ blocks of different sizes.

2. On piece B, draw vertical lines 2″ apart. Across the first four rows, draw horizontal lines 4″ and 8″ down from the top, as shown in figure B. Divide again the two upper blocks in the third and fourth rows into 2″ spaces. Cut the last block in half horizontally. Then draw lines from the center of one long side to the center of the other side. In this way, both sections are divided into two large and four small triangles.

3. Larger blocks are made easily from white pine 2″ x 4″. Use a try square to draw lines, first across the face, then down the front side. Three lengths, each

12′ long, will make a set of 33 blocks, divided as follows: six pieces 2′ long; eight pieces 18″ long; six pieces 12″ long; six pieces 6″ long; eight large triangles and two smaller ones.

4. Stain the blocks in different colors, and wax them.

Jigsaw Puzzles

Jigsaw puzzles are enjoyed by almost everyone. Simple ones will amuse boys and girls for hours at a time. Make them according to your own ideas.

Materials: Pencil and paper; colored pencil; plywood or wallboard; colored pictures or photograph prints; sandpaper; paste; brush; gray, blue, red, white, and yellow paint. To make the box in which to keep the puzzle, you will also need: orange crate; nails; tacks; glue; leather; decorated paper.

The Sailboat puzzle is designed for a

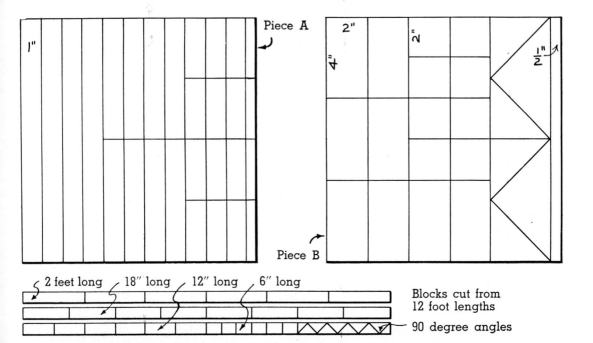

Older boys and girls can follow these plans in making blocks for the younger children.

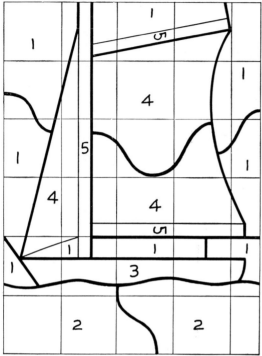

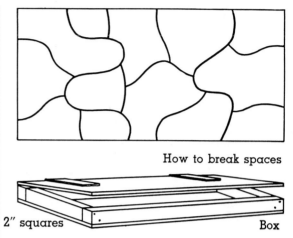

How to break spaces

2" squares   Box

You can make jigsaw puzzles which you and your friends can use on rainy days.

small child who will find it fun.

1. Draw the design on thin plywood or wallboard. Then saw with a thin blade. It is best to start sawing at a corner piece and proceed to the next piece until you cut out all the pieces.

2. Sandpaper all edges lightly.

3. Paint the *backs* of all pieces the same color. Paint parts numbered 1 gray; parts numbered 2, blue; 3, red; 4, white; and 5, yellow.

Your little brother or sister may like to fit the pieces together in a box to show to other admiring eyes, and to keep pieces from being lost.

The Box for the sailboat is made of two orange crate ends 9" long and ½" square, and two sides 13" long and ½" square. The top and bottom are both 13" x 10". Tack the bottom on. Attach

the top with leather hinges. Glue and tack the hinges to both top and back.

Other Puzzles are made by pasting colorful pictures to wallboard. Lines are drawn with a colored pencil before sawing. Be careful to avoid long points that might break off.

The personal touch in jigsaw puzzles will make gifts valued by young and old. What could be better than an enlarged photograph of a pet, or Dad's big fish, or a birthday party? Mount the picture. If it is for a grownup, saw it into smaller pieces than those made for children. Place the pieces in boxes covered with gay paper.

Humpty Dumpty Bean Game

Materials: Apple box; nails; pencil; brush; red, white, blue, and black paint.

1. Draw Humpty Dumpty on wood on the side of an apple box, and saw him out. Then saw out his open mouth.

2. Saw three pieces from the apple box, each 5" square.

This is a plan for you to follow to make the Humpty Dumpty bean box.

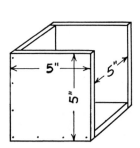

1" squares

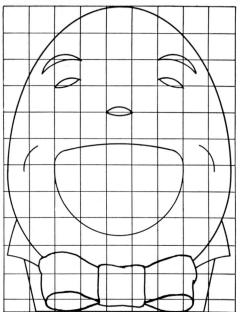

3. Nail the two sides to the bottom, as shown in the drawing.

4. Make a back piece that can be nailed on sides and bottom.

5. Nail Humpty to the front edge of the bottom of the box so that the bottom of the box is just below his mouth. This tips him back.

6. Paint the box and Humpty's tie bright red, his collar blue, his face white, and his nose and eyes black.

7. When the paint is dry, stand four or five feet away from him and see who can toss the greatest number of beans, one at a time, into his wide mouth.

Scat! Ringtoss

Materials: Orange crate; plywood; sandpaper; glue; nails; tacks; pipe cleaners; coping saw; brush and paints.

1. Draw the cat on wood from the end of an orange crate. Be sure the grain of the wood is running the long way of the tail.

2. The stand, or base, of the same material, can be left the full size of the crate end or it can be cut smaller as shown.

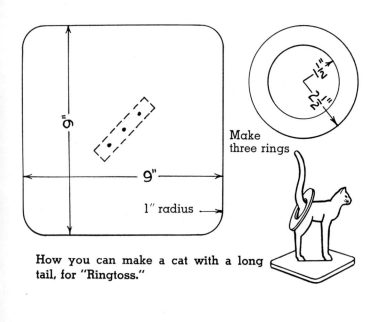

9"

9"

1" radius

Make three rings

How you can make a cat with a long tail, for "Ringtoss."

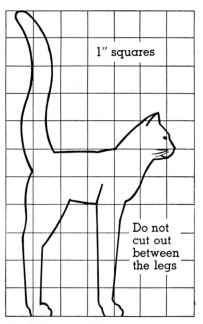

1" squares

Do not cut out between the legs

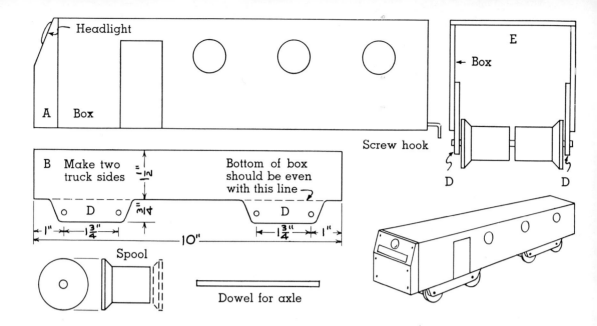

What boy does not want to make a toy train that he and his friends can play with?

3. File and sandpaper all edges.

4. Stand the cat upside down in a vise. Spread glue across the entire bottom edge, and nail the stand to it.

5. Saw rings out of plywood because this material will not break easily. Make at least three rings and paint them different colors.

6. Paint the cat black with yellow eyes and claws. Use gray paint for the section between the front and back paws. The base may be any color you like.

7. For whiskers, use pipe cleaners, wound together at the middle. When the paint is dry, tack the whiskers to the front of the cat's nose, and cut them to uneven lengths.

Turn to "Games for Indoors and Outdoors" to learn how to play Ringtoss, and how to make rings of rope and pegs of clothespins.

Toy Train

Materials: Orange crates and cheeseboxes; nails; glue; brads; ³⁄₁₆″ dowel; thread spools; screw hook and screw eye; brush and paints; and India ink if desired.

The cars and engine of this train are made from cheeseboxes, all the same size. The engine shown here has a slanted front.

1. To make the engine, saw a ¾″ block from an orange-crate end. Make the block as wide and as high as the box. Saw it to any slant you wish, and nail one end of a cheesebox to it.

2. Nail a circular block as a headlight in the center near the top.

3. Draw the truck sides, B, on wood from the sides of orange crates.

4. Bore ³⁄₁₆″ holes for axles.

5. Then saw the truck sides out.

6. Attach the truck sides to the inside of the box with glue and small brads. Only the portions D, holding the axles, should be below the line of the box.

7. Saw four pieces of ³⁄₁₆″ dowel, as long as the box is wide.

8. One spool is too short, and two spools are too long for wheels. Saw off one end of each spool so that two will fit, with just enough room to turn freely. You will need two spools for each axle, or eight for each car.

9. Make cars like the engine, but do not use a headpiece or headlight. Place a screw hook at the rear of the engine and each car. Place a screw eye on the other end of each car.

10. Paint your engine and cars the colors you wish. Doors and windows may be painted on, or traced on with India ink. One nine-year-old boy pasted gray paper for windows on his train.

Model Airplane

To make this airplane, use wood from the ends of an orange crate except for the motors, which are ¾″ dowel pins. If you have no dowels of that size, an old broom handle will do.

Materials: Orange crate; ¾″ dowel pins or broom handle; glue; small wire nails; sandpaper; brush and paint.

1. Saw all the parts out of the wood at the end of the crate.

2. Streamline the fuselage by round-ing all edges very carefully with a file.

3. Place the rudder upside down in a vise. Then glue the rudder and stabilizer (tail unit) together and strengthen with a small nail.

4. Glue and nail the tail unit to the rear of the fuselage.

5. Make the wings. If you desire a curve on the wings as in Figure A, make them in two sections. Nail on the lower section at the curve you want, using small wire nails. Otherwise, make the wing in a single piece as in Figure B.

6. Saw two sections, 1½″ long, off the dowel rod. Round off the nose of each with a file.

7. Cut slots across and down, as wide as the wing is thick.

8. Bore the holes in the centers of the propellers. Then saw the propellers out. Round the edges of the blades with sandpaper.

9. Hold the motors (dowel pins)

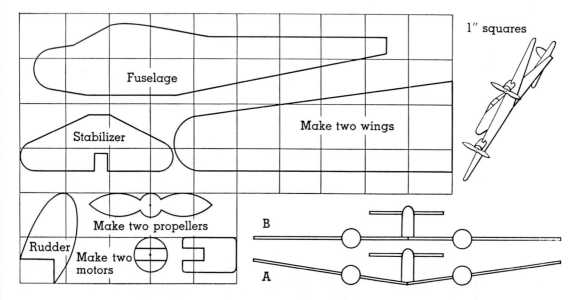

Use an old orange crate to make a model airplane from this plan.

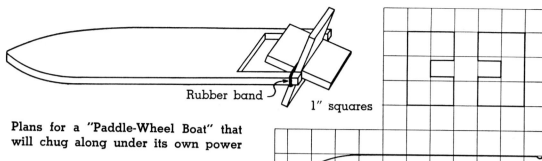

Rubber band 1" squares

Plans for a "Paddle-Wheel Boat" that will chug along under its own power

firmly in a vise and attach the propellers to the solid end of each.

10. Pour glue in the motor slots. Then fit them over the wings at equal distances from the fuselage. Your plane is now ready for a coat of paint.

Paddle-Wheel Boat

It is easy to make a toy paddle-wheel boat that will chug along under its own power.

Materials: Apple box or pine wood not more than ¼″ thick; rubber bands; glue; paint and brush.

1. Trace the pattern of the boat on the wood. The slot in each paddle should be the exact thickness of the wood you are using.

2. Saw the notches for the rubber band before making the inner cut on the boat.

3. Fit the two paddles together and test. Wind up backwards, let go, and see if any corners of the paddle hit the boat. Cut off any that do.

4. Glue the paddles together.

5. Then paint the boat. Use a different color for the paddles.

6. Try out different sizes of rubber bands to find out which makes the boat travel best.

Ring-on-the-Nose

Materials: Plywood; brush; pink, black, red, blue, or green paints; pencil and paper; cord.

1. Draw the policeman on 1″ squared paper and cut it out. Then trace the pattern on plywood.

2. Draw the ring with an outer diam-

eter of 5″ and an inner diameter of 2½″.

3. Saw out the policeman. Then paint his face and star pink; his hat, moustache, wrinkles, eye, and the handle black.

4. While the paint is drying, saw out the inside of the ring, then the outside. Paint it a bright color.

5. When both parts are dry, tie one end of a 28″ cord to the ring. Tie the other around the policeman's neck.

Hold the policeman in one hand, or let another player hold him. The ring on the policeman's nose must be caught five times out of five tries to win this game.

How to make a "Ring-on-the-Nose"

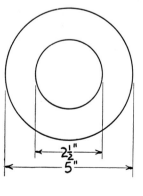

2½″
5″

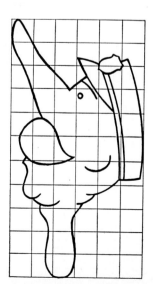

1" squares

Here We Go!

This is an amusing game that almost everyone likes to play. The game will be more interesting if your design shows places where you have been; for example, grandmother's house or your favorite picnic grounds.

Materials: A piece of wallboard or plywood 18″ x 14″ and one 6″ square; brush and green paint; nails; small wooden block; crayon; pencil, pen, and India ink; washer; buttons on cardboard; paste.

1. Paint the 18″ x 14″ board green.

2. While it dries, saw out a spinner of the same material 6″ in diameter. Nail it to a small wooden block underneath. This will serve as a handle. Do not put a nail in the exact center.

3. Divide the circle into eight sections, like pieces of pie. Mark the sections off with India ink or paint. Then write a number on each.

4. Draw an arrow on thin wood. Then cut it out and bore a hole in its center. Paint the arrow a bright color.

5. When the arrow is dry, put a washer between it and the circle. Attach all parts with a lath nail in the center of the circle, so that the arrow whirls freely.

6. Make four men, or counters, for each player. Make each set of four a different color. These may be small washers, painted buttons, or even cardboard colored with crayon and cut about the size of a dime.

7. When the large board is dry, paint or paste on it your design of a long, winding road. Make the starting place in one corner; the end of the journey

"Here We Go" is an interesting game which young and old enjoy playing.

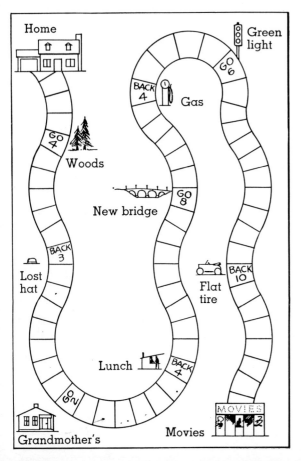

Percy H. Prior, Jr.

The boys are playing "Here We Go" which they have made. The boy on the left is holding the spinner which will tell how far he can move on the board.

in another. Mark off the sections. Let each GO and BACK section represent a place you know.

The rules are simple: Players take turns in spinning for a number to move men from HOME. They can finish with one man or get all four started on their way.

If you land on a section where another player has a man, his man is sent home to start over again. The one who first gets all his men to the end of the journey, wins.

Kites

Materials: Pine or spruce sticks; paper; scissors; string; rags; glue; plane; knife or three-cornered file.

1. Select two spruce or pine sticks, from ¼″ to ½″ square, and plane or sandpaper them until smooth.

2. Cut one stick 38″ long, the other, 28″.

3. Cut or file notches in the ends of the sticks so that the binding cord will not slip.

4. Find the exact center of the shorter stick. Cross it at right angles to the longer at a point 9″ from the top. By cutting shallow notches in each stick, you can fit them together more closely.

5. Glue the sticks together and lash them tightly with cord or fishline.

6. Connect the four ends with string, and pull the string tight. You now have a frame for your kite.

7. Press out a sheet of newspaper or wrapping paper with a warm iron. Lay the paper on the floor, and place the frame on top of it.

8. Draw a line 1″ beyond the frame all round it. Cut the paper along this line.

9. Cut off the corners, spread paste along the margin, and fold it over the string.

10. At points 6″ from the top and bottom of the longer stick, punch small

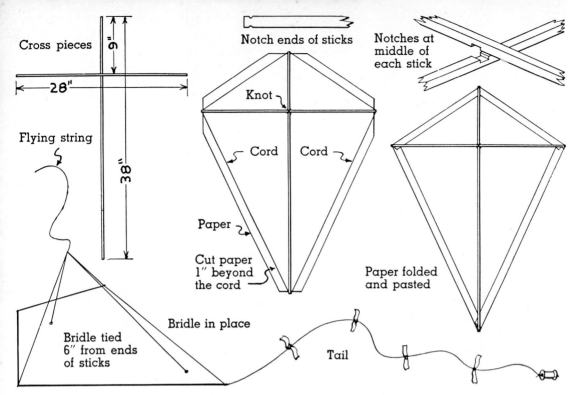

Making a workable kite to fly in the strong March winds is an exciting adventure.

holes in the paper. Wind a piece of string around the stick and run it through the paper at the top and bottom. Then tie the end to the lower part of the stick. This string should be about 28" long.

11. Attach another string to each end of the crosspiece with enough slack to allow the two strings to meet at a point just below the crosspiece. Now you have your bridle.

12. Attach the flying string to the center of the bridle.

13. Weights for the tail of the kite may be made either of rags or of paper. Cut the material into strips 7" x 5" and gather them in the center. Spread out the edges in the form of a bow tie. Then tie them on a string about one foot apart, and attach the tail to the kite. A small, light toy or a large spool may be used as an endweight for the tail.

14. Wind the flying string around a spool-shaped block of wood.

The Toys and Playthings you make by hand in your own workshop will give you a feeling of satisfaction in something well done. After you have made these you will doubtless think of many new, and perhaps more difficult, things to make. Soon, you may be making playthings of your own original design.

BOOKS TO READ

Jordan, Nina R. *Home Toy Shop.* Illus. by the author. Harcourt, 1937.

Lee, Tina. *How To Make Dolls and Doll Houses.* Illus. by Manning Lee. Doubleday, 1948. *What To Do Now.* Pictures and charts by Manning Lee; working models by the author. Doubleday, 1946.

Maginley, C. J. *Toymaker's Book.* Diagrams by Elisabeth D. McKee. Harcourt, 1948.

Taylor, Jeanne. *Child's Book of Carpentry.* Illus. by author. Greenberg, 1948.

COOKING
UP FUN

IRMA S. ROMBAUER
AND
JANE CRAWFORD TORNO

U & U

COOKING is still something of an art for it takes more than a can opener to make a cook. Boys, as well as girls, will enjoy "Cooking up Fun," especially when they find that it is easy to make such delicious foods as candy and various cool drinks. Modern gas and electric ranges, mechanical refrigerators, electric mixers, and various gadgets make cooking easy even for young persons. Irma S. Rombauer and Jane Crawford Torno are co-authors of *The Joy of Cooking*.

I T IS no wonder that you often find your way into the kitchen. This is one of the busiest rooms in the house. Cooking can be a wonderful adventure, for you can always experiment and make new dishes. Kitchens are workshops equipped with interesting tools and gadgets. Even babies like to play with the pots and pans. They fit together the pieces of a double boiler or a drip coffeepot, or nest the measuring cups. They pretend to cook and they imitate what their mothers are doing.

When you are big enough to hold a spoon and stir things, you can take part in the real fun of cooking. Your mother may have you begin by putting a sprig of parsley on the meat platter, or placing the maraschino cherry on the dessert. She may ask you to help break up the lettuce leaves for the salad, and the nut-

There are just two reasons for cooking— because you like to, or because you have to do so. Those who really like to cook have a great deal of fun.

meats for cakes and cookies. She may even ask you to shell the peas, and break off the tips of green beans.

There are many kitchen tools that you will need to know how to use. You snip up parsley and chives with the kitchen scissors. You scrape carrots, and even peel potatoes, with the vegetable scraper. If you have strong hands, you can use the nut cracker or squeeze oranges and lemons in the juicer. You can also put dry bread through the ricer or food mill. The meat grinder is even a better way to make bread crumbs. When the bread is ground, it may be sifted for fine and coarse crumbs.

But all cooks, young and old, should always be very careful in using the tools in the kitchen. If you are a beginner, it is especially important that your mother teach you how to use them. Your mother, or even your father, will be glad to be your companion for some of your first cooking adventures.

You will find that it is usual to sift

flour before you measure it. You do the same with sugar, if it is lumpy. You spoon flour and sugar lightly into a measuring cup, then level it off with a knife blade. But you pack brown sugar in firmly, just as you would pack damp sand in a mold.

First Cooking Ventures

After working with your mother in the kitchen for some time, the day will come when she will let you do some real cooking.

Gelatin Desserts. It is a thrill to be able to say, "I made the dessert." You may have this fun even before you are old enough to go to school, if you choose simple recipes. Among these are desserts made with flavored gelatin mixtures.

There is something magical about making one of these puddings. It is almost like doing an experiment in chemistry. A powder of one color turns to a liquid of a deeper color when hot water is added. The mixtures come in many different flavors, so there is also the fun of choosing the one you like best. To mix the gelatin, follow the directions printed on the package.

There are many ways to serve plain gelatin. You may chill it in several small molds or in one large one. Then you unmold it before serving. It may even be poured into a shallow pan. When it is firm, cut it into cubes to be piled into serving dishes. Or you may want to chill it in a bowl. Then when it is firm, put it through a ricer or a food mill. A gelatin dessert is attractive when prepared in this way. Usually, it tastes as good as it looks.

Gelatin Lollipops. Lollipops may also be made with gelatin mixtures. Jigger glasses or small jar lids may be used as molds. Fill them with plain liquid gelatin and place them in an empty freezing tray in the refrigerator. When the gelatin thickens, insert a match stick or wooden skewer. Freeze until firm. Remove them from the molds by running a knife around the edges. If no molds are available, teaspoonfuls of the mixture may be dropped onto the tray. Toothpicks are stuck in for sticks.

Fruited Gelatin. From 1 to 1½ cups of fruit may be added to plain gelatin after it has cooled and thickened slightly. Raw, or drained cooked or canned fruit may be used. Always cook fresh pineapple when you use it in gelatin. Canned pineapple may be used without heating because it has already been cooked. Sliced strawberries are delicious with orange gelatin. Bananas, oranges, and nuts are equally good with lemon gelatin.

These fruited gelatins may also be served as fruit salads. Unmold them on plates garnished with crisp lettuce leaves. Serve them with mayonnaise dressing.

Milk Shakes

Milk shakes are favorite drinks to serve for refreshments between meals. They are especially good for growing boys and girls. And, if served with straws, they can be as much fun as those you buy at the soda fountain.

Chocolate Milk Shake. This recipe will make four servings.

½ cup chocolate sauce (you will find this recipe with the ice-cream sauces.)

4 cups cold milk

Place the sirup in a deep bowl. Stir in the milk slowly. Beat the mixture well with an egg beater or an electric mixer. Serve it as soon as possible. If you are taking it outdoors, pour it into a large

This young girl is helping her mother by getting from the refrigerator things which are needed for making a cake.

Ewing Galloway

jar or clean milk bottles. Shake or stir it again just before serving, for the chocolate sirup will settle in the bottom if it stands too long.

Banana Milk Shake. This recipe is for six servings.

4 ripe bananas
1 quart chilled milk
2 tablespoons sugar
½ teaspoon vanilla
a few grains of salt

Peel the bananas and pull off the strings. Slice them thin into a large bowl. Then whip them with an egg beater until they are smooth and creamy. Add slowly the milk, sugar, vanilla, and salt. Beat the mixture until it is well blended. Serve it in tall glasses.

Eggnog

A glass of refreshing eggnog is almost a meal in itself. This recipe makes two servings. Use:

2 cups chilled milk
2 eggs
2 tablespoons powdered sugar or honey
½ teaspoon vanilla, or grated orange or lemon rind
freshly grated nutmeg

Place the eggs, sugar, and vanilla in a deep bowl. Beat them with an egg beater until they are well blended. Gradually add the milk, then beat the mixture again until it is frothy. Pour the eggnog into two tall glasses. Sprinkle the tops lightly with nutmeg. Serve at once.

To make an Orange Eggnog, add ¼ cup orange juice to the mixture when you add the milk.

A Practice Party

Everyone likes to have "company." Try serving lunch in your room at your own small table, with Mother as your guest. A practice party is fun for a rainy day. Set the table and help to make the sandwiches. Cut the sandwiches into small triangles or small squares. Garnish the plates with carrots, green peppers, or celery cut in sticks, slices, or rings. Pour the milk into a small pitcher so that you can pour it into the glasses yourself. You could serve applesauce or other cooked fruit for dessert.

For your parties and luncheons, it is well to know how to prepare sandwich fillings. Be sure the butter is soft before you spread it on the bread.

Easy-to-Make Sandwich Fillings

Peanut butter and honey or jelly
Peanut butter and raisins
Peanut butter and sliced banana
Cream cheese and jelly, jam, or marmalade
Sliced cold meat and chopped parsley
Grated carrot and raisins
Sliced hard-boiled egg and lettuce
Sliced tomato with cooked bacon and lettuce
Hard-boiled egg and lettuce, watercress, or chopped parsley

Tea Party for a Friend

After your practice party, you may want to try a tea party for one of your friends if your mother is willing. Early afternoon tea, between 3 and 3:30 o'clock, will not spoil your appetite for dinner if the refreshments are light. Half the fun is to plan and prepare for your tea party. How will you dress up your tea table? What will you serve that you can make yourself? In cold weather you might serve:

Malted Milk and Vanilla Wafer-Jelly Sandwiches. The sandwiches are made by spreading small vanilla wafers with jelly or jam. It is best not to make too many. Warm malted milk served in tea cups is delicious for afternoon tea. Follow directions on the package of malted milk. You can serve it from a teapot if you wish. Chocolate milk, which is sold like plain milk, also can be warmed for a tea party. Place a marshmallow in each cup for added flavor. For a warm weather party, you might prefer:

Fruit Juice and Cream Cheese-Watercress or Parsley Sandwiches. The fruit juice could be fresh, canned, or a mixture. Half grape juice, half water or ginger ale, with a dash of lemon juice makes a pleasant drink. So does lemonade. It is best to put it in a small pitcher. You may then pour it into the glasses. Be sure to allow for refills. Gay-colored straws, or sippers, will be fun to use for your drinks. They may be bought at grocery or dime stores, or at most paper supplies stores.

If the bread is already sliced thin, the cheese softened to spread easily, and the watercress washed and ready, it is easy to make the sandwiches. The bread is spread with the cheese, and sprigs of watercress or parsley or shredded lettuce are laid on top. Cut the sandwiches into small triangles or squares, or use a cooky cutter, if you like. You will get more fancy sandwiches from a loaf of bread if it is sliced lengthwise.

For Simple Entertaining

It is important to know how to entertain simply. If you get experience early, "having company" will never be a chore. You will learn, also, how to entertain unexpected company, and to serve whatever you have in the most attractive way. Here are some good recipes for simple refreshments.

Lady Finger Sandwiches. Split lady fingers lengthwise. Spread one half of the cut sides with jelly. Lay the other halves on top. Arrange them neatly on

Giles, Black Star

A measuring cup is one of the most important tools in the kitchen. Without it, you cannot hope to follow a recipe accurately and be a successful cook.

All the ingredients have been measured by this young cook. She is now mixing them before proceeding with her baking.

Spivey, Black Star

a pretty plate, like the petals of a flower.

Party Crackers. Heat the broiler to 375°. Butter small, square soda crackers. Remember to soften the butter first so that the crackers will not break as you spread them. After buttering the crackers, sprinkle each with brown sugar. Then sprinkle lightly with cinnamon. Place the crackers in a low baking pan. Slide them onto the broiler tray in the stove. If your stove does not have a broiler, place them in the oven. Watch them carefully while they toast to a crisp golden brown. Serve them hot.

Coconut Drop Cakes

1 ⅓ cups (1 can) sweetened condensed milk
3 cups (about ¾ lb.) shredded coconut
1 teaspoon vanilla
⅛ teaspoon salt

Grease a cooky sheet lightly with unsalted shortening. Light the oven and set the regulator for moderate temperature (375°). Place the milk, coconut, vanilla, and salt in a large bowl, and stir them thoroughly. Drop the mixture, a teaspoonful for each cooky, onto the greased cooky sheet. Leave a little space between the cookies so they will not run together in the oven. Place the sheet in the heated oven. Bake the cookies for about 12 to 15 minutes, or until they are

lightly browned. Remove them from the pan, while they are still hot, with a spatula or a small pancake turner. Place them on a cake rack, or on plates, to cool. This recipe will make about thirty cookies.

Using Kitchen Utensils

If you are old enough to go to school, you are usually ready to use the more complicated kitchen gadgets and appliances. You know how to open cans, make toast in the toaster, and how to control the electric mixer.

Start your knife work by first using a table knife to slice a banana or to peel and slice ripe peaches and pears. When you get the "feel" of it, you can use a regular paring knife, which has to be sharp to do a good job. Cut on a board, whenever possible. It is fun to cut up vegetables for soups and salads, or fruits for desserts. You may well be proud when you can cut bread or cheese in even slices. Boys are usually very good at this. It is fine practice for future carvers.

It takes a strong arm to cream butter and sugar for a cake or to beat egg whites for a meringue. Your mother would be

Tasting the mixture to see that everything is just right before it goes in to bake. The wide grin seems to say it is delicious, and could not be better.

Gendreau

glad to have you help at these tasks. At the same time, you will learn just how creamy the butter should be and how long to beat the eggs. Many a soufflé and angel-food cake has been spoiled by overbeaten egg whites. Cream that is beaten too much may turn into butter. These and other skills you learn by watching and doing.

You discover that cooking is more pleasant when you keep the work surfaces cleared for action. This means that you tidy up as you go along. You return everything to its proper place as soon as you have finished with it. Soiled dishes, mixing bowls, and pans are rinsed or put to soak, if they are not to be washed immediately. If you watch these details, the clean-up will be easy.

When you are tall enough, you may begin to use the stove. Modern stoves with their low ovens are especially suited to young cooks. If you have one of these stoves in your home, you will be able to try simple broiled and baked foods be-

fore you are ready for top-of-the-stove cookery.

Be sure that you know how to turn the stove off and on. Then scrub your hands, put on an apron, and have some good, thick pot holders handy.

Beginning Recipes for Stove Cooking

Baked Potatoes. Set the oven for 400°. Scrub the potatoes with a vegetable brush until they are absolutely clean. Dry the potatoes with a clean cloth or paper towel. Grease them lightly with butter, bacon fat, or shortening, to keep the skins soft. Place them on a rack in the heated oven. After 45 or 50 minutes, stick them with a toothpick or fork to see if they are soft. If the toothpick or fork sinks into the potatoes easily, they have cooked enough. They should be served hot from the oven. If you have to keep them warm, cut a gash in each one to let the steam escape. This will keep them from becoming soggy.

Baked Apples. Choose firm even-shaped apples. Wash them, then core them with an apple corer. The upper fourth of each apple may be peeled. Place the apples in a baking dish or pan. In the center of each apple put:

   1 tablespoon sugar
   ¼ teaspoon butter
   a few nuts and raisins

Into the bottom of the pan, pour 1 tablespoon of water for each apple. Bake the apples, with or without a cover, in a 400° oven for about 30 minutes, or until they are tender. Test them by sticking them with a straw, or toothpick. Baked apples are delicious served warm, with cream.

Making Your Lunch

When you know how to make sandwiches and heat a can of soup, you will be ready to prepare an entire lunch for yourself. With these, a glass of milk, and a piece of fruit, you will have a good lunch. All you need to do with most canned soups is to pour the contents of the can into a saucepan. Add a can of water, and stir it as you heat it. Making this kind of soup is a good top-of-the-stove venture. Another is:

Frying an Egg. Get out the smallest skillet you have, with a lid to fit it, a saucer, butter, and one egg. Place the egg in the saucer until needed, so that your egg will not suffer the fate of Humpty Dumpty. Eggs roll so easily that they should never be placed on a flat table top. Melt about a teaspoon of butter in the skillet, over low heat. While the butter melts, break the egg into the saucer. Tap it lightly, yet sharply, with the edge of a table knife, to make an even, crosswise break. Take the egg in both hands, with the break on the underside. Hold the edges of the break with the thumbs. Widen the break by pulling the edges apart far enough to let the egg slip out of the shell into the saucer.

The butter should be melted and hot, but not sizzling. Slip your egg from the saucer into the skillet. Cover the skillet with the lid. Be sure that your stove burner is turned low, for too much heat will give you a tough egg. Cook the egg until it is as firm as you like it, then sprinkle it with salt and either pepper or paprika. It would also be good with chopped parsley or chives sprinkled over it. Take the egg from the skillet with a pancake turner. A stubby, short-handled one is best for eggs. Sandwiches may be made of eggs cooked in this way.

How to Heat Canned Vegetables

Open a can of vegetables. Place the lid back on the can so that it will hold back the vegetable while you drain off the liquid into a saucepan. Place the saucepan on a burner, and let the liquid come to a boil. Continue to cook until it has boiled down about one half. Add the vegetable and a heaping teaspoonful of butter. Continue to heat it until the mixture comes to a boil. The rapid heating and boiling prevents the loss of vitamins. Taste it to see if any more salt is needed. You may add a sprinkle of paprika for flavor and appearance. Serve the vegetables in a warm dish. To warm the dish, fill it with hot water for a minute or two. Then dry it before putting the hot vegetable in it.

How to Cook Quick-Frozen Vegetables

Frozen vegetables may be kept for days in the freezing compartment of a refrigerator. Directions for storing and

Lawrence Thornton, Loder

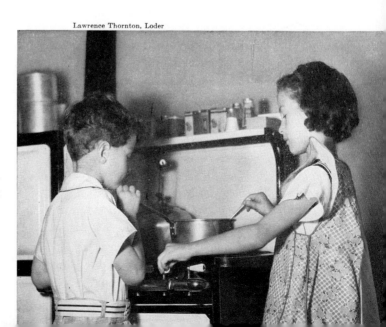

This brother and sister are making fudge. They are watching it as it simmers on the stove.

Titcomb, Black Star

Cutting out cooky dough in all kinds of shapes and sizes is a great thrill.

the drained vegetable into a warm serving dish. Melt 2 tablespoons of butter in a small saucepan or skillet. Pour it over the vegetable, and serve at once.

Broiled Hamburger Sandwiches

1 lb. ground beef
1 teaspoon salt
¼ teaspoon paprika or ⅛ teaspoon pepper
8 slices of bread
butter

Light the broiler, and set the temperature for 400°.

Place the ground beef, salt, and pepper in a large bowl. Stir the mixture well with a spoon. Toast the slices of bread on one side only. This may be done in the broiler, but the bread must be watched carefully so that it will not burn. Spread the untoasted sides of the slices with the meat mixture. Be sure to cover the bread completely with the meat, so the edges will not burn. Dot the tops with little dabs of butter. Place the sandwiches on the broiler rack close to the heat. On a gas stove, this would be about 3 inches below the flame. Leave the broiler door partly open. Broil the sandwiches for about 5 minutes.

Candies and Confections

The following recipes are for candies that are easy to make. Homemade candies can be used as presents. For gifts, pack the candy in inexpensive tin boxes with close-fitting covers. This will keep it fresh. Be sure to put waxed paper or cellophane between the layers.

Chocolate Fudge. Here is a foolproof recipe for making good fudge. It makes

cooking are given on all the packages.

Bring to a boil in a saucepan the amount of water called for. Add about ¼ teaspoon salt for each cup of water. Open the package and slide the contents into the pan. Be careful not to splash boiling water on your hands. Cover the pan with a close-fitting lid. Start counting time when the water comes to a boil again. Taste the vegetable when it has cooked the shortest time given in the directions. As soon as the vegetable is tender, it is done. Avoid cooking any vegetable too long. This makes it limp, and either tasteless or strong.

Some vegetables cook almost dry, and you may serve these with 2 tablespoons of butter on top. But if the vegetable has a good deal of cooking water left, pour the vegetable and water into a colander, or sieve, placed over a bowl. Save the water for future use in soup or gravy. It contains minerals and vitamins. Pour about 2 pounds of delicious candy. Use:

1⅓ cups (15-ounce can) sweetened, condensed milk
⅛ teaspoon salt
1 teaspoon vanilla
2 (6, 7, or 8 ounces) packages of semisweet chocolate
1 cup nut meats, broken into small pieces

Prepare your nut meats first. Grease a square, shallow baking pan lightly with butter. Place the milk, chocolate, and salt in the top of a double boiler over rapidly boiling water. Cook and stir these ingredients until they are thick. This will take about ten minutes. Remove the pan from the fire. Stir in the vanilla and nuts. Pour the fudge into the greased pan. Cool and place in the refrigerator for several hours. When it is firm to the touch, cut it into squares.

Peanut Brittle is easily made and will give you a crunchy, satisfying treat.

1 cup shelled peanuts
1 cup sugar

Oil a platter or shallow pan with vegetable oil. Sprinkle the peanuts evenly over it. Put the sugar in an iron skillet over a low burner. Stir the sugar constantly. It will gradually melt and change color. When the sirup is light brown, pour it over the peanuts. When the candy cools, break it into pieces. Other nut meats can be used instead of peanuts.

For a special treat, try crushing peanut brittle with a potato masher or a rolling pin, or grind it in a meat chopper using a coarse blade. Then sprinkle the crushed peanut brittle over ice cream.

Fondant is a reliable basic recipe to use in making several kinds of candy.

1 egg white
3 tablespoons cream
1 teaspoon vanilla
sifted confectioner's sugar

Place the egg white, cream, and vanilla in a bowl. Beat them until they are well blended, using either a wire whisk or an egg beater. Then add sifted sugar very slowly. Stir it in well, until the fondant is thick enough to knead or to work with your hands. Fold it over and over, as you might knead clay, until it is smooth and creamy. Cover it with a damp cloth and let it stand for one hour.

One of the pleasures of getting ready for Christmastime is making and decorating cookies cut in the shapes of Santa Claus, stars, and Christmas trees.

It may then be shaped into balls and rolled in cinnamon, or used to stuff dried fruits such as dates and figs. The fondant will remain fresh for some time if put in a tightly covered jar and kept in a cool place.

Chocolate Marshmallow Squares. You will have to decide for yourself whether these are cakes or candies. Perhaps they are a little of both. This recipe makes about 48 pieces, and, whatever you call them, you will find them a real delicacy. Use:

1 pound marshmallows
1 package (7 or 8 ounces) semisweet chocolate
3 tablespoons butter
½ teaspoon salt
1 teaspoon vanilla
2 cups crisp rice cereal or
1 cup cereal and
1 cup broken walnut meats

Grease a 9 by 12 inch shallow pan lightly with butter.

Melt the marshmallows, chocolate, and butter in a double boiler. Stir to blend well. Remove the pan from the fire and add the salt and vanilla. Place the cereal or cereal and nuts in a large greased bowl. Pour the chocolate mixture over it. Stir it well. Spoon it into the buttered pan, patting it to spread it evenly. When cool, cut it into 1 by 2 inch bars.

Coster, Black Star

To Serve Ice Cream

If you are serving bulk ice cream, and want to scoop it out in small balls, dip a round soup spoon in warm water and use it as a scoop. The ice cream will slip off the warm spoon without sticking. A tablespoon may be used in the same way but the ice cream will be in oval mounds instead of round ones. To serve brick ice cream in equal portions, first divide the brick in half, marking it lightly with a knife. Then divide each half into quarters or thirds. To make a smooth cut, dip the knife first in warm water.

Ice Cream Sauces

Strawberry Sauce may be used over plain cake, or in milk shakes, as well as on ice cream.

Strawberries
Sugar
Wash and hull the berries. Pour them into a deep bowl and crush them with a potato masher or the bottom of a clean pint milk bottle. Add sugar gradually until the berries are sweet enough. You can make a raspberry sauce by using raspberries.

Chocolate Sauce for Sundaes or Milk Shakes. This sauce may be served hot or cold. It will keep for several days in a covered jar in the refrigerator. This recipe makes about one cupful.

½ cup sugar
1 cup boiling water
1 ounce or square unsweetened chocolate, cut up
⅛ teaspoon salt
½ teaspoon vanilla
Place the sugar, water, chocolate, and salt in a saucepan. Stir them until the sugar and chocolate are dissolved. Then cook the mixture over low heat until the sauce is about as thick as sirup. Remove the saucepan from the burner. Let the sauce cool a little. Then add the vanilla and stir to blend it well. The sauce may be reheated in a double boiler. It will be thicker when it is cold.

A Picnic Lunch

After you have cooked one dish for lunch or dinner, you may soon want the adventure of preparing an entire meal. This will take careful planning. For a first attempt, it is best to serve foods which can be prepared well ahead of time. You could prepare the following first meal for the family. It could even be served as a picnic.

Deviled eggs
Lettuce wedges or carrot slices
Bread-and-butter sandwiches
Fruit
Milk shakes
Cookies
Make out a list of the groceries to be bought. Also, make a list of other things you need, such as plates, cups, forks, and napkins. Perhaps you could go to the store and pick out a bunch of fresh carrots or a head of lettuce. If you are planning a picnic, you will also need paper plates and cups.

The chocolate sirup for the milk

Acme

Peeling the potatoes for dinner is one of Mother's many chores. This kitchen helper has rolled up his sleeves and is determined to do a perfect job.

This girl is washing and drying the big sieve after putting some vegetables through it.

Anderson, Frederic Lewis

shakes could be prepared a day or two in advance. The eggs could be hard-boiled the day before. The picnic spot could be chosen, also the containers in which to carry the food outdoors.

Deviled Eggs. Place in a saucepan the number of eggs you think will be eaten. Cover them with cold water. Put the pan over medium heat and bring the water to the boiling point. Then lower the heat so that the water simmers. There will be small bubbles around the edge but the top of the water will not be rolling as it does in boiling. Allow twenty minutes to cook the eggs, after you reduce the heat. Then take the pan from the stove and place it in the sink. Let cold water run over the eggs until they are cool. This will keep the yolks from darkening around the edges. It will also make the eggs easier to shell. When the eggs are cold, shell them and cut them in halves, either lengthwise or crosswise. Remove the yolks, and place them in a separate bowl. Crush the yolks with a fork. For every 4 eggs add:

1 tablespoon milk, top milk, or mayonnaise
½ teaspoon lemon juice or vinegar
¼ teaspoon dry mustard
salt and paprika to taste

Taste the mixture to see if it needs more salt or a little more lemon juice. You could also add a little chopped parsley or chives, to give the eggs a different flavor. Celery seed, celery salt, or a little chopped cooked bacon or ham are also good additions. Use a teaspoon to heap the mixture into the white halves of the eggs. They will look even more appetizing if the tops are sprinkled with paprika and they are garnished with small sprigs of parsley. Wrap each egg in waxed paper or place the eggs on a platter and cover them with waxed paper. Chill them in the refrigerator until you are ready to serve them.

Carrot Slices. A large bunch of carrots will be enough to make four good servings. If the carrots are very young and small you can serve them whole. They can be washed, and scraped or peeled, the day before. Keep them in the refrigerator until ready to serve. Larger carrots can be sliced lengthwise into "ribbons," or sliced crosswise into "rounds." Wrap the slices in a damp cloth, or place them in a bowl of water in the refrigerator until serving time.

Lettuce Wedges. Wash lettuce and place it in the refrigerator until almost time for your meal. Then cut the head into four wedge-shaped pieces.

Saturday Lunch

Broiled wieners
Mustard; catchup; pickle relish
Carrot and green pepper strips
Bananas in orange juice
Hot buttered buns
Cookies

Again, you will plan ahead so that

Washing and drying the dishes after a meal. For willing helpers, this work can be real fun.

Paul Parker

there will be no hitches. Then, when your guests have all arrived, you will be able to say, "Come and get it!"

You might do the marketing for this party yourself on Friday afternoon. You will know how many wieners and buns to buy. You could select the carrots, green peppers, and bananas. Keep track of the change, and bring back the cashier's slip.

The lunch might be served at the kitchen table or in the breakfast nook, so that the cook will be close to the food for second or third servings. But, if you prefer, serve in the dining room.

The vegetables can be cleaned and cut into strips early in the morning. They will keep fresh if placed in the refrigerator in a quart jar and covered with cold water. They may be drained just before serving. Split the buns and spread one side with softened butter. If placed in a paper bag they can be reheated in the oven while the wieners are cooking.

At the same time, you could place the relishes, such as mustard, catchup, and pickles on the table. Your guests will like a choice. Be sure to have plenty of milk. Set the table early, and make sure that nothing is missing.

To prepare the wieners for broiling, use a pastry brush to paint each weiner with melted butter, bacon fat, or cooking oil. Then place the weiners on the broiler rack. Twenty minutes before lunch, start the oven and set the temperature control for 500°, "Broil," or "High." Ten minutes later, reduce the temperature to 350°, or to 375°, or medium heat. Slip the broiler rack into the broiler pan, and close the door.

The buns may be placed on a cooky sheet or baking pan. Allow five minutes in the oven to reheat them. When the wieners are a light brown on one side, pull the broiler pan part way out. Turn the wieners with a fork and spoon. As soon as they are browned on both sides, they are ready to serve. Turn off the oven heat. Line up the luncheon plates near the stove. Place a bun on each one, slip the wieners into the buns, and lunch is ready.

Bananas with Orange Juice. This simple dessert for your lunch may be prepared about a half hour beforehand.

4 bananas
2 tablespoons sugar
Juice of 2 oranges

Squeeze the juice from the oranges. Strain it into a glass or bowl. Add the sugar and stir to dissolve it. Taste it to see if it is sweet enough. If not, add a little more sugar. Peel the bananas. Then pull off the strings and slice them into a pretty glass bowl. Pour the orange juice over the bananas. Lift them gently with a fork until they are coated with the juice, then place the bowl in the refrigerator. Pineapple juice could be used instead of orange juice. This dessert looks even more tempting when decorated with maraschino cherries.

When you have learned how to plan and prepare a simple, nourishing meal, you are ready for an emergency. If your mother is away, you can step in with confidence and cook good meals.

As you grow older, "make your head save your heels." This is a good rule to keep in mind. Planning ahead will save many steps in getting a meal. You can prepare a meal calmly and easily if you have it clear in your mind what to do, and how to go about it. Hurry-scurry is tiring. It makes cooking difficult when it need not be so.

Food for Snacks

Perhaps food for snacks could be considered when the marketing lists are made out. In planning this, keep in mind inexpensive foods with which you can make dishes, rather than expensive ready-made foods. For late suppers or afternoon tea, there is nothing better than homemade drinks, and cookies, candies, sandwiches, or buttered popcorn. Your guests will enjoy helping to prepare the refreshments.

Special Dishes to Try

Hot Puffed Cheese Sandwiches. These sandwiches go well with a cup of hot cocoa after an evening of skating outdoors. To make 8 open-face sandwiches use:

1 to 1¼ cups grated sharp cheese (about ⅓ pound)
1 egg
3 tablespoons top milk or cream
a few grains salt
½ teaspoon paprika
8 slices of bread

Heat the oven to 375°. Prepare the grated cheese. You can do this ahead of time if you wrap the cheese in waxed paper and place it in the refrigerator. Beat the egg. Add the cream, salt, and paprika, and beat again. Put in the grated cheese. Then beat the mixture thoroughly with a fork. Toast the bread on one side only. Spread the cheese mixture on the untoasted side of the

Keystone

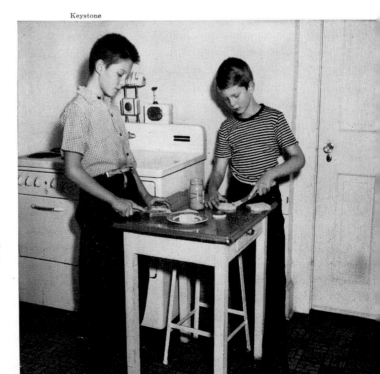

What boy has not taken his pal to the kitchen to get a snack!

bread with a small knife or spatula. Place the sandwiches under the broiler until the cheese is puffed up and slightly browned.

Barbecue Sauce. This sauce will go well with broiled hamburger sandwiches or broiled wieners. It is easily and quickly made and has a spicy taste.

    1 teaspoon prepared mustard
    2 teaspoons Worcestershire sauce
    4 teaspoons vinegar
    ¼ teaspoon black pepper
    2 tablespoons water
    1 tablespoon sugar
    6 tablespoons catchup
    1 tablespoon butter or bacon fat

Place all these, except the butter, in a bowl. Stir them well. Melt the butter in a small pan over a burner turned low. Pour the mixture into the pan of butter and stir the sauce until it is hot.

Breakfast in Bed

Some Sunday morning, if you would like to have a pleasant surprise for Mother, why not serve her breakfast in bed? Arrange the breakfast tray and make the sugar-cinnamon mixture Saturday evening. You are then off to a flying start. You could serve:

    Orange juice
    Scrambled eggs and bacon
    Cinnamon toast
    Coffee

Scrambled Eggs. For one average serving of scrambled eggs, you will need:

    2 eggs
    4 teaspoons cream or rich milk
    ⅛ teaspoon salt
    ⅛ teaspoon paprika
    1 tablespoon butter

Break the eggs into a bowl. Beat them with an egg beater until they are foamy. Add the cream, salt, and paprika, and beat again until blended. Melt the butter in a small skillet (about 7 or 8 inches wide) over a low fire. When the butter is melted, pour in the egg mixture. Stir it gently until the eggs are thick, but still soft and creamy. Serve them at once on a warm plate.

Baked Bacon. When you cook bacon

this way, you do not have to turn it. Heat the oven to 400°. Spread the strips of bacon on a cake rack or a grill for roasting meat. Place this in a baking pan, and set the pan on the middle rack of the oven. Cook it for about ten minutes or longer if you prefer it well done.

Cinnamon Toast. For 4 pieces of toast you will need:

    4 tablespoons sugar
    2 teaspoons cinnamon
    4 thin slices of bread
    butter

Heat the oven to 400°. Mix the sugar and cinnamon in a small bowl. Toast the bread on one side. Then take it from the oven and spread the other side well with butter. Then sprinkle the cinnamon and sugar mixture on top of the butter. Place the bread, sugared side up, on a cooky sheet or in a shallow baking pan. Place the pan in the heated oven for about 5 minutes, to melt the butter and heat the toast. Serve it at once.

Make the coffee as your mother does it. Have her help you with the amount of coffee and water. You will be pleased and so will she if you succeed in serving her a hot and tempting breakfast.

A Birthday Dinner for Dad

Roast beef
Green salad with French dressing
Browned potatoes
Lemon milk sherbet
A beverage
Crisp oatmeal cookies

This dinner calls for little last-minute preparation, and your mother will be glad to be your helper. The roast and potatoes (after they are boiled) will cook themselves in the oven. The salad dressing and the dessert can be made early in the day. You will make the gravy just before serving dinner. The salad could be tossed at the table.

Roast Beef. Select a cut of beef for roasting. Remove the meat from the re-

When all the dishes have been washed and dried, they must be put away neatly and carefully.

Gendreau

frigerator at least one hour before you begin to roast it, so that it will be at room temperature. Wipe the meat with a cloth wrung out of cold water. Place the roast, fat side up, on a rack in an open baking pan. Heat the oven to 300°. At this temperature, your roast will need about 18 to 20 minutes for every pound of weight for a rare roast; 22 to 25 minutes a pound for a medium roast; 27 to 30 minutes a pound for a well-done roast. If your roast is boneless, you should add 10 minutes a pound more. If it is small, use the longer time for cooking. If it is large, use the shorter time. For example, if you have a four-pound roast without a bone in it and wish to cook it well done, you should allow two hours and forty minutes cooking time.

Place the pan in the heated oven, but do not cover it. Add no liquid. Meat roasted by this constant-temperature method requires no basting. If you have counted your time carefully, you may forget about the meat until the time is up. If you open the oven door, you will only cool the oven and throw off the timing. When the time is up, prick the roast with a toothpick or a metal skewer. If the juice is red, the roast is rare. If it

is faintly pink, the roast will be medium-rare. If the juice is almost colorless, the roast will be well done.

When the roast is cooked, you can ask your mother to help you move it to a warm platter. Place it where it will keep warm. Strain the liquid in the pan into a small saucepan. Place the saucepan in a larger pan of ice water so that the fat will rise quickly to the top. Skim off the fat, and put 2 tablespoons of it in another pan over a low burner. Pour the remaining meat juice into a measuring cup. Add 2 tablespoons of flour to the fat and stir until blended. A wire whip is good to use for stirring gravies and sauces. To the meat juice, add enough water in which vegetables have been cooked, or water to which a bouillon cube has been added, to make 1 cup liquid. Stir constantly as you add it. Continue to stir until the gravy is smooth and comes to a boil. Turn down the heat. Taste the gravy. If it needs salt, add it in small quantities. You may also add pepper or paprika. If the gravy is pale in color, stir in 3 or 4 drops of brown coloring for sauces. Serve the gravy hot.

Browned Potatoes. Start to prepare

these about an hour and a half before dinner time. Choose small, even-sized potatoes. Scrub but do not peel them. Drop them into boiling water. Cook them until they are half-done. This is called "parboiling." It will take 15 to 20 minutes. Drain the potatoes. Cool them slightly, and remove the skins. Place them in the baking pan (not on the rack) with the meat. Spoon some of the fat from the roast over them. Sprinkle them with salt, and roast them with the meat for about one hour. Remove them with the roast to the heated platter.

Green Salad with French Dressing. You could wash the lettuce the day before the party. Select a firm fresh-looking head of lettuce. Cut out the core with a sharp knife. Hold the lettuce under cold running water so that the water will run into the head and between the leaves to force them apart. Wash the leaves carefully, and shake the water off. Wrap them in a dry tea towel and place them in the vegetable tray of the refrigerator to chill and crisp.

To make the dressing for a salad which will serve six people, you will need:

4 tablespoons salad oil
1 teaspoon salt
pepper
1 tablespoon vinegar, or lemon juice
1 clove garlic (if you like it)

Cut the clove in half and rub the bowl lightly with the cut surface, but do not leave the clove in the bowl. Place the oil, salt, and pepper in the bowl. Stir hard to blend it well. Add the vinegar or lemon juice and stir again. If you are preparing the dressing early, place the bowl in the refrigerator until serving time.

Stir the dressing again just before dinner. Break the lettuce leaves into the bowl. Use a large fork and spoon to toss the salad. To do this you turn the leaves over and over until each is coated with dressing.

Lemon Milk Sherbet. It is impossible to say how long it will take to freeze this dessert, because refrigerators vary. Your mother can advise you about yours. It may take 4 or 5 hours. This recipe makes six large servings. Use:

1 tablespoon unflavored gelatin
2 tablespoons water
3½ cups milk, or part milk and part cream
7 tablespoons lemon juice
1⅓ cups sugar

Place the gelatin and water in the upper part of a small double boiler, or in a bowl that will fit over a small saucepan. Soak the gelatin for 5 minutes. While it is soaking, heat some water in the bottom of the double boiler or in the saucepan. Place the gelatin mixture over the hot, but not boiling, water to dissolve the gelatin. Put the lemon juice and sugar in a large bowl. Stir until the sugar is dissolved. Add the gelatin. Add the milk slowly and stir the mixture until it is well blended. If the milk curdles, it will do no harm. Pour the sherbet into freezing trays. If you moisten the bottoms of the trays before putting in the sherbet, it will freeze faster. Place the trays in the freezing compartment of the refrigerator. When the sherbet is mushy, place it in a bowl. Beat it well with an egg beater or the electric mixer until it is creamy, but not melted. Put it back in the trays and allow it to freeze until firm. Beat it again before serving.

Crisp Oatmeal Cookies. This recipe makes about three dozen thin, crisp cookies.

1¼ cups quick oats
1½ teaspoons tartrate or phosphate baking powder or 1 teaspoon combination type (The label on the package will tell you the kind you have.)
½ teaspoon vanilla
½ cup brown sugar, firmly packed
¼ cup melted butter
1 small egg, beaten

Heat the oven to 350°. Place the oats, baking powder, and brown sugar in a bowl. Stir them to blend well. Add the melted butter and stir again. Beat the egg in a smaller bowl. Add it to the dry mixture. Then add the vanilla. Beat the mixture until it is well blended. Grease a cooky sheet lightly with unsalted shortening. Drop the mixture a small teaspoonful at a time onto the sheet. Leave plenty of room between the cookies to allow for spreading. Bake them for about 10 minutes. When you take them from the oven, let them stand for a minute or two. They will then be easier to remove from the pan with a spatula. Place them on cake racks to cool.

When you have learned how to prepare simple, wholesome dishes and serve good meals, you may want to try more elaborate dishes, pastries, and desserts, or think up some of your own. Before long, you will have many recipes, some of which you will want to keep. When you have tried out a recipe you like, copy it on a card, and file it in a recipe box. Look upon cooking as a game, and you will find that there is no end to the fun you can have.

BOOKS TO READ

Brown, Marcia. *Skipper John's Cook.* Illus. by the author. Scribner, 1951.

Clark, Garel. *Let's Start Cooking.* Illus. by Kathleen Elgin. W. R. Scott, 1951.

Freeman, Mae Blacker. *Fun with Cooking; Easy Recipes for Beginners.* Random House, 1947.

Hoffmann, Margaret Jones. *Miss B's First Cookbook; 20 Family-Sized Recipes for The Youngest Cook.* Photographs by Gerald Hunter. Bobbs, 1950.

Jordan, Mildred A. *Shoo-Fly Pie.* Illus. by Henry C. Pitz. Knopf, 1944.

Perkins, Wilma Lord. *Fannie Farmer Junior Cook Book.* Illus. by Martha Powell Setchell. Little, 1942. (Based on *The Boston Cooking-School Cook Book* by Fannie Merritt Farmer.)

ADVENTURES IN HANDWORK

MARTHA PARKHILL AND
DOROTHY SPAETH

Loder

THE FUN of making things is the creative joy of an artist. We can be artists in different ways. Making things is one kind of art. There is extra pleasure in making useful presents for your parents or playmates. Martha Parkhill and Dorothy Spaeth, authors of *It's Fun to Make Things*, show us how to make many things that are both useful and attractive. The tools to be used are simple, and the materials are easy to get.

No toy or plaything which comes from the store will give you as much joy and satisfaction as the one made with your own hands in your workshop.

YOU will be surprised at the number of useful and ornamental things you can make from odds and ends which you can find around the house. All you will need besides these are a few simple tools and the magic of your hands. Some of the things you will like to use yourself. Others will serve as gifts. Your friends will value these gifts the more because you will have made them. You can use the designs shown here if you prefer. But it will be more fun to create your own designs. Then you will have even more satisfaction in the finished product. It will be something all your own.

Where measurements are used, " will stand for inches, ' for feet, and x for by. For example, a piece of wood 4 feet long, 2 inches wide, and 1 inch thick would be 4' x 2" x 1".

Circle Cut-Out Pictures

Materials: Colored paper; paste; coins; pencil, crayon, or paint; scissors.

Circle pictures are easy to make, and can be finished in a short time.

What greater fun than to make circle cutouts and triangles from colored paper! You can paste these on a sheet of paper to make all kinds of interesting pictures.

1. Cut out several circles and triangles of different sizes from colored paper. Quarters, nickels, and half dollars may be used as circle patterns.

2. Paste the circles in various designs on a sheet of paper of different color as shown in the illustration, or in designs of your own.

3. Add tails, eyes, and other lines with pencil, crayon, or paint.

Round Fan

Materials: Paper; pencil and crayons; paste; scissors; saucer; tongue depressor or flat stick.

1. Trace two circles on heavy paper, using an old saucer as a guide.

2. Cut out the circle.

3. Draw a design on each circle.

4. Color the designs with crayons.

5. Spread paste on the undecorated surface of one circle.

6. Place a tongue depressor or a flat stick on the pasted circle. Leave about two inches of the stick protruding for a handle. Place the unpasted circle on top of this.

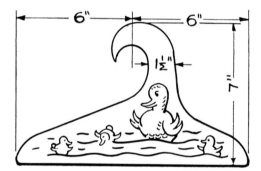

How to make an attractive coat hanger

7. Place the completed fan under a heavy weight until dry.

Folded Fan

Materials: Crayons; heavy paper. The paper should be at least three times as long as it is wide, and about 6″ x 18″ is a good size. If your paper is not long enough, add another piece of paper the same width. The joining will not show in the folds.

1. Draw and color a design on each side of the paper.

2. Starting at one end of the paper, fold the paper the first time towards you. Then fold it away from you. Make each fold about ½″ in width. Repeat the folding until all the paper is folded.

211

A decorated round fan

3. While the paper is still in the folded position, crease the folds well. Bend the bottom of the fan about 1″ for a handle.

Child's Coat Hanger

It is much more fun to hang up your clothes if you have attractive hangers that you have made yourself.

Materials: A heavy piece of cardboard—12″ wide at the base and 7″ deep; paint (any paint which does not rub off is suitable); pencil; ruler; paste; scissors.

1. Draw the outline of the hanger on your cardboard, using the measurements given in the illustration. Be sure the part left for the hook is in the center so that the hanger will balance.

2. Cut out the cardboard along the line you have traced. If the hanger does not seem strong enough, cut an extra strip of cardboard for reinforcement on the back of the hanger.

3. Paint the hanger.

4. When the paint is dry, decorate the hanger with painted designs. You may wish to paint your own name on the hanger. This will be most helpful if you have brothers or sisters. Other possible designs are also shown.

A folding fan with color design

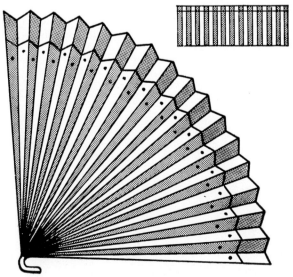

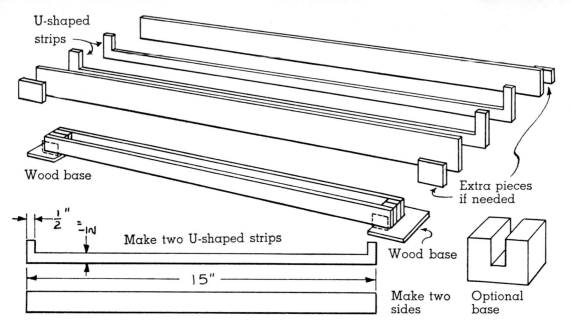

U-shaped strips

Wood base

Make two U-shaped strips

$\frac{1}{2}''$

15"

Extra pieces if needed

Wood base

Make two sides

Optional base

A holder like this in which you can put playing cards can be easily made.

Playing-Card Holder

A holder like this one makes it easier for you to handle playing cards.

Materials: 4 strips of heavy cardboard 15" long, and 2" wide; 2 pieces of wood 1½" to 2" square, ¼" to ½" thick; glue; paint (any paint will do); sandpaper; pencil; ruler; saw.

1. Cut four strips of cardboard, each piece 15" long and 2" wide.
2. From one of the strips cut out the center portion. Leave ½" on either end and on the bottom as shown in the diagram. This makes a U-shaped strip.
3. Repeat with a second strip.
4. Glue one of the U strips to one of the uncut strips so that the bottom and edges meet exactly. See diagram.
5. Glue the second U strip on top of the first U strip, so that the bottom and side edges meet exactly.
6. Glue the last cardboard strip on the U-shaped strip. Let it dry under a weight. As you will see, the U strips seal the bottom and side edges. They form a pocket to hold your cards.
7. Cut two pieces of wood about 2" square. The thickness of the wood depends more or less on the scraps available—¼" is thick enough. However, a thicker piece serves the purpose as well.
8. Sandpaper the two pieces of wood until smooth.
9. Glue one piece of wood to each end of the cardboard holder as shown in the illustration. If you find the cardboard holder is too narrow to stick firmly to the wood, two or more extra pieces of cardboard may be glued to the outside of the holder at the bottom corner. Be sure to match the bottom edge exactly. This will give you a wider gluing surface.
10. When the glue is dry, paint the entire holder. Decorate the holder with painted designs when dry.

Instead of the two wooden square bases glued to the holder, two slot bases may be made. But this type requires the use of a knife.

Christmas-Tree Decorations

Much of the fun of Christmas is in looking forward to it and in planning bright decorations. Homemade decorations for your tree will seem like old friends as you take them out of their box and hang them up each year.

The Cherub is simple to make. After you have made this, you will be able to make other decorations.

Materials: Heavy white wrapping paper; tracing or tissue paper; red and green paper; gilt or yellow paper (gold foil from a candy box may be used); paste; crayons, water-color paint, or colored chalk; pencil; scissors.

1. Trace the face and wings of the cherub on a piece of heavy white paper and cut them out. Draw the eyes, nose, and mouth of the face, and color. Give the cheeks a touch of red.
2. Trace the hair of the cherub on gilt or yellow

HOW TO MAKE A CHERUB

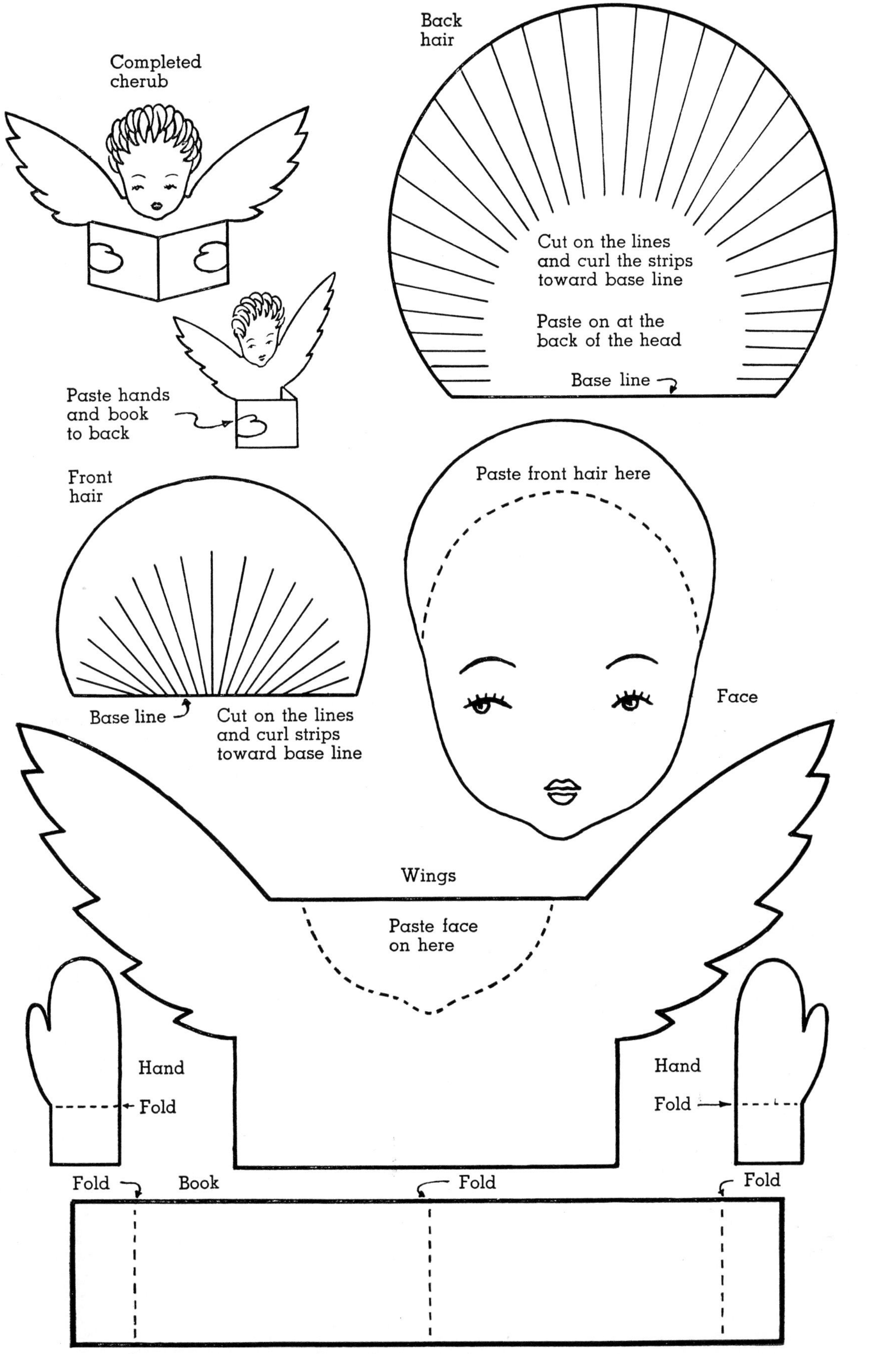

Completed
cherub

Back
hair

Cut on the lines
and curl the strips
toward base line

Paste on at the
back of the head

Base line ⟶

Paste hands
and book
to back ⟶

Front
hair

Paste front hair here

Base line ⟶ Cut on the lines
and curl strips
toward base line

Face

Wings

Paste face
on here

Hand

Fold ⟶

Hand

Fold ⟶

Fold ⟶ Book

Fold ⟶

Fold ⟶

Heavy silver or gold paper
rolled in shape of a cone

You will find it easy to make angel decorations for your Christmas tree.

paper. Cut the lines for the hair. Curl the strips by pulling them over a dull knife blade or the edge of a ruler. Or you can roll them around a pencil. Paste the hair in place with the large piece on the back of the head, and the small piece on the front.

3. Trace the mittens on a piece of red paper, and the book on green paper. Cut out and paste in place (see illustration). The book is pasted to the body. The mittens are pasted on the back and bent forward to give the appearance of holding the book.

4. Paste a ribbon on the back of the cherub to hang it to the tree.

See how many different kinds of cherubs you can make. Use the same basic pattern, but cut different wings and hair.

Angel. To make a full-length angel, cut a cone-shaped piece of gilt, silver, or bright-colored paper. Then fasten it together in the back with a wire paper clip or staple. A long, rolled tube of paper

to which the head is glued runs to the bottom of the cone and is held in place by a wire paper clip. The arms and wings are pasted to the back of the cone. A small tube of bright paper is glued to the hands for a candle.

Tin-Can Building Blocks

Castles, windmills, lighthouses, and many other toy buildings can be made with tin-can building blocks.

Materials: Tin cans of many different sizes; wall can opener; paint (any kind will do); paintbrush; heavy paper or cardboard; cork; hammer; nails; lollipop sticks.

1. Use a wall can opener, or any can opener which leaves the edges smooth, to remove one end of each of the tin cans. Use cans of all sizes.

2. The cans may be painted or left unpainted. Doors, windows, letters of the alphabet or pictures may be painted on. Or they may be cut from colored paper and pasted on.

3. Towers such as those on the castle and windmill are cut from a paper circle. Heavy paper

Cut out a
circle to form
a cone-shaped
roof

How you can use tin cans to make windmills, castles, and lighthouses

Decorating bottles and glasses can be a most interesting way to use your time.

or cardboard can be used. Cut the circle to the center. Then draw the edges together to form a cone. Fasten them together with a paper clip or paste. The platform of the lighthouse is made of a piece of cardboard. Colored paper pasted on lollipop sticks will serve as flags. The cardboard windmill is fastened on with a lollipop stick. Use a cork at either end to hold stick and windmill in place. The stick is put through a hole in the can, which has been made with a hammer and nail.

By using your own imagination, you can build many kinds of castles from these blocks.

Bottle and Glass Decorations

Materials: Ruler; pencil; scissors; household cement; glasses or bottles; a scrap of cloth; knife; colorless nail polish or clear lacquer. Fancy trimming tape, called *gimp*, used for upholstery binding and in art shops, may be bought at art supply, hobby, and upholstery shops, and most large stores.

1. Use a ruler and a pencil to draw a guide line around the glass where you wish to start winding the trimming. This will keep the first band of gimp straight.

2. With your scissors, slice off the starting end of the gimp for a slant of about one inch (see illustration).

3. Use a scrap of cloth to smear a light coat of cement on the glass wherever you wish to wind the gimp. Some glasses look best with only a few rows of gimp. Others look well with several inches.

4. Start winding with the slanted end at the bottom of the space you are decorating. Hold the straight edge of the gimp down, with the

cut side fitting close to the second row. Wind smoothly and close to the finished row. Push the gimp together as you wind.

5. When you have covered the space desired, cut the end of the gimp to a point. Then fit the cut edge snugly to the preceding row (see illustration). If you wish to change colors in winding the gimp, always cut the gimp on a slant for both the beginning and end. Butt the slanting ends tightly together.

6. Use a knife to scrape off any dry cement that has run over on the glass.

7. Apply a coat of clear lacquer or colorless nail polish to protect the gimp from water.

Gimp is the most satisfactory material for this use. The colors are good and it goes on smoothly. However, colored string, binders' twine, paper cording, and raffia may be used. See the illustration showing how to begin and end the winding of these materials.

Lapel Ornaments

Materials: Felt scraps; cotton; needle; colored embroidery thread; pencil; tracing or tissue paper; pins; scissors; yarn for braided cord.

1. Draw or trace the outline of the mitten shown on a piece of paper. Cut it out.

2. Using this as a pattern, pin or hold it in place on your felt. Cut out four felt pieces.

3. The mittens shown have white felt strips on the backs. Cut two similar strips of felt, embroider them with colored thread, and sew to the backs of the mittens.

You can make pretty mittens to decorate your jacket on a cold winter day.

4. Using an overcast, or over-and-over stitch, sew the palm and back of the mittens together. Contrasting or matching thread may be used. Leave a small opening through which cotton may be stuffed. Use only enough cotton to give a slightly rounded effect to the mitten.

5. Attach the mittens together with a cord of braided yarn.

Lapel ornaments take a small amount of felt. Any old felt article of pretty color will contain enough felt to make many lapel ornaments. Dogs, horses, fish, hearts, and other figures are attractive when made with felt. In some cases, it looks well to overcast the edge of the ornament with raffia.

These lapel ornaments can also be made from leather.

Felt Pictures

Materials: Colored felt scraps such as old felt hats and banners; paste; pencil; scissors; crayons or paint; drawing or manila paper for mounting felt picture; picture frame, or glass cut the right size for framing picture; velvet ribbon, bias tape, or Scotch tape.

1. Draw a design very lightly on the paper on which you are to mount your felt picture. Make the design larger than the picture shown. Be careful not to smudge the paper. This drawing is merely to guide you in pasting the felt picture.

2. Trace your design, this time on heavy paper. This tracing is for your pattern.

3. Cut carefully around your pattern. Be sure to follow the outline exactly.

4. Now cut the pattern into sections as shown in the illustration.

5. Color the face which you have drawn lightly with paint or crayon. Paint the eyes and mouth after the face is dry. Paint the hair last.

6. Decide what color of felt you wish to use in your picture. For example, the girl's hat and mittens can be red, the bodice and shoes black, the apron yellow, and the skirt blue. Use your pattern sections to cut the felt pieces.

7. Spread the paste evenly on the paper where the felt is to be pasted. Use your finger or a fine brush. Now paste the felt pieces in place. Push them together where they join, so that there is little seam showing.

8. Outline the skates with a soft pencil.

9. Place a flat, heavy weight over the entire picture until the paste is thoroughly dry. This will keep the felt pieces smooth.

10. Frame your picture with a wooden frame. Or, if you wish, you may back your picture with a piece of cardboard. Then cover the picture with glass, and frame with a velvet ribbon, bias tape, or colored adhesive or Scotch tape. If ribbon or tape is used, it is glued around the front and back edges of the picture. This frames it in front, and binds the glass to the picture.

Nursery-rhyme characters and peasant designs make attractive felt pictures, because of the bright colors which may be used.

Felt Lapel Purse

Here are directions for making two lapel purses, one of felt and the other of

Follow these plans to make the felt picture of the skating Dutch girl.

Bonnet

Mittens

Upper skirt

Shoes

PATTERNS

Bodice

Lower skirt

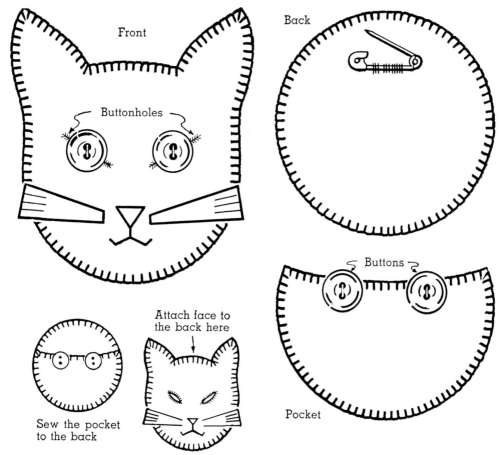

These plans show you how to make a pussy-cat purse out of felt.

leather. The designs can be interchanged. Either one may be made of leather or felt as you wish.

Materials: Felt of an old felt hat, steamed flat; two buttons for eyes; pencil; paper; straight pins; safety pin; needle and thread; scissors.

1. Trace on paper the patterns shown in the diagram. Trace one pattern for the face, one for the back, and one for the pocket of the purse.

2. Pin the patterns on pieces of felt and cut them out.

3. Cut a small triangular piece of felt for the nose. Use a contrasting color.

4. Cut two long triangular pieces of felt for the whiskers. Slash the ends with scissors to make a fringe. Use a contrasting or harmonizing color of felt.

5. Now make the face. Cut slots for buttonhole eyes and edge with a buttonhole stitch. Sew on the small, triangular nose. Embroider the mouth and sew on the whiskers. Make a buttonhole stitch around the outside of the face except the portion between the ears. (See the chapter, "Sewing for Fun," which shows how to make a buttonhole stitch.)

6. Make the pocket. First, make a buttonhole stitch across the top edge of the pocket. Then sew on two buttons for the eyes so that they correspond to the buttonholes on the face.

7. Attach the pocket to the back with a buttonhole stitch. Outline the entire edge of the back except the portion between the ears.

8. Sew the face to the pocket side of the back. Attach it with a buttonhole stitch to the portion between the ears.

9. Sew a safety pin on the back above center so that the purse will not tip when pinned on.

Use colors that will harmonize with your coat, or hat. One color combination could be: red felt face, back and pocket; white eyes, whiskers, and stitching around the edge; green nose, mouth, and stitching around the eyes.

Leather Lapel Purse

Materials: Scrap pieces of different colored leather; gimp or leather lacing (about three times the length to be laced); snap fastener; household cement; leather punch; pencil; paper; safety pin; scissors or a leather knife; lacing needle; snap button fastening set; but, if you have none, the snaps may be put on at a shoe repair shop.

If you do not wish to invest in leather tools, you can use substitutes. A paper punch or a nail with the point filed off, and a hammer, may be used instead of a leather punch. Instead of a lacing needle you may paint the end of your lacing, or dip it in glue or nail polish to harden the point.

1. Trace on paper the patterns from the design. You will have thirteen pieces—the back, pocket, head, jacket, two arms, two hands, two eyes, two whiskers, and a nose. Use leather in different colors. In cutting the jacket, allow an extra piece at the top as shown by the dotted lines on the drawing of the bunny's face. The bunny's face is cemented to the extra piece allowed at the top.

2. Cut out the paper pattern pieces.

3. Clip the patterns on the pieces of leather with paper clips. Then trace around them with a pencil.

4. Cut the leather where you have marked, using scissors or a leather knife.

5. Cement the head on the jacket and let it dry.

6. Attach the snap fastener and snap. Be sure they are in matching positions. Otherwise, they will not meet when the purse is finished.

7. Lace the pocket to the back. Do not allow the leather or gimp to twist while you lace it. Also, lace it so that the right, or smooth side, of

You will enjoy making this bunny lapel purse from scraps of leather.

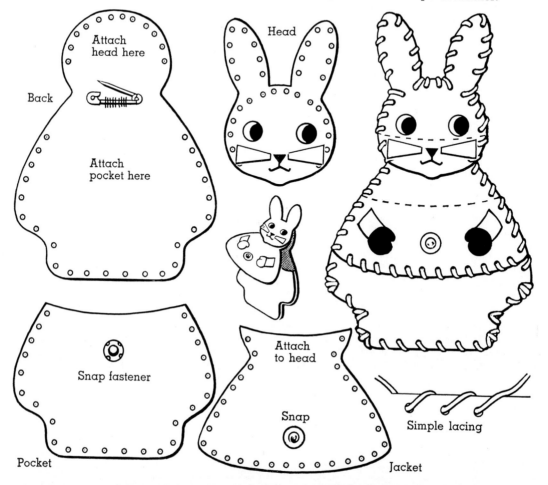

Back

Attach head here

Attach pocket here

Head

Attach to head

Snap

Pocket

Snap fastener

Simple lacing

Jacket

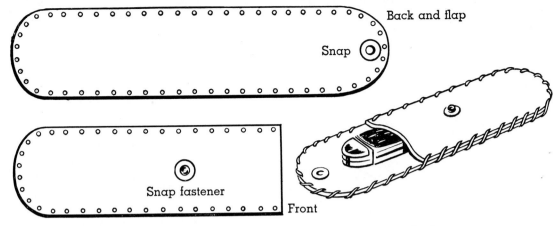

Back and flap

Snap

Snap fastener

Front

This leather pocketknife case is especially designed for use by boys.

the thonging is the side that shows. Before you start lacing, take the end of the thonging you will use and, for about two inches, lay it along the edges which you are to lace together. Then lace as shown. When you have reached the end of the lacing, be sure to take the end of the leather thonging and run it under the last four or five lacings. This will keep the lacing from pulling out. In the corner holes, make two or three lacings as pictured.

8. Outline the front piece with a simple lacing stitch. Join it to the back piece at the sides of the head and between the ears. See the diagram.

9. Cement the eyes, nose, whiskers, arms, and hands into place. If you wish to paint these parts in, you may do so with leather dye, which comes in several colors.

10. Sew a pin on the back.

Pocketknife Case

Place your knife on a piece of paper and draw a pattern. Make the pattern ½″ larger all around than the actual size of the knife. Make another pattern for the underside of the case. Round it off 1″ longer than the other, to allow for a snap fastening. Lay the pattern on soft leather. Cut the case out. Then finish it the same as the leather lapel purse.

Shellcraft

No cutting or shaping of material is necessary for shellwork. Instead, you select from among the shells the size and shape you want. You will find as you work that one idea leads to another. The best shells come from Florida. There are many types and sizes. Small shells may also be gathered at the seashore or near large inland lakes. Good shells to start with are tiny cup shells, garfish shells, lucine shells, and baby conch or whelk shells for flower centers.

If you gather your own shells they can be cleaned with one part water and one part household bleach. Let the shells stand in this liquid for several hours. Rinse and dry.

Coloring the Shells. If you buy shells, it is best to buy them already colored. They can be bought in about twenty-

Shells gathered along the shores of lakes and oceans can be used in many ways.

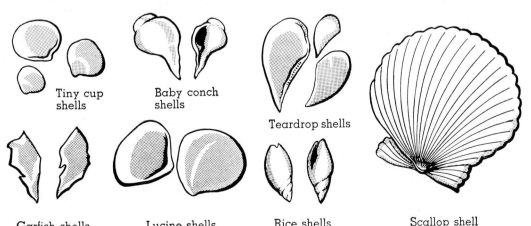

Tiny cup shells

Baby conch shells

Teardrop shells

Garfish shells

Lucine shells

Rice shells

Scallop shell

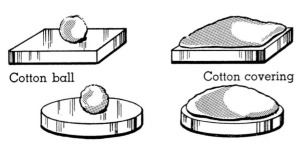

Cotton ball   Cotton covering

Use cotton when you want to give the earrings a rounded or padded effect.

five different shades and colors. Shells may be colored with household tinting dye. Or they may be painted with oil paints. Another method of coloring is to put the shells in a strainer and dip them in enamel paint which has been well thinned with turpentine. Art supply stores carry a lacquer used especially for tinting shells. It comes in many colors and gives the shells a lusterlike finish.

After your design is put together, you may touch it up with oil paint, enamels, or colored or India ink. The lines of flowers, or the eyes of animals and bird

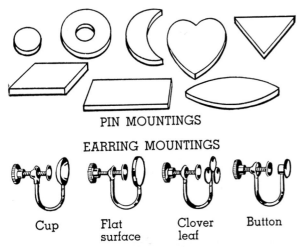

PIN MOUNTINGS

EARRING MOUNTINGS

Cup   Flat   Clover   Button
         surface   leaf

These mountings can be purchased at dime stores and used in making lapel pins and earrings from colorful shells.

designs, may be drawn. Clear lacquer or colorless nail polish may be used to paint the finished article. This preserves the colors. Home-dyed shells are likely to fade.

Shell Earrings

Materials: Tweezers; clear household cement; cotton; shells; pencil; paper; knife; clear lacquer or colorless nail polish; mountings, depending on type of earring back; earring backs, purchased at dime stores or art supply stores. If the earring back is not large enough to take your design, use a mounting, and cement it to the back of the earring. Mountings come in different shapes. They are made of plastic. See illustration.

1. Select the shells to be used. Lay out or draw the design first.

2. Cement a small amount of cotton on the backing. The cotton holds the shells in place.

3. Cement the shells into place in the cotton, and arrange them according to the design you have planned. Handle the shells with tweezers. Keep the tweezers clean of cement by wiping them off with a cloth. Dip the end of each shell in a little cement before putting it in the cotton.

4. When dry, touch up with oil paints, enamel, or ink. Draw the flower lines and shadings.

5. If you have used a mounting, a separate front or face, cement the mounting to an earring back. Be sure to fill the cup with cement so that there are no air bubbles.

6. Paint the shells with clear lacquer or colorless nail polish if desired.

In making designs, flowers may be completed first and placed in the design. Where there are several flowers, it is wise to complete one flower before setting it in the design. Then the flower need not be used if it does not turn out well. To make a separate flower, rub a very little vaseline or oil on a piece of glass. Place a drop of cement on this. Let it set for a few seconds and then form your flower in it. Dip the end of each shell in cement before you place it. When the cement is dry, remove the flower from the glass with a razor blade. Then cement it to your backing.

If you wish a rounded or padded ef-

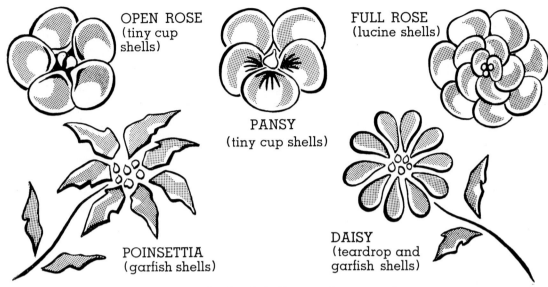

OPEN ROSE
(tiny cup shells)

FULL ROSE
(lucine shells)

PANSY
(tiny cup shells)

POINSETTIA
(garfish shells)

DAISY
(teardrop and garfish shells)

How you can use different kinds of shells to make flower decorations.

fect for the earrings, first cement a ball of cotton in the center of the backing. Next cut a piece of cotton the size and shape of the backing. Cement this on the backing and turn the edges under. See illustration.

Pins, bracelets, barrettes, button shanks, and other backings and mountings can be bought in a number of sizes and shapes. Backings and mountings may be cut with scissors from plastic, and a pin catch or safety pin can be cemented on the back. Do not use too much cement as it will make the plastic warp.

Forming Roses. To make roses use cup shells, lucine shells, gar shells, baby whelk, or baby conch for a center. To make an open rose, use five baby cup shells the same size, with either the smooth or the hinge side up. Place the shells in an overlapping circle. Use the tweezers to dip the parts in cement, and place in a drop of cement. Place a

baby conch shell or baby whelk shell in the center. Use green gar shells for leaves.

To make a full rose, use lucine, cup, and gar shells. Begin from the outside and make an overlapping ring of seven small lucine shells. Inside this, make an overlapping circle of five small lucine shells. Place two baby cup shells inside this facing each other. Pinch the whole rose together. Use gar shells for leaves. Full roses may also be made from a number of baby cup shells. Begin on the outside of the circle and work inward. Pinch the whole rose together.

Poinsettias may be made of garfish shells, and baby conch shells. Dip the shell ends in cement and place in a drop of cement, with points out. Use about seven shells to form a circle, leaving a small space in the center. Fill the space with a few yellow baby conch and whelk shells.

Pansies may be made of cup shells or lucine shells. Use five shells for each

Unusual shell decorations for a matchbox cover, ash tray, and candy box

Candy or nut can

Matchbox metal cover

Nut dish or ash tray

flower. Place two standing up in the back of the cement drop, hinge down. Place two shells in front of these with a small space between. Place the fifth shell in front, cup up and lying flat. Paint pansy markings on the shells. The darker shells should be on top.

Daisies may be made of teardrop shells, or baby whelk or conch shells. Place the points of the teardrop shells toward the center, making a circle with the center free. Use baby whelk or conch shells for centers. Garfish shells may be used as leaves.

Shell Decorations

Use tweezers to handle the shells. Dip one end of each shell in household ce-ment and put it in place to make desired decorations.

Matchbox Cover can be made and dec-orated in a variety of styles.

1. Cut and bend a piece of metal so that it fits around three sides of a safety matchbox. Leave the rough surface of the wooden box free for striking matches.
2. If desired, paint this metal cover with en-amel paint. Then let it dry.
3. Decorate with shells. Paint the background design with oil paints or enamel to complete your design.

Decorated Cans. Short coffee cans, peanut cans, or any low tin can or glass jar with a cover makes a good candy, stuffed date, or nut box.

1. Enamel the can and cover, and let it dry thoroughly before you follow the next direction.
2. A handle may be put on the lid by pound-

Place cards

Tally

Name
1.   5.
2.   6.
3.   7.
4.   8.

Merry Christmas

Gift card

Beautiful greeting cards, place cards, and tallies can be made with shell decorations.

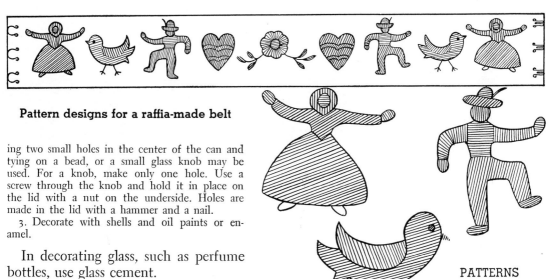

Pattern designs for a raffia-made belt

PATTERNS
FOR A BELT

ing two small holes in the center of the can and tying on a bead, or a small glass knob may be used. For a knob, make only one hole. Use a screw through the knob and hold it in place on the lid with a nut on the underside. Holes are made in the lid with a hammer and a nail.

3. Decorate with shells and oil paints or enamel.

In decorating glass, such as perfume bottles, use glass cement.

Cards and Ash Trays are among the many other things which can be decorated with shells. Place cards, greeting cards, and tallies are easy to decorate in this way. Nut cups and ash trays can be made by using one scallop shell for the dish. The hinge part may be decorated with smaller shells. To decorate cards:

1. Use a good grade of heavy paper or light cardboard.

2. Cut your paper the desired size. It is wise to buy your envelopes first and cut the cards to fit.

3. Decorate with shells, water colors, or oil paints.

Raffia or Yarn Belt

This will make an attractive belt to wear with many costumes.

Materials: Webbing 2" wide; lining material 2" wide and same length as webbing; colored raffia, or bright colored wool or string; pencil; paper; pins; heavy needles; scissors.

1. Cut the webbing the desired length for your belt.

2. You may prefer to draw your own rather than to use designs shown here. Draw the figures you wish to use on a piece of paper and cut them out.

3. Pin the paper figures on your belt in the places where you wish them. Pin the one you

wish to go in the center of the back first. Then pin the two front figures in place. Have these about 1½" from the ends of the belt. Now place the other figures so that the spaces between them are equal.

4. Trace around the figures which you have pinned in place on your belt. If your webbing is light colored, you may do this with a soft lead pencil. If your webbing is dark, use a white pencil.

5. Now fill in the figures with yarn or raffia, using a simple over-and-over embroidery stitch. The stitches should be made to run in different directions to show different parts of the body. Various colors may be used for the figures. The man's hat could be red, his face tan or flesh-colored, his shirt yellow, and his trousers green.

6. When you have finished embroidering the figures, turn under the front edges in a hem. Then line the inside of the belt with your lining material. The edges should be turned under first. Then the lining may be sewed on with small stitches. Use thread the color of the material.

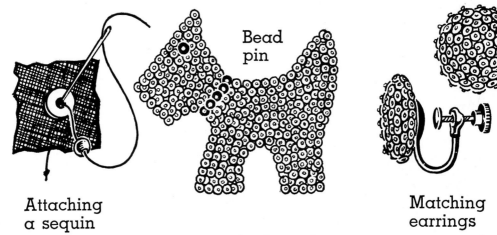

Bead
pin

Attaching
a sequin

Matching
earrings

How you can use sequins and glass beads to make pins and earrings to match

7. The belt may be fastened with large hooks sewed on the front edges. Or it can be laced together with the same kind of yarn you have used in embroidering the figures.

Sequin or Bead Pin

Materials: Felt, which may be from an old hat, as near the color of the beads or sequins as possible; sequins; small glass beads; cotton; No. 16 bead needle; heavy thread; pencil; paper; straight pins; pin backs, which may be purchased at dime stores, general stores, hobby shops, or art supply stores. It is not essential to have pin backs; if you wish, you may use a safety pin as a pin back.

1. Trace your design on felt, repeating the design twice. If dark felt is used, trace around with a white pencil or chalk.

2. Cut out the traced designs.

3. Sew the two pieces of felt together. Use an overcast stitch. Leave a small opening in the top into which to stuff cotton. Use only enough cotton to give a slightly rounded effect. Close the opening with an overcast stitch.

4. Cover one side of the felt design with small beads or sequins. Place them close together. If sequins are used, anchor each sequin with a small bead as shown in the illustration. If you make the dog design, use contrasting colored beads or sequins.

5. Sew a pin back or a safety pin on the back. Two figures or pieces may be attached to each other with a chain, making a chatelaine as shown.

For earrings to match the pin, use a cloth-covered button and a cup-shaped earring back. Contrasting colors in sequins or beads may be placed around the outside of the button. When covered with sequins, cement the button to an earring back with household cement.

Attractive colors for the dog pin or chatelaine are pale blue sequins anchored with bright *iridescent* beads. The eyes, collar, and earring border may be gold sequins.

Making Birdhouses, Birdbaths, and Feeding Stations

A birdhouse is a wonderful way to invite birds to make their homes and raise their families near you.

Many boys and girls, however, are disappointed in their first attempts in making birdhouses. Perhaps the most common mistake in building birdhouses is to make the entrance hole too small or too large for the bird you expect to live in the house. If the entrance to a wren house is too large, an English sparrow may move in. If it is too small, not even a wren can enter. Again, the hole is often placed too close to the floor. A mother bird sitting on her eggs likes to be hidden, and the baby birds should be protected from drafts.

You should never build two-family houses for birds. Nor should you place birdhouses too close together. Birds, with the exception of purple martins and a few others, like privacy. Nesting houses should not be placed nearer than thirty feet apart. Tin cans or metal houses should never be used. Wrens may nest in them, but a tin can gets too hot in summer, and the heat may kill the young birds. Birdhouses, even when built properly, often remain empty if they are put up too late in the season. The best time to make them is in the fall or winter. In the northern states, they should be ready for the birds before March 1. Houses for most birds should be placed on poles or on the trunks of trees below the lower branches. Put them well out of the reach of cats. A

funnel-shaped girdle of tin around a tree, or strands of wire around the trunk, will prevent cats from reaching the bird-house.

Rain and cold winds in summer usually come from the North. For this reason, the birdhouse door should face southeast. No perch is necessary. Unless the wall is very thin, the entrance hole should have an upward slant so as to keep out the rain. It should be protected further by an overhanging roof. A peaked roof should have a tin or building paper weatherstrip along the ridge. Birds like sunshine, but not too much. No birdhouse should be placed where the afternoon sun will beat down on it. A birdhouse also needs a little ventilation and drainage. A few small holes bored in the sides just under the roof will provide ventilation without drafts. Another small hole in the middle of the

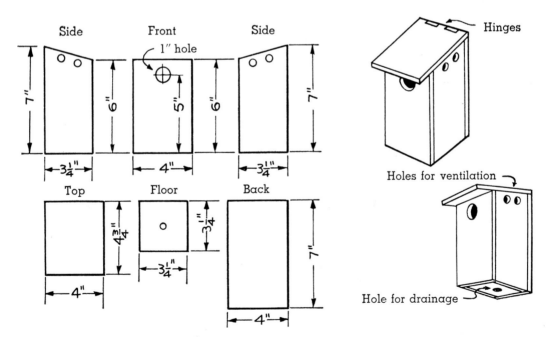

Follow these plans to make a wren house with a sloping roof.

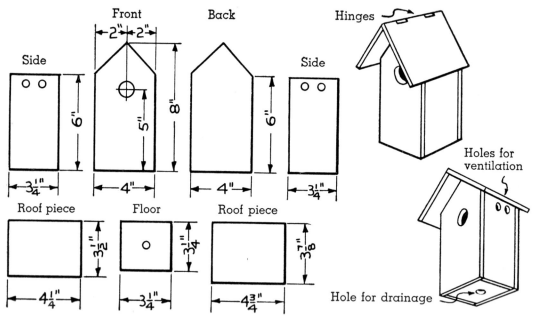

This type of neat wren house is one which has a peaked roof.

floor will provide a means of drainage.

There are more than fifty kinds of birds in the United States that will nest in boxes or in open brackets and pavilions. Each box, or house, should be built with a special bird in mind. Robins, phoebes, catbirds, song sparrows, brown thrushes, and barn swallows will nest in open boxes. The crested flycatcher, which often builds its nest in abandoned woodpecker holes, will nest in a rustic box. This may either be rounded and made of birch bark, or four-sided and made of slabs of wood with the bark left on. Boxes of this kind also will attract the redheaded and downy woodpecker and the flicker. The floors of houses for these birds should be covered about an inch deep with sawdust, chips, fine shavings, or ground cork. A fairly sunny spot is the best location for these birdhouses. The chickadee, the titmouse, and the nuthatch also like homes that look like trees. The chickadee nests near the ground. Titmouse and nuthatch boxes are placed higher. Bluebirds also seem to prefer a rustic house. Boxes for tree swallows and phoebes should be close to water. Wrens are the least fussy of all birds, and will nest in almost any kind of box if the opening is the proper size.

Birdhouses, if attached to the trunks of trees, should hang below the leaves. If they are pitched slightly forward, it helps to keep out the rain. In the fall, after the birds have left their nests, the boxes should be opened and cleaned. The old nests should be taken out and burned. In order to open them for the annual housecleaning, either the roof or one of the sides should be hinged, or fastened on by hooks. If the boxes are made of smooth wood, the inner walls should be roughened, grooved, or cleated. If this is not done, the young birds may have trouble in climbing out.

Tools and Materials. You will need a saw, hammer, screw driver, plane, pliers, chisels, brace and bit, pencil, ruler, nails, and screws. A small table vise and a hand scroll saw will also be helpful. You can use any soft wood about an inch thick. This can be covered with strips of bark. You can make use of chalk boxes and cigar boxes. If your birdhouse is not the rustic kind, you can stain the wood a dark brown, or green. Stain is better for this purpose than paint or varnish, as it looks more like the natural color of bark.

Wren Houses may be built in any one of several designs. The simplest kind will look something like a mailbox. This can be made of smooth pine wood. Floor dimensions, 3¼″ x 3¼″; sides, 3¼″ x 7″ x 6″; back, 4″ x 7″; front, 4″ x 6″; top, 4″ x 4¾″. The entrance hole should be ⅞″ or 1″ across—about the size of a quarter. The hole should be placed 5″ above the floor. If the house is to have a peaked roof, the sides can be 3¼″ x 6″ each. The front and back will then have to be shaped at an angle to fit the roof. The peak of the roof should be 2″ above the sides. This design can be varied, allowing the sides to slant inward something in the manner of a corncrib. You can add a tiny chimney to the house if you like. Rustic wren houses can be made from slabs for sides, front, and roof. One attractive model is triangular in shape as seen from the side. The floor slopes upward to meet the strip of bark used for the roof. The entrance hole is at the side. Another type of box is lantern-shaped, with a conical or candle-snuffer roof. It can be hung from the lower branches of a tree. If you live in the South, you can also hollow out a gourd. Dry and varnish it, and cut an entrance hole before hanging it on a tree.

The following table, taken from a United States Department of Agriculture bulletin, will give you an idea of the dimensions of boxes for various birds.

BIRDHOUSE MEASURES

BIRD	FLOOR INCHES	DEPTH INCHES	ENTRANCE ABOVE FLOOR INCHES	DIAMETER OF ENTRANCE INCHES	HEIGHT ABOVE GROUND FEET
Bluebird	5 x 5	8	6	1½	5 to 10
Robin	6 x 8	8	open	open	6 to 15
Chickadee	4 x 4	8 to 10	6 to 8	1⅛	6 to 15
Titmouse	4 x 4	8 to 10	6 to 8	1¼	6 to 15
Nuthatch	4 x 4	8 to 10	6 to 8	1¼	12 to 20
House Wren	4 x 4	6 to 8	4 to 6	1	6 to 10
Bewick's Wren	4 x 4	6 to 8	4 to 6	1¼	6 to 10
Carolina Wren	4 x 4	6 to 8	4 to 6	1⅛	6 to 10
Tree Swallow	5 x 5	6	2 to 5	1½	8 to 12
Song Sparrow	6 x 6	6	open	open	8 to 12
House Finch	6 x 6	6	4	2	10 to 15
Crested Flycatcher	6 x 6	8 to 10	6 to 8	2	8 to 20
Redheaded Woodpecker	6 x 6	12 to 15	9 to 12	1¼	6 to 20
Downy Woodpecker	4 x 4	8 to 10	9 to 12	1¼	6 to 20
Hairy Woodpecker	6 x 6	12 to 15	9 to 12	3	12 to 20
Flicker	7 x 7	12 to 15	9 to 12	2	12 to 20
Phoebe	6 x 6	6	open	open	8 to 12

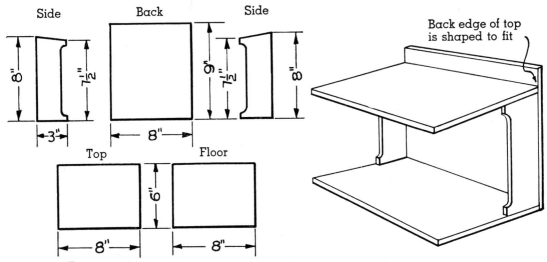

Side Back Side

Back edge of top is shaped to fit

Top Floor

An open shelter or bracket can be made from rough lumber without difficulty.

Bluebirds, wrens, tree swallows, crested flycatchers, and purple martins are likely to prefer a house set on a pole. Tree swallows and martins like to feed over water. Their boxes should be placed twenty feet or more from buildings and trees. Chickadees, titmice, nuthatches, downy and hairy woodpeckers are woodland birds. But they may often be attracted to gardens and orchards if houses are provided. Purple martins live together in large flocks. A purple martin house can be more easily purchased than made. It is always an apartment house, with two or three stories, and as many as twenty-four compartments. It is set on a long pole. The martins usually return to the same house every spring.

Robins, catbirds, barn swallows, brown thrashers, and phoebes build their nests in open shelters.

These open shelters or brackets are not difficult to make. Rough lumber or slabs may be used. The simplest type consists merely of a floor, a backboard, a roof sloping downward, and rounded-out sides. The floor should be about 8″

wide and 6″ deep, and the backboard should extend 1″ or 2″ above the roof. It can then be fastened to the side of a house under the eaves, or placed in the crotch of a tree. Another kind of shelter is in the form of a little summerhouse or pavilion. This has a peaked roof supported by four posts, one at each corner. Robins need mud with which to build their nests. A small mud puddle near the shelter will supply the birds with plaster. Most birds will have no trouble finding twigs, feathers, moss, and other material for nests. But if you wish to aid them, scatter bits of string, yarn, and cotton over the lawn where they can find them. String should be cut into short lengths. Otherwise, a nest builder might become entangled in it.

Birdbaths. A birdbath in your yard will be an extra invitation for your bird friends to visit you. Birds need water to bathe in, to drink, and to mix with clay for their nests. You will be amused by their bathing antics. You can watch the birds easily if the bath is not too far from your windows. A fancy birdbath is not necessary. A shallow earthenware dish will even do. It should not be more than 2½″ deep.

If set in the ground, it should be in an open space as a safeguard against prowling cats. You may be able to supply it with a constant trickle of water from the garden hose. If not, the dish should be refilled with fresh water every morning. It would be best perhaps to mount the saucer on a post 3′ or 4′ high. The bottom and edges of the dish should be slightly roughened to give the birds a firm foothold. Another simple birdbath can be made of a flat stone scooped out and mounted on a pillar of small stones cemented together. A large boulder with a shallow hollow at the top will serve as well.

Feeding Stations. An empty coconut shell with a hole cut in it may be all you will need in the way of a feeding station. The shell may be suspended from an overhanging branch of a tree. Or a wooden tray one foot square, with a raised ledge around it, may be fixed to the sunny side of a wall. If the top and sides are covered, it will prevent the food from being blown or washed away. Small holes drilled in the corners of the shelf will permit any water to drain away. A tray of this kind may be built to fit into a window sill. Hold it in place with wires running from the outer edge to the window frame. By protecting the food with chicken wire, you can keep the squirrels from it. If you like, you can divide the shelf into compartments for various foods such as grain, bread crumbs, and dried sunflower seeds. Glass sides and roof may be added, and, with these, you will be better able to watch the birds eat. Often if a feeding station is put up early in the fall, your summer

visitors will remain with you all winter.

Sundial and Weather Vane. Before clocks were invented, people used sundials to tell them the time of day. Sundials may be ornamental as well as useful. On an 8″ x 10″ base or dial face draw a semicircle, or half circle, and divide it in half. Mark the dividing point 12. Nail it loosely to the flat top of a three-foot post, and turn it so that the figure 12 faces north. Cut a thin piece of wood into a right-angled triangle, with one side 6″ in length and another, 4″. Fasten it with one nail upright to divide the dial face in two, with the point facing south. At 12 o'clock, turn it so that it makes no shadow, and drive in another nail. At 1 o'clock, note where the shadow falls on the semicircle, and mark it 1. Do the same with each hour of the morning and the afternoon. Then fasten the base securely to the post.

If you have a garage or a tool house in your yard, a weather vane on the roof-tree will give it a finishing touch. It will tell you from which direction the wind is blowing. You can use a scroll saw to cut the figure out of soft wood 1 inch thick. Cut out a duck, a rooster, a fish, or perhaps an elephant. Bore a hole in the bottom edge and insert a metal rod. Attach the rod to the peak of the roof, and you will have a weather vane.

If you have planted sunflowers or a mulberry bush in your garden, and have built one or two birdhouses and a feeding station, you will have done about all there is to do in the way of attracting birds. But there will always be many new adventures in the art of handwork:

So, build a little birdhouse in your head;
Keep mentally alert, and do your best,
Until an idea, winging,
O'er land and sea comes singing,
And in your little birdhouse builds its nest.

BOOKS TO READ

BEIM, JERROLD. *Tim and the Tool Chest.* Illus. by Tracy Sugerman. Morrow, 1951.

CARLSON, BERNICE WELLS. *Make It Yourself: Handicraft for Boys and Girls.* Illus. by Aline Hansens. Abington-Cokesbury, 1950.

JORDAN, NINA RALSTON. *Holiday Handicraft.* Illus. by the author. Harcourt, 1938.

LEWIS, ROGER (pseud. for ZARCHY, HARRY). *Weaving.* Knopf, 1953.

POWERS, MARGARET. *Book of Little Crafts.* Chas. A. Bennett Co., Peoria, Ill., 1942.

ROBINSON, JESSIE. *Things to Make from Odds and Ends.* Illus. by the author. Appleton, 1945.

SCHNEIDER, HERMAN and NINA. *Science Fun with Milk Cartons.* Illus. by Jeanne Bendick. McGraw, 1953.

ZARCHY, HARRY. *Let's Make a Lot of Things: Crafts for Home, School and Camp.* Illus. by the author. Knopf, 1948. *Let's Make More Things,* 1943.

PUPPETS AND MARIONETTES

ALICE M. HOBEN

Harold M. Lambert

PUPPETS AND marionettes have an interest that appeals to young and old. They are easy to make and will furnish endless fun and opportunities for creative play. Alice M. Hoben, author of *The Beginner's Puppet Book*, describes in this chapter how to make and use these delightful playthings.

For thousands of years, puppets have brought pleasure to children and grown-ups in almost every part of the world.

NOBODY knows who invented puppets or when and where they were first used. But these clever-looking little actors have been found in Egyptian tombs that were more than three thousand years old. In India, there were puppets which were made of ivory and gold. Puppets were widely used by persons in acting out Bible stories during the Middle Ages. A number of them were used to act out the story of the Virgin Mary. For that reason, some of them became known as marionettes, or "little Marys." Puppets

have been used in performances before kings and emperors in royal palaces, and before monks in their dim monasteries. Scholars, poets, and artists have made puppet shows their hobbies. And famous composers have written lively music for these animated dolls.

Few hobbies can give you more pleasure than the making of puppets and the staging of puppet plays. You can take up this hobby by yourself. Or you can interest your friends and organize a puppet theater group for the purpose of giving shows. As a "puppeteer," you can use your imagination freely. In staging puppet shows, you can entertain others as well as yourself. You can begin by making two or three puppets and giving a simple play. Even if you only give your show at home, with a doorway or a window as the stage, you will have plenty of fun. You can invite the members of your family, or some of your schoolmates to the show.

Perhaps you will want to make a puppet stage that can be folded up and carried around. Your group could give a performance in your school, in the church recreation rooms, or in a park field house. You could take your show to a children's hospital ward and give an entertainment. You could even raise money with your show for the Red Cross or for crippled children. Puppets also make welcome birthday or Christmas gifts. Even a single puppet can keep you amused for hours when you are on a long trip, and can find little to do.

Kinds of Puppets

There are several kinds of puppets. Some are easier to make than others, and each kind is worked in a different way.

Hand Puppets, which are the easiest to make, slip over the puppeteer's, or operator's, hand. They are also called *fist*, or *mitten*, puppets. They consist simply of a head and a loose garment something like a nightgown. Usually they have no legs, or, if they do, the legs are limp and dangling. The index finger of your hand fits into a hole at the bottom of the puppet's head. Your thumb and your middle finger fit into the sleeves. By wiggling the thumb and the two fingers, you can bring the puppet to life.

You will be delighted at the number of things you can make a hand puppet do. He can nod or wag his head. He can wave his arms and clap his hands. He can scratch his head and brush his

Front   Back

KNOTTED HANDKERCHIEF PUPPET

Yarn hair

Painted face

PAPER-BAG PUPPET

A hand puppet can be made readily by knotting a handkerchief and draping it around your hand. A painted paper-bag puppet is just as easy for you to make.

First and second fingers cut off glove

Cardboard legs and feet

Finger position in glove

Paper figure glued to glove

Rag-doll top, skirt open in back. Elastic band at waist

GLOVE PUPPET   FINGER PUPPET

A glove or finger puppet will provide you with hours of jolly entertainment.

clothes, sit down in a chair, or take a bow. He can turn the pages of a book or even climb a tree. He bunny-hops rather than walks across the stage, and a twist of your wrist gives him a jaunty swaying motion. Put one of these puppets on each hand. Then give those around you some fun by making the two wrestle or box.

The simplest form of hand puppet is a knotted handkerchief draped around your hand. The knot takes the place of the head, but the puppet has no arms.

You can make a paper-bag puppet in a few minutes. Take a small paper bag and draw a line across one side of it about a third of its length from the top. Between this line and the top, paint or draw a face. You can use colored crayons. Glue some yarn on top for hair. Gather in the bag at the neck, where the line has been drawn, and tie a string loosely around it. Then slip your hand

into the bag, and you have a funny-looking puppet.

Glove and Finger Puppets are first cousins of the hand puppet. The first and second fingers of an old glove are cut off either half way or all the way. Glue a figure which you have cut out to the back of the glove. Slip your hand into the glove. Your first and second fingers make the legs. With the thumb and other two fingers curled into the palm of your hand, you have a wonderful little dancing doll.

Another finger puppet can be made by making a rag doll from the waist up. The skirt must be wide enough so that you can slip your hand into it at the back. It is sewed to the body at the front and left open at the back. Sew a strip of elastic to the top of the open part of the skirt. This will hold it tightly around your hand. Roll two pieces of cardboard into tubes and glue them firmly. They should fit over the first and second fingers of your hand. These make the puppet's legs. If you like, you can paste small paper shoes at the bottoms of the tubes. You can also place wires in the arms of the puppet. These can be bent in any position you wish. For operating, your hand rests against the back of the doll.

Rod Puppets are usually cutouts mounted on rods at the side or at the bottom. They can be shoved across the stage or raised to the stage level by rods. They can be made with flat, wooden bodies and jointed arms and legs. They can be worked by rods attached to the heads or bodies. And they can also be worked by finer rods, such as umbrella ribs, attached to their hands and feet. Jointed rod puppets can be very lifelike. Rod puppets make especially good animals. Puppet stage scenery is also often moved in and out by rods.

Shadow Puppets are cut out of cardboard or some other heavy material, and attached to wooden sticks. When held between a strong light and a screen, their shadows are thrown on the screen. These puppets have one advantage over the others. By changing the position of the light or the puppets, you can make a single puppet take on many sizes and shapes.

Making Heads

Heads are the most important parts of puppets. Puppet heads should be large compared to their bodies, and are usually made about four inches long. You can carve puppet heads out of balsa wood or model them in plasticine, plastic wood, or papier-mâché. You can also make them in plaster molds. You can use a doll's head, a rubber ball, or even

an apple. An old tennis ball with a hole cut in it for your finger will make an excellent head. Paint eyes, nose, and mouth on it. An apple should be cored and varnished if used for a head.

Cloth Heads. You will need the following materials for making cloth heads:

cloth or stocking; needle and thread; scissors; cotton; cardboard; rubber bands; embroidery yarn; string; felt; shellac; show-card paint.

To make a simple head, take a ball of cotton about four inches across. Punch a hole in it the length of your index finger. Roll a strip of cardboard into a cylinder as big around as your index finger. Hold the cardboard together with rubber bands. Poke it into the hole in the cotton ball. Wrap a stocking heel or a square of cloth around the ball, and gather it in at the bottom. Outline the eyes, nose, and mouth with embroidery yarn. Or, if you wish, bits of cloth of different colors can be sewed in place for the eyes, nose, mouth, cheeks, and eyebrows. Ears can be made of felt and sewed to the head. Finally, paint the head with clear shellac and touch up the face with paints.

Wooden Heads. To make wooden heads, you will need the following materials:

block of balsa wood, pine, spruce, or cedar; knife; augur; plastic wood; glue; paint; brass tacks; paper and pencil; carbon paper; orangewood stick.

First, decide on the kind of head you wish to carve. A picture in a book may serve as a model. Take a block of soft wood about three inches square and four or five inches long. It will be easiest merely to carve out an egg-shaped head. You can carve a wooden neck if you wish. Bore a hole in the bottom about three-fourths the length of your index

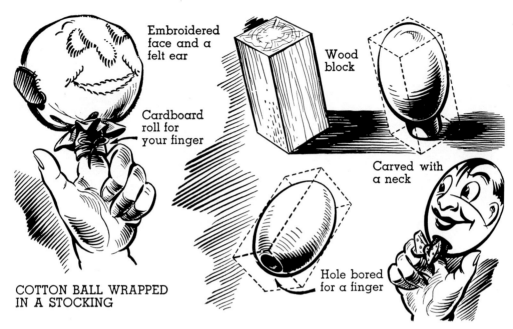

Embroidered
face and a
felt ear

Cardboard
roll for
your finger

Wood
block

Carved with
a neck

Hole bored
for a finger

COTTON BALL WRAPPED
IN A STOCKING

A puppet's head is important. It can be made from wood, cotton, or lead.

finger. Or you can omit the neck, and bore the hole in the bottom of the head.

Using the picture as a guide, cut out a paper pattern of the face. Then trace the eyes, nose, and mouth on the egg-shaped block with carbon paper.

Paint the face white and allow the paint to dry. Paint in the features, using blue or brown for eyes, red for the nose and mouth, and pink for the cheeks. Blur the paint on the cheeks slightly with your fingers. The hair, too, can be painted, unless your puppet is to have a wig or a cap. You can, however, make the nose, mouth, cheeks, and ears from plastic wood which you mold on the wooden head. The eyes, nose, mouth, and ears can be made of colored cloth and pasted on the head. Brass tacks may be used to make shiny eyes. Eyebrows, eye sockets, and lips may be carved if you prefer.

Papier-Mâché Heads. You will need the following materials:

wallpaper paste; water; newspaper; oil paint or water colors; cardboard; rubber bands.

A papier-mâché head is not difficult to make, and it always looks well on a puppet. It should be made extra large, because the material shrinks in drying. Two cups of wallpaper paste will be enough for several heads. Into this mixture pour little squares of newspaper, about 1½″ in size. Knead the mixture with your hands until it is thick enough to keep a shape. Make a cardboard tube to fit your finger. You can hold the tube together with rubber bands. Then build an egg-shaped mass of your paste and newspaper mixture around the tube. Let the mass dry before you paint in the features.

Plastic Wood Heads. For this purpose,

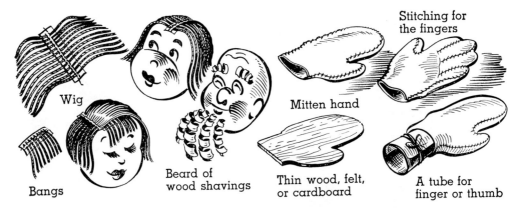

Wig

Bangs

Beard of wood shavings

Mitten hand

Thin wood, felt, or cardboard

Stitching for the fingers

A tube for finger or thumb

Wigs and beards help to make your puppets look like real actors.

you will need the following materials:

plastic wood or sawdust; glue; paint.

Plastic wood or wood-pulp heads are made in the same way as papier-mâché heads. You can make your own plastic wood by mixing sawdust with glue until it is thick enough to mold.

Finishing Your Puppets

Wigs and Beards. To make wigs and beards, you will need the following materials:

yarn for hair, or other material such as shredded rope, cellophane, wood shavings; metal pot cleaners; cloth; needle and thread; scissors; glue.

Your puppet will need a wig if you do not paint its hair. And perhaps you will want to make a mustache or whiskers as well. Hair and beards can be made of many materials, including yarn, shredded rope, cellophane, wood shavings, metal pot cleaners, chenille thread, and soft leather cut into strips.

To make a wig, lay strands of yarn, or other material you use for hair, along a strip of cloth about 1½″ wide. The strip should be long enough to reach from the hairline on the brow to the back of the neck.

Sew the yarn to the cloth in two parallel seams close together. The seams will make the part. The part may be in the middle or at one side of the puppet's head. Glue the cloth strip around the puppet's head. Then, dampen the yarn and curl it around a pencil, if you wish your puppet to have curly hair.

Hands. To make the hands, you will need the following materials:

cardboard, cloth, felt, or oilcloth; needle and thread; cotton, kapok, or tissue paper; glue.

A puppet's hands, as well as its head, should be made extra large. They may be cut out of cardboard, thin wood, felt, or oilcloth. The hands may be glued or sewed to cardboard cuffs. The cuffs, in turn, are sewed to the ends of the sleeves.

Hands, also, can be made in the form of mittens. Make them out of several layers of cloth or felt, or stuff one layer with cotton. The mittens can be stitched to look like fingers. Fine wire or hairpins twisted into the shape of hands and fingers can be bound at the wrist with tape.

Costumes. Hand puppets are usually dressed in baglike cloth garments three inches wide and four inches long. The bag may be gathered at the neck and fastened to the tube into which your finger is inserted. A necktie may be added. A jacket with sleeves may be sewed to the garment.

The right-hand sleeve is the one in which you place the thumb of your right hand. This sleeve is sewed in about one inch from the neck. The other sleeve is sewed an inch lower. For a puppet worn on the left hand, the sleeve on the right side is the one sewed lower.

Trousers may be sewed to the waistline, or beltline, of the garment, and loosely padded. If legs are used, the puppeteer should wear a sleeve of the same material to hide his arm.

Animal Puppets. All sorts of funny animals such as elephants, pigs, ducks, wolves, and rabbits, can be made in much the same way as other puppets. The heads can be made of papier-mâché, and you will want a baglike garment for the body, even if you use fur. You can make the body of cloth and glue on bits of fur.

Scraps of felt stiffened with glue can be used for horns and beaks. Bright-colored beads or buttons make good

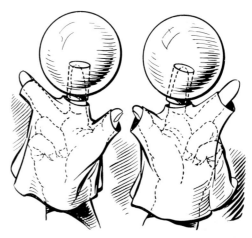

Costumes for your puppets are made of loose cloth garments which you may adorn to make them more interesting.

eyes. For some of your animals you may even want to make clothes.

Hand Puppet Stage

Unless you want to use toy furniture for your play, hand puppets need no platform for a stage. A window sill, if it is high enough from the floor to hide the operator, will serve well for a performance. An open doorway, draped or boarded up part way, can also be used.

A draw curtain can be strung on a

Press Syndicate

This clever group made a stage by fixing up an old carton.

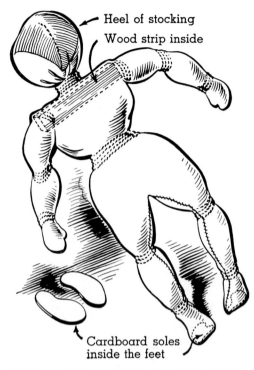

Heel of stocking

Wood strip inside

Cardboard soles inside the feet

Old stockings will be found useful in making some excellent marionettes.

rod, or even on a string, tacked to the doorway. You can use safety pins to attach the curtain to the string so it will slide easily.

A table or a packing box draped with a cloth can be used as a stage. A portable stage can be made of a three-panel screen. The center panel should be about 3 feet wide. The two side panels may be 2 feet wide. You can make an opening at the top of the center panel 24 inches by 18. You can decorate the front with paint, crayons, or colored paper. The screen can be folded up easily and carried around. Other helpful directions for making a screen may be found in the chapter, "Making Toys and Playthings."

Scenery and Lighting for a puppet

show should be simple. The backdrop, or curtain, should merely suggest the place, indoors or outdoors, where the action takes place. You can decorate it yourself with paints or crayons. You can also paint in furniture if you wish. Scenery, cut from cardboard, may be fastened to sticks and shoved on and off the stage. The light should come from above. A goose-neck desk lamp, set on a small table in front of the stage, will make a good light.

Marionettes

Jointed puppets, worked with strings from above the stage, are known as marionettes. Their heads can be made in the same way as those of hand puppets. Their bodies can be flat or rounded, but the rounded bodies are better. You can make a funny little marionette out of six peanuts. Select a small, round peanut for the head, a long one for the body, and four others for the arms and legs, and sew them together. Attach a thread to the top of Mr. Peanut's head, and you can make him dance.

Another simple marionette can be cut out of cardboard. Draw a pattern first on plain paper. Make the head and neck 2 inches long, and the body, 3½ inches, tapering in at the waist. The arms and legs should each be cut in separate pieces. The arms should be about 3½ inches long, and the legs, about 4 inches. Make holes through the joints. Fasten the parts together with spreading brads. These can be bought at any store that sells paper supplies. Be sure to fasten the brads loosely enough to allow your puppet to move freely.

A stocking can also be used to make a marionette. Cut off the foot, leaving only the heel and the leg. Then stuff the heel to form the head. Gather in the stocking below the head and tighten it with five or six rows of stitches. Now you have a neck.

A strip of wood three inches long placed crosswise underneath the stitches makes the shoulders. Gather the stocking at the waistline with several rows of stitches. Stuff it above and below the waistline. If legs are desired, slice the stocking up the middle and sew the sides together, making stitches at the knees and ankles. Stuff the legs.

Insert cardboard soles 1½ inches long, add cotton stuffing, and sew up the toes. Now you have the feet. Arms can be made separately out of any material. The material should be gathered to form elbows and wrists, and attached to the ends of the shoulder rod.

Paint the eyes, nose, and mouth, or attach a mask. Then dress the marionette.

Controls. Marionettes are worked by strings running from various parts of their bodies to a T-shaped holder held in the puppeteer's left hand. Some holders, or controls, have two crossbars. Others are double T's, held together by a peg where the pieces cross. For a simple control, use two flat strips of wood 2 inches wide. Make one 6 inches long, the other 8 inches long. Glue or tack the pieces together in the form of a T. Use the 8-inch strip as the top of the T, and the shorter one as the handle.

Place small screw eyes at each end and at the center of the crossbar, and at points halfway between the center and the ends. Also place one at the end of the shorter bar.

From the center screw eye of the crossbar, run a thread or strip of fishline about 20 inches long to the back of

Front   Back

Strings for working marionettes are attached to a T-shaped holder. This is held in the puppeteer's left hand and tilted at various angles as he works.

the marionette's head. Attach it above the center. Connect lines at each end of the crossbar with the knees. From the screw eyes midway between the center and ends of the crossbar strings, attach the marionette's elbows. The cord at the end of the handle runs to the marionette's back, above the waist.

To adjust the strings, have someone hold the marionette upright on a table as you attach the string to the head. Then hold the control so that the marionette stands with the string alone. Attach the other string so that they are tight as the marionette stands motionless. Another crossbar may also be used to operate the marionette's feet.

You will soon learn how to make the

marionette perform by tilting the control at various angles and by pulling on the strings with your free hand.

The Stage for marionettes needs a floor. If a doorway is used, a shelf may be placed at a convenient height from the floor. At a point about 18 inches above the stage, the doorway should be draped or boarded up. This will hide the puppeteer from the audience. A low window sill can also be used as a stage. The shield can be made of wallboard, or cardboard, and decorated.

An orange crate or a small packing box open at the top and at one side makes a good stage. A shield high enough to hide the puppeteer, who stands or sits at the stage level, can be fastened to the box at the open side. Cut out an oblong piece the height and width of the stage, leaving two narrow strips at the sides where the shield may be fastened to the box.

Plays for Puppets and Marionettes

If you are planning a puppet show, you should select your play before making the little actors. Many interesting puppet plays have been written. But you can write your own or base one on a favorite story. Select a play with only a few characters. Then you can make your puppets to fit these characters.

If you select a story for your play, you can make up the lines as you go along. Or you can write them out and read them. Your play should not last more than fifteen or twenty minutes. In the chapter, "Playmaking and Play-Acting," you will find directions for writing or adapting a simple play. You could have a master of ceremonies, perhaps in the form of a clown, to announce the acts.

A phonograph can supply the music, but this should not be so loud that it drowns out the words of the actors. Sound effects are easily produced off stage. Tapping two coconut shells on a table will sound like a horse galloping. BB shot dropped on a drum head will sound like rain. Rolled on the drum head, they will sound like thunder.

Puppets and marionettes are especially interesting to make, because their personalities depend entirely on you. It is up to you to bring them to life.

BOOKS TO READ

ACKLEY, EDITH FLACK. *Marionettes; Easy to Make; Fun to Use.* Illus. by Marjorie Flack. Lippincott, 1929.

BUFANO, REMO. *Book of Puppetry.* Edited and compiled by Arthur Richmond. Illus. by the author. Macmillan, 1950.

FORNAM, HELEN, and WHEELER, BLANCHE. *Let's Make a Puppet.* Webb, St. Paul, Minn., 1947.

JAGENDORF, MORTIZ ADOLF. *The First Book of Puppets.* F. Watts, 1952.

LEWIS, ROGER (pseud. for ZARCHY, HARRY). *Puppets and Marionettes.* Knopf, 1952.

PELS, GERTRUDE JAECKEL. *Easy Puppets; Making and Using Hand Puppets.* Illus. by Albert Pels. Crowell, 1951.

STEINER, CHARLOTTE. *Pete's Puppets.* Illus. by the author. Doubleday, 1952.

SEWING
FOR FUN

CATHERINE CORLEY ANDERSON

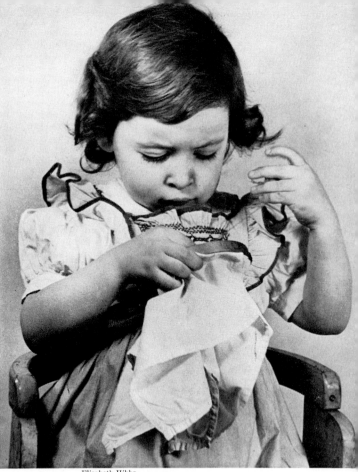

Elizabeth Hibbs

SEWING IS not only one of the most interesting, but also one of the most useful, hobbies for boys or girls. It can be done in odd moments, or while listening to a radio program. Catherine Corley Anderson is the author of *Make It Yourself* and other books and articles, and was formerly artcraft instructor for the Chicago Park District. She tells you, in words and illustrations, how to use needle and thread to make such things as rag dolls, stuffed animals, and Indian costumes.

HAVE you ever strung bright-colored buttons on a thread to make a necklace? This is one way to get used to handling a needle and thread. Pull the thread through the eye of the needle until the two ends meet. Then tie a knot in the two threads. Select a button with a small hole so that the knot will not slide through. Push the needle through the hole in the button, and slide the button

There is no end to what you can make with needle and thread. There are new things to make and old things to make over. This girl is embroidering.

along the thread until it meets the knot. String together as many buttons as you like, cut the thread, and remove the needle. Then tie the two ends of the chain together.

Sewing on Buttons

One of the first and most useful things to know about sewing is how to sew on a button. It is easy to sew one on all by yourself. Thread the needle, double the thread, and knot it as you did before. For the first buttons you sew on, select ones with only two holes because they are easier to attach.

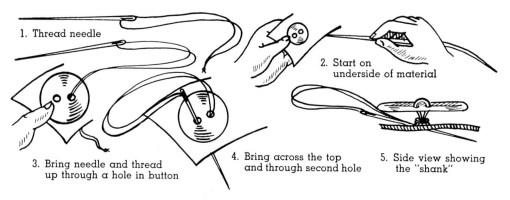

1. Thread needle

2. Start on underside of material

3. Bring needle and thread up through a hole in button

4. Bring across the top and through second hole

5. Side view showing the "shank"

Boys and girls will find it useful to learn how to sew on buttons well.

Start the needle on the underside of the material at the place where you want the button. Pull the needle and thread through until the knot catches in the cloth. Put the needle through one of the holes in the button, and let the button slip all the way down the thread. Then put the needle through the other hole and back through the material. Pull the thread through. Now run the needle through the material at the spot where it first went in, so that it will come through the first hole in the button. Poke the needle down through the second hole, and pull the thread through. Do this five or six times. Make a knot on the underside of the material by taking three small stitches, one over the other, and cut off the thread.

Buttons with four holes may be attached by sewing first two holes on one side, then two on the other. You can also sew them from corner hole to corner hole, crossing the threads in the center. To make a stronger fastening, wind the thread tightly around the thread between the cloth and the button to make a "shank." Then make a knot on the underside.

Picture Sewing

Materials: A square or rectangle of muslin or old sheeting; a large needle; bright-colored embroidery thread or yarn; carbon paper; pencil; scissors.

Most boys and girls like to do picture sewing. Perhaps you can draw a picture directly on a piece of cloth by using a pencil or crayon, but drawing your picture on paper may be easier. Place carbon paper on a cloth and place a sheet of paper on top of the carbon. Pin the paper and carbon to the cloth. Draw or trace a picture of a dog, a cat, a monkey, an elephant, a house, or even a simple landscape with trees, hills, and clouds. Then take off the paper and carbon. Thread your needle. Double the thread and knot the ends. If you are making a landscape, use thread of different colors, green for the grass, pink for the clouds, blue for the hills.

Hold the cloth in your left hand. Start with the knot on the underside in the lower right-hand part of the picture. Pretend that the needle is a little worm tunnelling through the garden. It sticks its head in and out, and pulls its tail behind it. Follow the lines of the drawing with large, in-and-out stitches. These are called "running" stitches. When you have stitched around the drawing, make a knot on the underside, and cut off the thread. Hang your picture up, so that everyone can admire it.

Learning to use the scissors is also part of learning to sew. Start with round-bladed scissors, and cut bright-colored scraps of goods. It will be easier to cut a straight edge if you cut a small notch in the edge of the goods, and pull out a thread from the center of it. This will leave a space, or line, in the material, which you can follow with your scissors. Now you can cut out the material for the sewing pictures.

By using colored threads on old cloth, you can make interesting pictures of an animal, house, or other object.

It is always easier to cut material when it is lying flat on a table. Slip the material between the blades of the scissors. Hold the scissors so that the blades are straight up and down, with the lower blade resting on edge against the table. Keep this edge against the table as you cut. Keep the table covered with oilcloth or newspapers to protect its surface.

Table Runners, Place Mats, Napkins, Doll Covers

Materials: Your sewing picture; burlap or other coarse material; pins; needle and thread; colored embroidery thread.

After you have made a sewing picture, perhaps you would like to hem the edges to keep them from fraying. Then your picture may be used as a table runner or doily, a napkin or place mat, or a doll cover.

Clip off the corners of the material, as shown in the drawing. Turn up the edge ¼"; then turn up again ½". Pin and baste the edges, one edge at a time. A basting stitch is a large running stitch which you use to hold the material in place. Then complete the hem with a running stitch of colored thread. Rip out the basting stitches.

Another easy way to make table runners, napkins, and place mats is to cut them out of clean burlap or other coarsely woven material. Pull out at least six threads from the edges on all four sides of the material. This will give a fringed edge which does not need to be hemmed. Decorate with rows of even stitching. Use thread of different colors. The rows may follow the edges in a border, or they may be placed unevenly in a plaid pattern. They may also be crossed in large checks. You could make a small lunch cloth in this way, with small napkins to match. This luncheon set would make a useful and attractive gift.

Useful table runners, place mats, doilies, and even napkins are easy to make.

Beanbag and Stuffed Animals

Materials: Strong cloth; pins, needle, and coarse thread; scissors; dried beans or peas. For animals, use scraps of felt or soft leather; cotton or kapok; yarn or embroidery floss; small buttons.

It is easy to make a beanbag. Cut a piece of strong material 8" x 5". Fold it in the center crosswise so that it is 4" wide and 5" long. Pin it in several places to keep it from slipping. Start ½" from the upper right-hand corner and sew down along the right side and across the bottom. Make your stitches ½" from the edge.

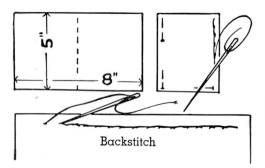

Backstitch

How you can make your own beanbag

Use a backstitch. Make it by taking a backward stitch on the upper side of the material. Then bring the needle through the underside, and up in front of the back stitch. This locks the stitches together, and makes a stronger seam than the running stitch.

Turn the bag inside out and pack loosely with dried beans, peas, or tiny pebbles. Turn the top edges in toward each other, about ½" from the edge, and pin and baste together. Then overcast the top edge. To do this stitch, bring the needle from the underside of the bag through to the upper side. Carry the thread over and over the edge. Space the stitches about ¼" apart.

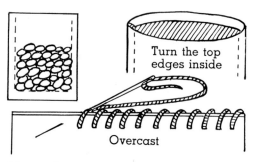

Turn the top edges inside

Overcast

This is how you overcast the top edge with a neat over-and-over stitch.

You can cut the beanbag in the shape of a cat, duck, or rabbit. Make the ears and paws of the animal out of scraps of felt. Make a side view of the duck, and make its bill and feet of felt. Insert the felt pieces between the two layers of cloth before sewing. Be sure the animal's paws or feet, ears, and bill are in the right places. They should face inward. Then, after you sew the seams and turn the beanbag right side out, these parts will stand out from the sides as they should. Leave an open space at the top for stuffing. Stuff, then close the opening with overcasting.

Stuffed Animals. Make the pattern larger for stuffed animals if you wish. Stuff with kapok or small, white rags. Use buttons for eyes, and make the nose

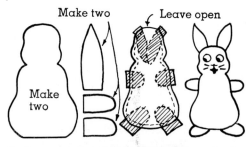

Make two   Leave open

Make two

Make two

It is easy to make stuffed animals by sewing scraps of old felt together.

and mouth of yarn or floss. Or use scraps of felt for eyes, nose, and mouth. Cut a little felt jacket and put it on the animal to dress it up.

Marble or Jack Bag

Materials: Heavy cloth; needle and thread; scissors; pins; cord or braided yarn; small safety pin.

Make a marble or jack bag in almost the same way as the beanbag. Cut the material 11″ x 7″. Fold down the center crosswise so that it is 7″ long and 5½″ wide. Sew up two sides with the backstitch. Turn down the top ¼″. Fold over again 1″. Pin and baste. Hold the top of the bag in the left hand with fingers inside the bag, to make sure you will not sew the two sides of the top together. Sew a hem with a small running stitch about ¼″ from the top of the bag.

Make a second row of running stitches about ½″ below the first. The space between the two rows of stitching is to be used for a drawstring which will close the top of the bag. Turn the bag right side out.

A marble bag which you have made yourself comes in handy in the springtime.

Carefully cut a small hole in the top layer of goods in the center of the drawstring space. Tie a small safety pin to the end of a strong cord or braided yarn, about 15″ or 20″ long. Push the pin and cord through the hole and around the space between the lines of running stitches. Remove the pin, pull the ends of cord together tightly, and tie in a bow.

If you wish, you may decorate the bag with bright buttons or felt flowers. You can even stitch a picture, or your name, in colored thread.

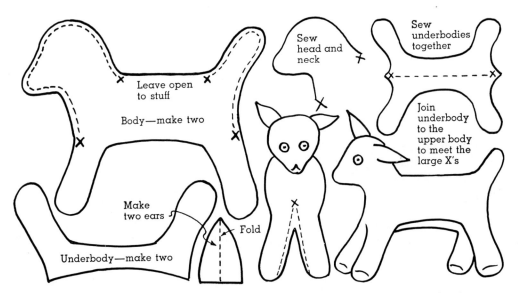

Follow these patterns and you will be the proud owner of a stuffed lamb.

Lambikin, a Stuffed Lamb

Materials: Terry cloth, or soft toweling; cotton or kapok; needle, thread, and scissors; two small black buttons.

This soft, wooly little lamb, named Lambikin, is easy to make, for there are only three parts. Cut each part on doubled cloth, so that there will be two of everything. Sew the two parts of the underbody together along the center line. Pin and baste the two parts of the upper body together from x to x. Leave the center back open for stuffing.

Now sew the upper body to the underbody as shown. Turn the material right side out. Stuff firmly with cotton or kapok. Turn in the open edges at the center back, and overcast firmly together. Sew a black button on each side of the head for eyes.

Cut out the ears. Fold each ear down the center, and sew along the curved edge. Turn right side out, and stuff loosely. Turn the open edges in and baste. Sew the ears to the sides of Lambikin's head. Its ears will then flop when it walks.

A Stuffed Pussycat

Materials: Cotton cloth or oilcloth; needle, thread, and scissors; cotton or kapok; colored embroidery thread.

Cut the two sides out of cotton material or oilcloth. If you use cotton cloth, sew it around the edge on the wrong side. Leave a space for stuffing. Then turn right side out, and stuff firmly. Sew the open space together. Embroider eyes, nose, and mouth.

If you use oilcloth, overcast the edges, leaving a space for stuffing. Stuff, and overcast the opening.

Coco, a Stuffed Clown Doll

Materials: Paper and pencil; old muslin sheeting or sugar sack; colored material for ruffles; pins, needle, and thread; scissors; two small black buttons; two small red buttons; crayon; red yarn.

Coco looks as if he had just stepped out of the circus! Cut a paper pattern like the drawing, but make it a little larger than you want the doll to be. Allow ½″ all the way around for seams.

Pin the pattern to a double piece of material, and cut out. Backstitch the two sides together, leaving an open space at the top for stuffing. Turn inside out. Stuff with cotton, kapok, or small white rags. Overcast the sides of the opening together.

Sew on buttons for eyes, nose, and mouth. Color the cheeks with red crayon. Add scraps of red yarn for hair. Cut a wide cone from the muslin for a cap. Fold it over and sew along one edge. Turn inside out, and stitch in place on Coco's head. Make pompons of yarn for the top of the cap and for buttons. You can find out how to make pompons in this chapter under "Trimmings."

Cut strips of colored material 2″ wide and 8″ to 12″ long. These strips are to make ruffles around Coco's neck, arms, and legs. Fold in half lengthwise, and gather with a large running stitch. To gather, pull your thread so that the material puckers into gathers. Fit the gathered side of the ruffles around Coco's neck, arms, and legs, and sew tightly in place.

Sammy, a Stocking Doll

Materials: Pencil and paper; a man's plain cotton or woolen sock; gingham cloth; cotton, kapok, or rags for stuffing; two white buttons; red, black, or brown yarn; large needle and heavy black thread; scissors; string; cardboard; bias tape.

You will like Sammy, for, whatever happens, he always comes up smiling.

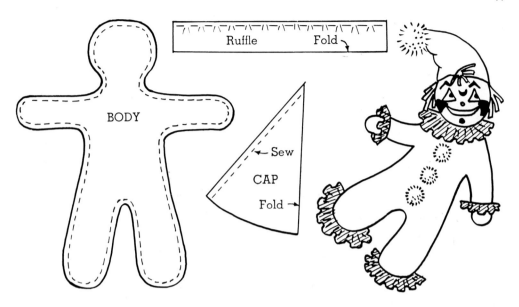

These patterns show you how to make a stuffed clown doll.

Cut off the foot of the sock. This will make Sammy's head and body. Stuff the toe solidly with rags, cotton, or kapok, for about 3½″. Tie a strong cord or thread around the stocking at this point to form the neck.

Cut a 1″ slit on each side of the sock, just below the neck. These are for the armholes.

For arms, from one edge of the leg part of the sock, cut a piece about 9″ long, and 1½″ wide on the fold. Use a backstitch to sew about ½″ in from the long edge on the open side. Turn the piece inside out, and stuff it with cotton or rags. Tie each end tightly. This long, narrow piece makes both of Sammy's arms. Do not cut it in half.

Pull the arm piece through the slits in the sides of the sock. Allow each side to extend for about 3″. At the bottom, or heel part of the sock, cut a slit through both thicknesses up the center for about

3½″. These parts will make Sammy's legs.

Stuff the body above the legs.

With strong thread or matching yarn, overcast the inside edges of the legs. Stuff the legs more lightly than the body, so that they can move. Tie the ends tightly.

Sew two small, white button eyes in place with black thread. Make a little black x with thread or yarn, for a nose. Embroider a red mouth with yarn.

To make Sammy's hair, wind black or brown yarn thickly around a piece of cardboard 6″ long and 3″ wide. Slip the yarn off the cardboard and tie it loosely through the center to hold it in place. Place the yarn on Sammy's head. Then overcast through the whole thickness of the yarn at the center and through the stocking head. Cut off the holding yarn. Trim the ends and spread to cover Sammy's head.

Sammy's Clothes. To make clothes for Sammy, enlarge the patterns for blouse and overalls. Sew along the seams with a backstitch. Hem all edges neatly. Use bias tape for overall straps. Sew one piece on each side of the overall top at the back. Then cross the straps over Sammy's shoulders and sew in front.

Susie

Materials: Pencil, paper, and carbon paper; cotton cloth; printed material; silk; a strip of felt; pins, needle, thread, and string; colored yarn or embroidery thread; scissors; cotton or kapok; black oilcloth, plastic, or cardboard.

Susie is sure to be a favorite doll. Make a pattern first on paper. The head, arms, and body are in one piece. Place the pattern on two thicknesses of material.

Make the legs of two rectangular pieces. Cut double width. Fold the legs lengthwise, and sew with a backstitch on the sides and bottom. Leave the top open for stuffing.

Sew the two sides of the head, arms, and body with a backstitch, leaving the lower side open. Turn the legs and body right side out, and stuff with cotton or kapok. Turn in the edges at the bottom of the body, and baste each edge. Overcast the top of each leg, and pin it in place between the basted edges.

Baste the legs in place. Remove the pins. Overcast the legs to the body. Overcast the remaining basted edges together.

Susie's Clothes. Cut out a paper pattern for Susie's dress. Follow the picture shown. Try the paper pattern on Susie to see if it fits. You allow ½″ for seams, and 1½″ for the hem. Be sure to make the pattern large enough. Lay the pattern on a doubled piece of printed cotton material, with the shoulders on the fold. Then cut.

Sew the side seams on the wrong side of the material with a small, running stitch. Turn up the hem ½″. Turn it up again 1″, and baste close to the top of the last turn. Sew with a plain hemming stitch. Turn right side out.

Turn the material under ¼″ around the neck and armholes. Cut tiny snips around the neckline, before turning the material under. Pin and baste. Make a ¾″ wide ruffle for the neck, and a 1½″ ruffle for each sleeve. Make the ruffles the same as for Coco, the clown. Pin and baste them in place. Sew to the material with a small running stitch.

Bonnet. Cut a paper pattern large enough to fit Susie's head. Pin the pattern on a doubled piece of material. Pin the straight edge of the pattern on the fold of the material. Cut out the bonnet. On the right side of the material, turn the edges in about ½″ toward each other, and baste together. Finish with a buttonhole stitch in a differently colored yarn or embroidery thread.

A buttonhole stitch is much like the overcast stitch, except that after you insert the needle through the material toward you, you bring the thread around under the needle from right to left to form a loop. Pull the needle through this loop and tighten the thread. Place the next stitch about ¼″ away from the first stitch, and keep all stitches about ¼″ in from the edge.

Finger crochet two strings with which to tie the bonnet. You can find out how to finger crochet in this chapter under "Trimmings."

Shoes. To make shoes for Susie, cut two ovals out of black oilcloth, plastic, or cardboard. Cut a top for each shoe. Then place the two ends of each shoe top together, and make a seam ½″ from

HOW TO MAKE A STOCKING DOLL

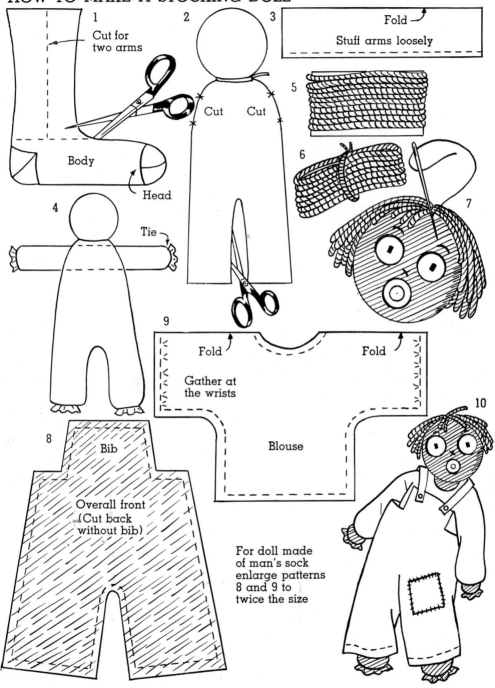

1 Cut for two arms

Body

Head

2

3 Fold — Stuff arms loosely

Cut   Cut

5

6

4 Tie —

7

9 Fold — Gather at the wrists   Fold —

Blouse

8 Bib

Overall front (Cut back without bib)

For doll made of man's sock enlarge patterns 8 and 9 to twice the size

10

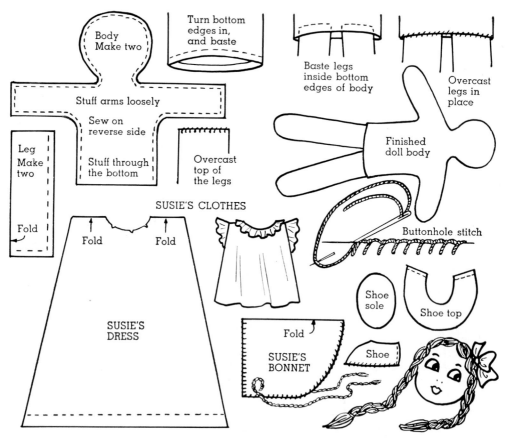

Body Make two

Turn bottom edges in, and baste

Baste legs inside bottom edges of body

Overcast legs in place

Stuff arms loosely

Sew on reverse side

Leg Make two

Stuff through the bottom

Overcast top of the legs

Finished doll body

SUSIE'S CLOTHES

Fold

Fold   Fold

Buttonhole stitch

SUSIE'S DRESS

Shoe sole

Shoe top

Fold

SUSIE'S BONNET

Shoe

"Susie" is another type of doll you will find interesting to make.

the edge. Baste the sole and shoe top together. Overcast the edges together. Place on Susie's feet.

Finishing. Embroider Susie's eyes, nose, and mouth. Or you may cut them out of felt, and sew them in place. Make a thick braid of yellow yarn to hang down on either side of her face. Use six strands of yellow yarn, about 3′ long, for each part of the braid. How to braid is shown in this chapter under "Trimmings." Sew the braid to the top of Susie's head. Tie on her sunbonnet.

Design other patterns for Susie's costumes.

Caps

Materials: Heavy material such as felt or burlap; needle, thread, and scissors; paper and pencil; embroidery thread.

Here is a basic pattern for caps which you may cut out of cloth. Cut at the lower dotted line if you wish to turn up the bottom one fold. Cut off at the upper dotted line if you do not wish to hem the bottom.

Trace the pattern on heavy paper and cut it out. Fold the material so that you can cut two sections at once. If you are using felt, do not fold, because it is too thick to cut more than one section at a time. Pin the pattern to your material, and cut out six triangular pieces. Pin and baste these together. Sew with a back-stitch. Spread seams out flat.

If you are making a burlap cap, make a buttonhole stitch around the edges of each seam to keep the seams from ravel-

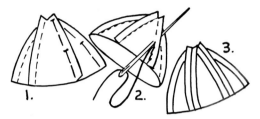

Pin and baste the sections together.

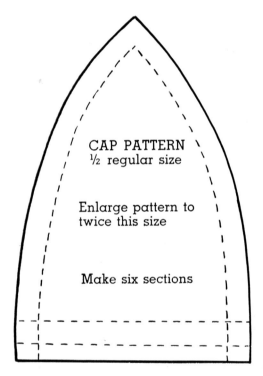

CAP PATTERN
½ regular size

Enlarge pattern to twice this size

Make six sections

A pattern to follow in making each of the six sections of the cap.

ling. Trim the cap to match your belt. Sew a button to the top center, or make a bow of crocheted yarn or felt to sew on top.

If you wish to turn up the bottom of your felt cap to make it stronger, use a "pick-up" or hemming stitch, because of the thickness of the felt.

To make the hemming stitch, put the needle through the material between the cap and the hem, bringing the needle toward you. The knot will be inside the hem and will not show. Start about ⅛″ from the edge. Pick up one thread from the cap section with the needle, sewing from right to left. Bring the needle through from the underside of the hem and tighten the thread. Space stitches about ¼″ apart. Pick up one thread from cap section, and continue as before. When you come to a side seam, spread the two parts out so that they lie flat inside the hem.

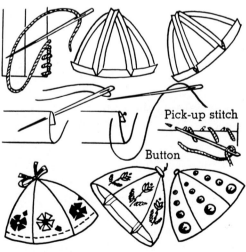

How you can make a burlap cap

Purses and Bags

Materials: Burlap, old woolen scarf, taffeta from an old dress, or attractive cotton cloth; lining material; pins, needle, and thread; yarn; felt; button; snaps; plastic ring or old bracelet.

Purses to match your cap and belt sets are easy to make.

Burlap Envelope Purse. Cut a piece of burlap about 15″ long and 8½″ wide. Measure 5½″ from the bottom and turn it up at that point to form the sides of your purse. Pin and baste the sides together. Then sew sides with burlap thread pulled from the material. Use a backstitch.

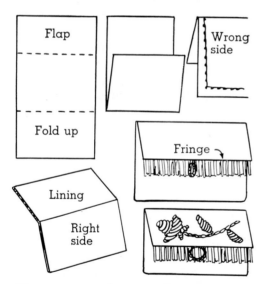

These patterns show you how to make a fringed envelope purse from burlap.

Material extending beyond the sewed sides is the flap. Pull out four to six threads from the three edges of the flap to make a fringe finish.

Cut the lining material the same size as the purse. Sew up the sides the same way, using sewing thread.

Crochet or braid a short length of burlap thread or yarn for a loop to fasten the purse. Sew it to the center of the flap.

Turn the burlap right side out and insert the lining. Turn in the edges of the flap lining and slipstitch to the edges of the burlap. A slipstitch is much like the "pick-up" stitch for hemming. Insert the needle between the lining and burlap, so that the needle and thread come through the lining toward you. Pick up one or two threads from the burlap with the needle. Bring the needle back and pick up one or two threads from the edge of the lining where it is turned under. Continue around the flap.

Turn down the flap. Measure the position of the loop and sew a button in place on the side of the purse. Trim the purse with running stitches of bright yarn or with embroidered yarn flowers.

Felt Purse. You can make a felt purse without lining. Use the same pattern as for the burlap purse. Turn up the sides and pin them in place. Sew the edges together on the outside with yarn, using a buttonhole stitch. Finish the flap with a buttonhole stitch. Sew snaps in place on the flap and side for closing. Cut a nar-

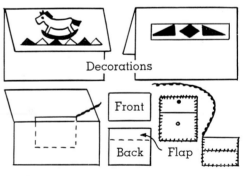

A decorated purse made from felt

row strip of felt and sew it to the back of the purse at each end for a handle.

You can trim the purse with felt flowers, or other designs, such as initials, or funny animals. If you wish to make a pocket inside your purse, cut a rectangle about 3" x 4". Slipstitch the sides and bottom to the inside back of the purse before sewing up the sides.

Make a coin purse by cutting a rectangle a little smaller than your 3" x 4" pocket. Cut another rectangle 2" deeper, to allow for a flap. Pin, baste, and sew the two sides and bottom. Turn down the flap and sew the snaps in place. Finger crochet or braid a narrow cord. Sew one end of the cord to the corner of the coin purse, and the other end inside your purse.

A Stiff Purse can be made by slipping a piece of buckram or pliable cardboard between the lining and the purse before joining the flaps. Cut the stiffening a little smaller than the purse pattern.

Trimmings

Simple Braiding. Braided yarn, cord, or lacing may be used for many things, such as purse strings, belt ties, blouse neck fastenings, cap strings, and mitten cords. Three-strand braids are simple to make. If a thicker braid is desired, use

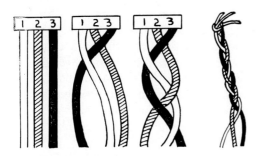

Three-strand braids can be used to make ties, mitten cords, belts, and other things.

six or nine strands. Divide into three equal parts to braid. Use scotch tape to fasten three strands of the material you wish to braid to the edge of a table. Bring No. 3 strand over No. 2, which brings No. 3 to the center. See drawing. Bring No. 1 over No. 3, making No. 1 the center. Continue bringing the right-hand strand over the center, then the left-hand strand over the center. Tighten the cords firmly or loosely as desired, but always evenly. When finished, remove the tape and tie a knot at both ends of the braid.

Finger Crocheting is another way to make cords and ties. Use the same materials as for braiding, and as many strands as you wish, but keep them all together as a unit.

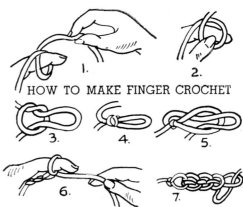

HOW TO MAKE FINGER CROCHET

Cords and ties can be made very simply by crocheting with your fingers.

Wind heavy yarn or string around your left first finger, to form a loop. Slip the loop off your finger. Bring the right-hand thread in a loop through the first loop and tighten it.

Bring the right-hand thread through the second loop, forming a third loop.

Tighten, and continue to the length you wish. To end, slip the loop off your finger, bring the right-hand thread through the last loop, and pull tight.

Pompons make attractive decorations for many articles you will sew. Use them on your caps, purses, gloves, slippers, blouses, dresses, and on the ends of crocheted or braided cords.

Cut two cardboard circles about 2¼″ in diameter. Cut a circular hole in the center of each, about ½″ in diameter. Slit the cardboards on one side. Place them together, matching the slits. Keep the slits to the right, and wind yarn from right to left around the two cardboards.

Slip the yarn through the slits each time you bring it around. Continue winding until the circle is firmly and closely wound with yarn.

Slip a scissors blade between the edges of the two cardboards, and clip the edges of the yarn all the way around. Separate the cardboards slightly.

Place a strong thread between the cardboards and around the yarn which comes through the center holes. Tie the ends of the string tightly around the yarn.

Slip off the cardboards and fluff out the pompon. You will be surprised at its fluffy roundness.

Indian Costume for Boys

Materials: Burlap, flour sack, or cotton cloth; newspaper, and wrapping paper; crayons; pins, needle, thread, and scissors. For moccasins: Soft leather or felt; a punch; leather lacing or cord.

It is great fun to play Indian, especially when you make your own costume. You can make the top part, or tunic, from gunny sacks, dyed flour sacks, or cheap, brown cotton material. Make a headband of cloth. Cut pieces of paper, and color them like feathers. Sew them to the headband. Use your own khaki overalls for trousers.

To make the tunic, first cut a newspaper pattern. Cut a hole about the size of your head in the center fold of a double sheet of newspaper. Cut a 5″ slit in the newspaper from the back center of the hole. Put your head through the opening with the slit in the back. This is the neck opening. Pull the newspaper down around your shoulders.

Ask someone to hold the sides of the newspaper around your arms and then along the sides. Mark the sleeves and sides with pins. Be sure to allow plenty

Make two

1.
2.
3.
4.
5.
6.

HOW TO
MAKE
A POMPON

You can use pompons on caps, gloves, purses, and on many other things.

of space for seams and a loose fit. Your mother can be a great help with this.

Now remove the newspaper carefully. Smooth it out and cut the sleeves and sides as marked with the pins.

Sew the seams on the wrong side of the material with a strong thread and a large needle, using the backstitch. Allow ½″ for seams. Make a strong knot at the beginning and at the end.

Turn the material right side out. Cut ½″ slits for fringe. Make the fringe about 2″ deep around the bottoms of the sleeves and tunic. But STOP CUTTING 1″ away from both sides of all seams.

Use crayons to decorate the tunic in Indian designs. Indians used zigzag lines, diamonds, triangles, squares, and straight lines. Some of their designs look like birds, animals, and people.

Cut a cloth band 3″ wide and 1″ longer than it takes to fit around your head. Fold the band lengthwise and sew it together on the wrong side along the top edge. Turn the band right side out. Hold the ends together and pin them ½″ from the edge. Then sew them with a backstitch. Turn right side out. Decorate the band with crayons in Indian designs.

You can cut feathers from colored drawing paper or from wrapping paper colored with crayons. Sew the feathers to the band about 2″ apart. Cut another strip of cloth or paper 2″ wide and 15″ long. Sew one end of this to the back of the headband. Sew feathers along this band to hang down your back.

Indian Moccasins. Stand barefooted on a piece of paper and draw a line around the outside of one foot. Now, make a line 2″ outside the first line all the way around. Draw an oval, also, on

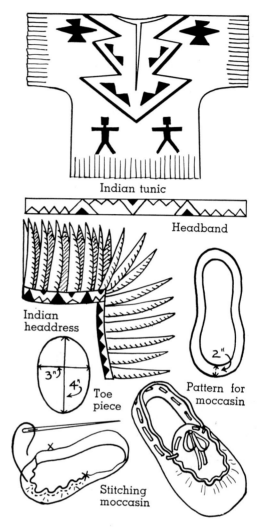

Indian tunic

Headband

Indian headdress

Toe piece

Pattern for moccasin

Stitching moccasin

These patterns will be helpful to you in making a colorful Indian costume.

paper. This should be 4″ long and 3″ wide. Now you have the pattern for your moccasins.

Cut out the patterns. Pin them to a piece of soft leather such as chamois used for cleaning, and cut them out. Felt may be used instead of leather. Cut two of each piece.

Start at point X. Use a strong needle and heavy thread to sew around the edge of the bottom piece of the moccasin. Sew about ½" from the edge. Continue to X on the opposite side. Gather the leather to form the toe of the moccasin. Measure on your foot before making the knot in the thread. If the moccasin seems loose, pull the thread, making the gathers tighter. If it is tight, loosen the thread before making the knot to fasten the gathers.

Fit the oval piece into the toe. Pin it in place, and sew it into the bottom part, from X to X, around the front of the moccasin. Sew on the outside.

With leather or paper punch, punch holes ½" apart and ½" from the edge, around the top edge of the *back* of each moccasin. Continue the holes across the top of the oval centerpiece.

Pull leather lacing, felt stripping, or braided cord through the holes, starting at the center front of the oval piece. Continue around the heel, and end the lacing at the center front. Leave the ends of the lacing long enough to tie in a bow. Tighten the lacing to fit.

Glue an inner sole of correct size inside the moccasin. These moccasins make comfortable lounging slippers and wonderful gifts. You can decorate them by sewing on beads if you wish.

How to Use the Sewing Machine

After you have learned to sew by hand, you may want to learn how to use the sewing machine. Ask your mother to show you how to use the machine. A sewing machine saves time, and does more even stitching than you can do by hand. Whether you have an electric machine or a treadle model, the operation and threading are somewhat the same.

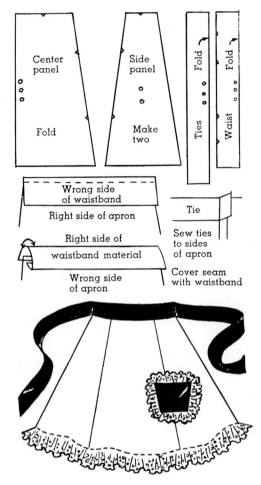

An apron which beginners can make

The treadle machine has a foot pedal which you must push up and down. Place both feet in the center of the treadle, with the left foot slightly higher than the right.

The electric machine is usually worked by knee pressure against a lever, or by arm or foot pressure. You regulate the speed of the sewing by the amount of pressure.

You will want to learn first how to

thread the machine. Different machines require different threading. Your machine will have directions for its use. But it will be easier for you to learn if your mother shows you how to sew with it.

Place a piece of material under the sewing foot to practice. Mother will show you how to raise and lower the sewing foot, which protects the needle. Let the bobbin, or bottom thread, and the top thread extend about 4″ beyond the needle.

Start the machine by pressure which will start the big wheel at the right moving, and the needle going up and down through the material. Always be sure to lower the sewing foot before starting to sew.

Use even pressure to keep the wheel running smoothly. Guide the material beneath the sewing foot. Practice until you can control the line of sewing, and keep it straight. To stop sewing, stop the pressure.

To turn the material under the sewing foot, release the lever to raise the sewing foot, but keep the needle in the material. Turn the material, lower the sewing foot, and continue sewing. BE VERY CAREFUL never to get your fingers in the way of the needle.

Practice until you can handle the machine well. Practice stopping and starting the machine, and turning the material.

Aprons

Materials: Paper and pencil; scissors; cotton cloth—used, or leftover material, or flour sacks; thread; rickrack tape for trimming.

Aprons are easy to make, and are always useful. A simple one, for beginners, can be made of used material, such as bleached or dyed flour sacks, or leftover cloth.

Cut paper patterns for the center and two side panels. Allow ¾″ on each side for seams, and at least 2″ on the bottom for a hem.

Baste the two side sections to the center panel, one on each side. Then sew on

How you can make a sweetheart apron

APPLE POCKET

Cut two
for each
pocket

Sew around three
sides. Then turn
right side out.
Turn bottom edge
in. Stitch on
right side.
Leave top
open.

Making an apron with a fruit design

material in view. Turn apron to the outside. Allow about 2″ width for waistband on the inside, and 2½″ on the wrong side. Turn ½″ of the waistband under on the wrong side, and baste and sew along the seam.

You can use cloth of another color for the waistband and ties. Appliqued flower or fruit design in the same material as the ties and band, or a ruffled pocket make attractive trimmings.

You can make another apron with shoulder straps and bodice. Trim with rickrack, binding, or eyelet ruffles.

You can make a sweetheart apron from one yard of white material, plain red material for ties and pocket, and some red rickrack. It will be just the thing to wear if you are hostess at a Valentine party.

Bolero

Boleros add a bright touch to any costume. Only two parts are needed for the paper pattern. Cut out a back and try it for size. Cut two sides from a pattern laid on doubled material. Allow 1″ all around for seams.

Baste and sew sides and back together at shoulders and down the sides. Bind the neck and sleeves. Also bind the front and around the bottom. If the bolero is made of heavy material, trim it with felt flowers and wool embroidery. If you make it of cotton, sharkskin, or rayon gabardine, for summer, trim it with pretty buttons or appliqued designs. Appliqued trimming is another bit of cloth attached with an overcasting, or buttonhole, stitch.

To bind an edge of material, use bias binding tape or cut your own bias binding from a piece of your material.

To cut on a bias, fold a large square of

the sewing machine, on the wrong side of the material. Allow about 4″ of thread to extend beyond the material before breaking the thread at the end of the seam. Always allow about this much thread at the beginning of a seam, also. The thread ends can then be tied together to strengthen the seams.

Make paper patterns for the waistband and ties. These should be cut on the fold. Fold the ties lengthwise on the wrong side of the material. Pin, baste, and then sew along one short side and along the long edge. Turn right side out. Place the waistband wrong side up along the top edge of the right side of the apron. Baste in place. Sew on the machine.

Fold the waistband up over the seam, bringing the right side of the waistband the material from corner to corner to form a triangle. The material along the fold will be on the bias. Cut along this fold. Then cut a band about 1″ wide. Cut more strips along the same lines. Join bias strips together on the straight of the material, and sew to make longer strips. If you make bias strips, you will need your mother's help in sewing them together.

Place the tape against the edge to be bound, with the right side of the tape against the right side of the cloth. Stitch ¼″ from the edge. Turn under the other edge of the tape if it is not already finished. Then fold tape over the edge,

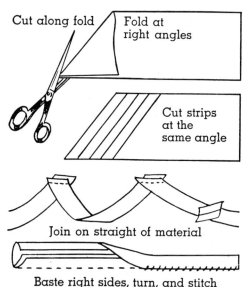

Cut along fold / Fold at right angles

Cut strips at the same angle

Join on straight of material

Baste right sides, turn, and stitch

How you can learn to cut on a bias

stitching it at the seam. Binding is often used as a neat finish for necks, neck openings, open armholes, and sleeve bottoms.

Facing is almost the same as binding, except that a wider piece of bias material is used, and it is cut from the material you are using. Facing is used for finishing necklines, dress openings, and fronts of blouses, dresses, and coats.

Common Seams

Basting. Large, even stitches about ½″ long are used to hold material until it can be stitched permanently. We call these basting stitches. Basting a hem or a seam makes it much easier to sew an even seam or make a hem the same width. After the stitching is done, the basting threads are pulled out.

Plain Seam. This is made by sewing two sides of material together. To finish, press the seam flat. To prevent ravelling,

Make one back

Make two side fronts

Bind all edges (inside of bolero)

Patterns for making a bolero

a plain seam may be pinked on both edges with pinking shears. You can also overcast on each edge with small, firm stitches. Or the raw edges may be turned under and sewed on the sewing machine close to the edge, if the material is thin. This way of finishing seams is too bulky to use on thick materials, such as wool or corduroy.

Hemmed Fell Seam. Trim one edge of a plain seam to ⅛″ size. Fold the other edge under and bring it over to cover the first edge. Hem by hand. This seam is used on light fabrics, such as washable silks and rayons and sheer cottons.

French Seam. This is a narrow, strong seam used on sheer materials. Sew the seam on the right side of the material. Trim seam to ⅛″. Turn to the wrong side of material, and machine or hand stitch to enclose the seam.

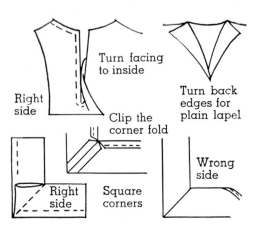

Directions for making a common seam

Flat Fell Seam. Cut one seam down to ⅛″ width. Fold the other edge over to enclose the first edge and machine-stitch it flat to the material. This is a strong seam for use on tailored and play clothes. A flat fell seam cannot ravel,

because all its edges are turned in and stitched under. That makes it an excellent seam for clothes that have to stand hard wear, but it cannot be used on heavy or bulky materials.

Top Stitch Seam. This is the seam usually used to join a waist and skirt. Turn one edge under the amount of the seam allowance, and baste. Lay this piece on the line of the seam allowance for the

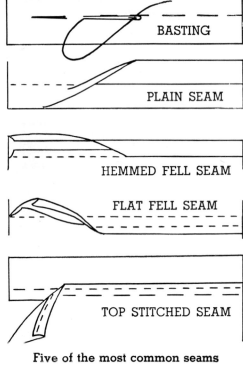

Five of the most common seams

other piece to be sewn. Pin and baste close to the folded edge. Sew on the sewing machine.

You will find that the fun of sewing is never-ending, for there are always new things to make and old ones to make over. Perhaps you will even become so skillful that you can make your own designs.

BOOKS TO READ

Ackley, Edith Flack. *Dolls to Make for Fun and Profit*. Illus. by Telka Ackley. rev. ed. Lippincott, 1951.

Chapman, Jane A. *Girl's Book of Embroidery*. Illus. by Walter Chapman. Greenberg, 1953.

Jay, Edith. *Child's Book of Knitting*. Illus. by Lucile Newman. Greenberg, 1952.

Jordan, Nina Ralston. *How to Sew*. Illus. by the author. Harcourt, 1941.

Karasz, Mariska. *Good Housekeeping See and Sew; A Picture Book of Sewing*. Illus. by Christine Engler. Lippincott, 1943.

MAKING
MUSICAL
INSTRUMENTS

DAVID DUSHKIN

Freida Zylstra

EVERY INSTRUMENT described and pictured in this chapter has been made, tested, and played by boys and girls. You will be surprised how much fun it is to make musical instruments, and how much real music you can get from them. David Dushkin established and directed the Dushkin School of Music at Winnetka, Illinois. In this chapter, he tells how to make simple instruments that will give you hours of pleasure.

Ever since early times, people have enjoyed making and playing their own musical instruments. This girl has just about finished making a xylophone.

LEARNING to make music can be fun if you do not make work of it. You learn to talk before you learn to read. In the same way, you can learn to play a musical instrument before you can read even a note of music. Learning to make music in that way is fun. It is even more fun to make your own musical instruments.

You know how interesting it is to take things apart and put them together in a different way. By doing this, you may even succeed in making something entirely new. There are many things to be found around the house, or in the neighborhood, from which you can make musical instruments. Bottles and bottle caps, drinking glasses, saucepan covers, cigar boxes, pieces of inner tube, wire, rubber bands, glue, and other odds and ends will supply you with the necessary materials.

People have made and used musical instruments from the earliest times. Drums have been made from hollow logs and skins, and many people have danced to their rhythm. Drums have

262

also been used for calling tribes together, and for sending messages in much the same way that we send telegraph messages. Medicine men of different tribes have used rattles made of gourds, animals' teeth, and shells.

As people grew more civilized, they invented wind instruments. Among these were the trumpet. They invented stringed instruments like the lyre, which is a simple harp. Most of these instruments were so simple that they might well have been made by children.

You, too, will make simple things at first. But if you have a box of tools and clever hands, you can make better musical instruments than some of the old ones. And you will have no end of fun learning to play them. As your skill improves, you will want to visit museums and study some of the musical instruments of long ago. By doing this, you may get ideas for making new ones of your own.

In making musical instruments, tuning them, and playing them, your hands will become more skillful, your eyes and ears more keen, and your mind more alert. Also you will become a good listener. And a good listener can usually become a good musician. The easiest musical instruments to make at first are those which produce music by beating, rattling, or rubbing.

Kinds of Instruments

All sound is produced by vibration, or quivering. But different kinds of instruments produce these vibrations in different ways. The sound of percussion instruments is produced by striking them. For example, when you beat a drum you set up vibrations of the tightly stretched drumhead. You can see these vibrations

if you watch the movement of a little sand sprinkled on the drumhead.

The musical vibrations of other percussion instruments such as the tambourine, cymbals, xylophone, and chimes are all produced by striking in various ways. With a string instrument such as the Hawaiian melody-maker, or a violin, the sound is produced by making the strings vibrate. The music of wind instruments such as a shepherd's pipe or a trumpet is made by vibrations of the column of air inside the instrument.

In directions for making the following instruments, " will stand for inches, ' for feet, and x for by. For example, a piece of wood 5 inches long, 3 inches wide, and ⅛ inch thick would be 3" x 5" x ⅛".

Percussion Instruments

Tom-Tom

Tools: Scissors; pliers; can opener; small paintbrush.

Materials for drum "shell": A large tin can such as a potato chip or coffee can, or a wooden pail, small keg, or coconut shell. For drumhead:

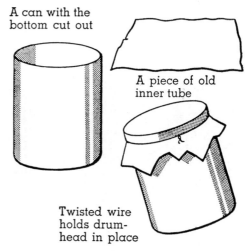

A can with the bottom cut out

A piece of old inner tube

Twisted wire holds drumhead in place

You can make a fine drum from a used coffee can and an old inner tube.

A piece of inner tubing, cloth, or parchment; a piece of soft wire; airplane dope; cord; adhesive tape.

If you use inner tubing, stretch it over the shell head and hold it in place by twisting the wire around the overlapping edges about 1″ below the top. When the wire is tight enough to hold the rubber in position, pull the edges of the inner tubing down to make sure the drumhead is tight and smooth. Then give the wire a few additional twists and bend the ends against the side of the shell. You may decorate the shell if you wish.

If parchment is used for the drumhead it must first be soaked in water. Then stretch it into position as you would rubber tubing. Parchment will shrink as it dries, making a tighter head.

If cloth is used, spread several coats of airplane dope over it to stiffen it and give it a mellow tone. Let each coat dry before applying the next one.

If the bottom of the can, keg, or pail you are using for a drum shell is removed, you can have two drumheads laced together with cord. If you lace the heads together, strengthen the edges with adhesive tape. Be sure to have the

holes for the cord at least 1½″ from the edge of the drumhead.

Drumsticks. A wooden dowel, ½″ thick and 8″ to 12″ long, makes a good drumstick. An excellent tapper which can be used, also, to play chimes, can be made by sticking a ³⁄₁₆″ dowel into the hole in a Fuller ball. This small rubber ball may be bought at any hardware or plumbing supply store.

Tambourine

Tools: Scissors; hammer; small punch or drill.
Materials: A pair of embroidery hoops; piece of cloth or parchment; airplane dope; six bottle caps; a few thin nails.

You can make a pretty tambourine with strong, smooth cloth and a pair of embroidery hoops. Separate the hoops and spread the cloth over the smaller one. Then press the outside hoop over the cloth and the other hoop. Gently

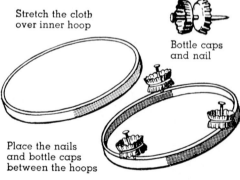

Stretch the cloth over inner hoop

Bottle caps and nail

Place the nails and bottle caps between the hoops

This diagram shows how you can make use of six bottle caps, cloth, and an embroidery hoop to make a tambourine.

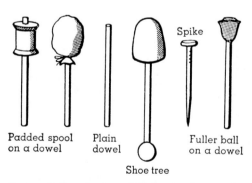

Spike

Padded spool on a dowel   Plain dowel   Fuller ball on a dowel

Shoe tree

Drumsticks of many kinds can be made to suit your own particular taste.

pull the loose ends of the cloth until the surface is tight. Give the cloth three or four coats of airplane dope to shrink and harden it. Trim the cloth edges close to the hoop.

If parchment is used, it must be soaked in water and placed in the hoops while wet. Drying stretches and hardens the parchment.

Six bottle caps with a hole punched or drilled in the center of each will make three sets of jingles. The holes can be punched by placing the caps on a block of wood and pounding a nail through the tops. Place the caps, top to top, on the tambourine. Then mount them loosely on the frame with thin nails. Pound the nails into the crack between the two embroidery hoops.

Jingle Rattle

Tools: Hammer; small drill; pliers.
Materials: Nail; wooden dowel or small stick; wire; bells.

String the bells on a wire. Then put the wire ends into a handle made from a wooden dowel. Or use a small stick, in

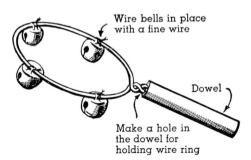

Wire bells in place with a fine wire

Dowel

Make a hole in the dowel for holding wire ring

How you can make a jingle rattle

one end of which a small hole has been drilled, for a handle. If you have no drill small enough, you can make the hole by pounding in a small nail and pulling it out. If the hole in the handle is too large to hold the wire, drive a nail in along the side of the wire to grip it.

Saucepan Cymbals. Saucepan covers, struck together with a glancing blow,

have helped out many a home orchestra with their pleasant clang. Decorate them with tassels of colored string or yarn attached to the center handles.

Castanets or Clappers

Tools: Hammer; saw; drill for drilling ⅛″ hole.
Materials: Plywood, or other wood, about ¼″ thick, 2″ wide and 19½″ long; stick of ¾″, or smaller, half-round 2″ long (a round wooden stick cut in half lengthwise); two flat head nails 1½″ long.

Cut the strip of plywood into two pieces. Make one piece 10″ long and the other 9½″ long. In the shorter piece, drill two ⅛″ holes. These should be ½″ from each side and 4¾″ from each end. Now set the half-round across the center of the longer strip of plywood. Place the short strip over the half-round so that the holes come exactly over the top of it. Then drive your nails in through the half-round and the plywood beneath it. Leave the heads of the nails sticking up 1⁄16″ above the upper piece of plywood so that it can swing freely. The points of the nails can be bent over with a hammer or clipped off with a pair of cutting pliers and smoothed with a file.

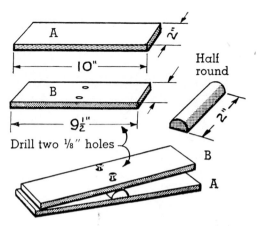

Half round

Drill two ⅛″ holes

Make your own castanets or clappers

To play the instrument, hold the long strip in your hand and clap out the rhythms by shaking the wrist.

Sandpaper Blocks. These blocks, with one face of each covered with sandpaper, make the swishing sound often heard in orchestras. They may be oblong or square, so long as they are easy to hold. The sandpaper may be glued or tacked on. Strips of soft leather or firm cloth, such as bed ticking, may be tacked to the backs for handles.

Triangle. If you have a vise, you can make a musical triangle. Use a solid metal rod about 1/4" thick. Clamp part of the rod in the vise and hammer it into the shape of a V, with one arm of the V longer than the other. A 6" rod bent in this shape and held by a string tied at the bend will give clear, musical tones when struck. If you wish, you can use a longer rod. After making the first bend, clamp the other end of the rod in the vise and hammer it down to form a triangle.

When it is played, it is best to suspend the triangle from a string. The fingers should be quite close to the triangle so that it does not swing too wide when it is struck. It should be tapped lightly with a heavy nail or some other suitable object.

Musical Glasses can easily be prepared to give pleasing music. Collect glasses of different sizes and set them in a row on several thicknesses of cloth. Thin glasses will ring in the clearest tones. Play by tapping the glasses lightly with a stick. Arrange the glasses with the lowest sounding ones at the left, and the highest sounding ones at the right. Add a little water to some of the glasses if you want to lower the pitch. As soon as you have a scale of several notes, you can play tunes.

Musical Bottles. Instead of glasses, you can use bottles to make a pleasant, tinkling sound. Hang them in a row from

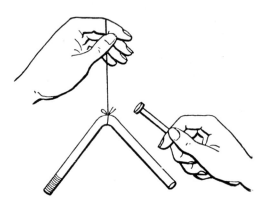

A musical triangle is easy to make.

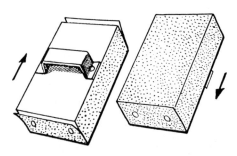

Sandpaper blocks for orchestra use

a frame. Tune them to different pitches by pouring various amounts of water into them. Tune the first one on the left to lower or middle C on the piano. The next bottle should be a note higher, and so on. To make your scale you can experiment with bottles of different sizes. To play, strike with the Fuller ball tapper described under *Drumsticks*.

Musical Flowerpots. You can get good music from flowerpots hung upside down, like bells, from a crossbar. Select flowerpots of different sizes to give different tones. Tie a knot at the end of a heavy cord. Then run the cord from the inside of each pot through the hole at the base. The knot will hold the flowerpot. Fasten the other end of the cord to a crossbar of wood. The cord can be tied around the bar or to a nail driven in the wood. The tone of any pot

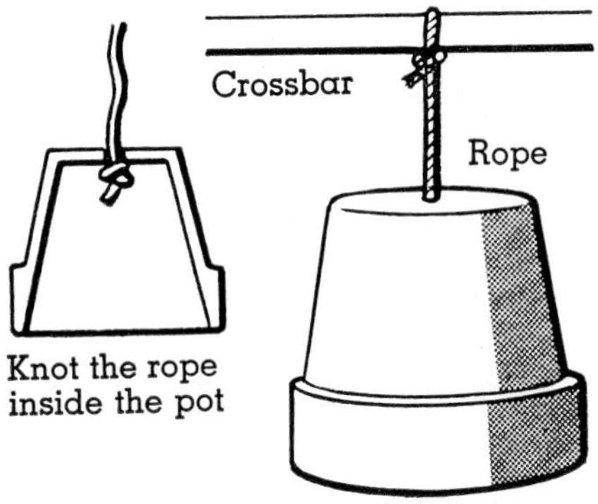

Making good music with flower pots

may be lowered by coating the inner surface with plasticine. To play, strike with the Fuller ball tapper described under *Drumsticks.*

Chimes can be made of metal tubing or thin pipe. Cut the metal into pieces of different lengths. Then drill a small hole through each tube, about 1″ from the top. Put a string through the holes and hang the tubes from nails driven in a crossbar. You can raise the pitch of any of the tubes by cutting a small slice off the lower end. You can lower the pitch by filing some metal off the side. To play, strike the chimes at the top. Use the tapper described under *Drumsticks.*

Xylophone

Tools: Saw; hammer; ¼″ drill.

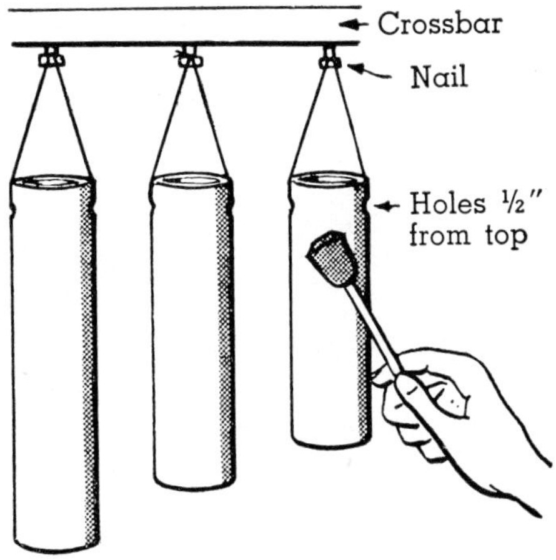

Chimes can be made from metal tubes.

Materials: Doorstop lumber; about 12 feet of cardboard or plywood; two strips of wood, 2′ x 1″ x 1½″; dowel; nails; felt weather stripping.

Doorstop lumber is the easiest material to use for making keys, or bars, for this excellent instrument. The lumber comes in strips about 1⅜″ wide and ½″ thick. Be sure it is at least ½″ thick, because it may sound rather dead if it is too thin. Cut strips of doorstop lumber into 15 pieces. Make one each of the lengths given below. Measure from the top of each length after it has been cut, and mark the proper nail-hole positions with a pencil.

BAR LENGTH	POSITION OF NAIL HOLE (from top of bar)
13″	3¼″
12¼″	3 1/16″
11⅝″	2 13/16″
11″	2¾″
10″	2½″
9¾″	2 7/16″
9⅜″	2 5/16″
8⅞″	2 3/16″
8⅜″	2 1/16″
8″	2″
7⅝″	1⅞″
7⅛″	1¾″
6¾″	1 11/16″
6⅜″	1 9/16″
6″	1½″

Next, drill the nail holes, as marked, with a ¼″ drill. Be sure you have the correct nail-hole position for each bar length. Be careful to center the holes.

Now make the xylophone frame. For this you need a base of cardboard or plywood about ¼″ thick, 23″ long, and 8″ wide. You also need two strips of wood 2′ long, 1″ thick, and about 1½″ wide. Draw two lines along the strip of plywood or cardboard, slanting toward each other. Make the lines 6½″ apart at the wide end and 3″ apart at the narrow end. Turn your board upside down and set the 1″ wood strips for the uprights at the same slant as your lines. Be sure they are set along the lines in such a way that

nails driven through the line into the strip will go through the center of the strip. Now nail securely. Turn the frame over so that the 1″ uprights are on top. Glue or tack to the top of each a narrow strip of felt weather stripping.

Now put your wooden bars on the felt. Place the longest at the left and the smallest at the right. Mark the bars in the center with the letters of the scale: C, D, E, F, G, A, B, C, D, E, F, D, A, B, and C. Now drive a 1½″ flat head nail through the ¼″ nail hole in each bar. Be sure to drive the nail through the felt and into the upright beneath. Leave about ½″ of the nail sticking up above the bar. Keep about ⅛″ space between

How you can use doorstop lumber in making a xylophone

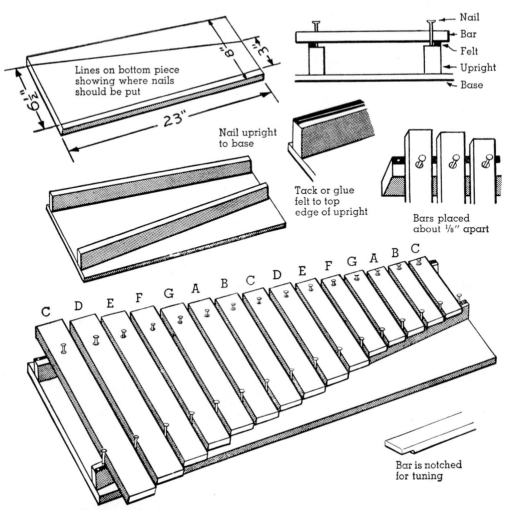

Lines on bottom piece showing where nails should be put

Nail upright to base

Tack or glue felt to top edge of upright

Bars placed about ⅛″ apart

Nail
Bar
Felt
Upright
Base

Bar is notched for tuning

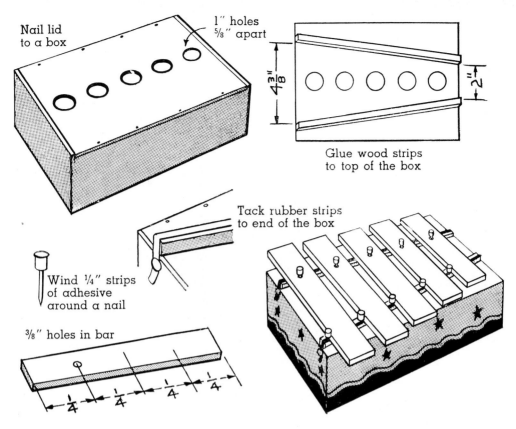

Follow these diagrams in making a sound box for these chimes.

the bars when you drive your nails. On the other upright you also drive nails into the felt, but *between* the bars. These nails will prevent the bars from touching or slipping sideways when they are played. Shellac or lacquer the bars if you wish.

For each tapper, use a ¼″ dowel about 8″ long, and a small block of wood about 1″ x ⅝″ x 1½″. Drill a ¼″ hole in the center of this block. Then push the ¼″ dowel into it. If the fit is loose, glue the dowel in place.

Now you are ready to tune your xylophone. Strike Middle C on the piano, and then tap the longest bar with your tapper. If this bar sounds a little below C, cut off a sliver with your saw. Be sure not to cut too much. If this does not bring the note up to pitch, cut off a little more. If the bar sounds too high, turn it upside down and make a little saw cut

across it in the center. Tune each bar until you have a scale of two octaves.

Dinner Chimes

Tools: Metal saw; wood saw; hammer; scissors; file; two drills.

Materials: Cigar box; twelve 1½″ flat head nails; a few ½″ nails; two strips of rubber inner tubing or other elastic about ⅛″ wide and 6″ long; adhesive tape; four thumb tacks; glue; two strips of wood about ¼″ square and 9″ long; a strip of flat, hard aluminum or soft steel about 3′ long x 1¼″ x ⅛″.

If you can get an ordinary cigar box, it will make a good sound box, or resonator, for these chimes. If not, first make a small box about 9″ x 5½″ x 2″ or 3″ high. Before attaching the lid, drill five 1″ holes lengthwise along the center of it about ⅝″ apart. After the holes are drilled, the lid may be placed on the box and attached with glue and the ½″ nails. Now glue two thin wood strips to the lid of the box. At the left, place the strips 4⅜″ apart (inside measurement) and 2″ apart at the right. Attach narrow rubber strips along the top of each wood strip. Use a thumb tack at each end to hold them in place. If your elastic is long enough, place the thumb tacks on the sides of the box. Wind a few turns of adhesive tape, ¼″ wide, just below the heads of the nails you will use to hold the bars in place. The bars are made by cutting the metal strip into the following lengths:

1 each: 8¼″ long
7¼″   "
6⅝″   "
5⁹⁄₁₆″ "
5¹⁄₁₆″ "

If you are careful in cutting these bars, you will have scarcely any tuning to do.

Now drill a ³⁄₁₆″ hole in each bar, centering it about one fourth of the distance from the end. Put the bars in position, the longest at the left, over the holes in the box lid.

Use a Fuller ball tapper, described under *Drumsticks*. With this tapper, gently strike the bars. To tune, compare them with the notes C, E, G, C, E on the piano. If they are in tune, drive the nails into the holes. Also drive nails between the metal bars, on the opposite side, to hold the bars in position.

If any of the bars are flat, or below pitch, shorten them by filing the end before attaching them. If they are too sharp, or high in pitch, file across the center of the underside of the bar. Decorate the box if you wish.

Wind Instruments

Pipes o' Pan. Long ago, it was discovered that a set of tubes of different lengths could be fastened together side by side, and played upon to produce a simple tune. This was supposed to be the favorite instrument of Pan, the goat-like god of ancient Greece.

In making this instrument, you can use bamboo tubes open at one end, small bottles, empty cartridge shells, or tubes made of stiff paper. They should either be of different lengths or they should be partly filled to different levels with modeling clay. Fasten these tubes together between strips of wood clamped tight with thumb screws. Or you can put them between heavy sheets of cardboard to which the tubes are tied, taped, or glued.

To play, blow across the open ends of the tubes.

Musical Comb. Merely wrap a sheet of tissue paper around a hair comb and sing into it. You can feel the paper vibrating against your lips, and it will tickle them a little, but a comb orchestra is always fun.

Stringed Instruments

Grunter. This noisemaker is modeled

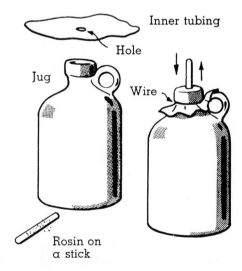

Making a noisemaker from a jug

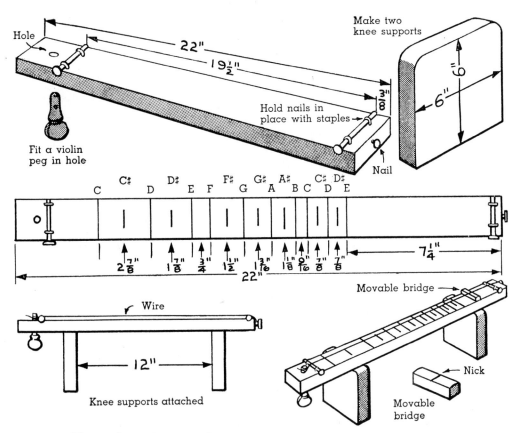

These plans show you how to make a Hawaiian melody-maker.

after those the Dutch children use during their Christmas festivities. Cover the open neck of a jug with a strip of inner tubing. Stretch it tight and fasten it to the neck with string. Then coat a small, round stick with rosin. This may be bought in music or hardware stores. Thrust the stick through a hole in the center of the rubber. As you pump the stick up and down, a grunting sound will come from this instrument.

Squawker. Punch a hole through the center of the bottom of a tin can. Tie a small piece of wood to the end of a string, and thread the other end through the hole. Rub the string in rosin. Pulling your hand the length of the string makes a screeching sound which is magnified by the hollow can. It sounds like a squawking chicken.

Hawaiian Melody-Maker

Tools: Drill for a ⁵⁄₁₆″ hole; saw; hammer; file.
Materials: Two 4″ finishing nails (or ordinary nails of about the same thickness); four small staples; six 1 ¾″ finishing nails; strip of 1″ wood 22″ long; two pieces of 1″ wood about 6″ square; standard violin peg; piece of steel wire at least 2′ long, or a steel viola or violin string (not wound).

Drive one of your smaller finishing nails partly into the end of the long strip of wood. Leave the nail head standing out about ¼″. In the center of the other end of the board, 21″ from the end where the nail was placed, bore a ⁵⁄₁₆″ hole. Fit your violin peg into this hole so that the tiny hole in the peg comes just above the surface of the wood. The peg should fit tightly. If the hole is too small, you can enlarge it with a small, round file. Use staples to fasten one of your heavy nails across the board about ⅜″ from the end where the nail was placed. This will serve as one bridge. The other bridge, formed by the other heavy nail, should be stapled into position 19½″ from the first bridge. Now mark the note lines, spacing them as shown in the diagram. Make black lines for the natural notes of the scale and red lines for the sharps or flats.

Next, nail the board to the knee supports, the 6″ blocks of wood, so that you can hold the instrument securely in your lap while playing. Use finishing nails and place the supports about 12″ apart on the underside.

To string, make a loop, if one is not already there, at one end of your steel wire. Place it over the nail first driven into the end of the board. Run the other end of the wire through the small hole in the tuning peg. Turn the peg two or three times to secure the wire string.

Use hardwood or plywood to make your movable bridge, with which you will play this melody-maker. The bridge should be ⁵⁄₁₆″ square and 1¾″ long. Slant the top of this bridge slightly with your file, so that the string will only touch it in the center of the right-hand side. A nick made with a penknife or file where the string crosses the bridge will keep the string from slipping, and thus will improve the tone.

To play, pluck the string with the finger or thumb held near the bridge. Slide the movable bridge along the board by holding it between the thumb and middle finger of your other hand. If the notes are not perfectly in tune, your bridge may be a little too high or too low.

After you have made some of these musical instruments, you may want to interest your friends in making others. What fun it would be to form a small orchestra! And, perhaps, you could even give a concert.

BOOKS TO READ

AVERY, KAY. Wee Willow Whistle. Illus. by Winifred Bromhall. Knopf, 1947.

BALET, JAN B. What Makes an Orchestra. Oxford, 1951.

BERRY, ERICK (pseud. for BEST, ALLENA CHAMPLIN). One-String Fiddle. Music by Lillian Webster. Illus. by the author. Winston, 1939.

DUSHKIN, DAVID. Fun with Flutes. Illus. by Alfred D. Stergis. Univ. of Chicago Press, 1934.

HUNTINGTON, HARRIET E. Tune Up; The Instruments of the Orchestra and Their Players. Illus. with photographs by the author. Doubleday, 1942.

LACEY, MARION. Picture Book of Musical Instruments. Illus. by Leonard Weisgard. Lothrop, 1942.